INTRODUCTION TO INTERNATIONAL BUSINESS

SECOND EDITION

REVISED PRINTING

AF769642

GEB3375

Dr. Hoon Park

University of Central Florida

Kendall Hunt
publishing company

Kendall Hunt
publishing company

www.kendallhunt.com
Send all inquiries to:
4050 Westmark Drive
Dubuque, IA 52004-1840

Revised Printing 2012

ISBN 978-1-4652-0736-4

Printed in the United States of America
10 9 8 7 6 5 4

BRIEF CONTENTS

Part A: Theories in International Business

CHAPTER 1. INTRODUCTION

Political Environment

Global political environment can profoundly influence overall international business environment through its impact on the volume and patterns of cross border transaction. There has been a dramatic change in the world's political environment over the last couple of decades. The collapse of the Soviet Union and the failure of Communism led to a great deal of instability and uncertainty in the global political system.

The world's political system that we used to have before the collapse of the Soviet Union was known as a "Bipolar System", in which we have two major political systems - the communist system led by USSR and the democratic system led by the U.S. and its allies. Fortunately or unfortunately, this bipolar system was lost as a result of the failure of the communist system. The communist system and Soviet Union, that used to support the bipolar system, could not be sustained anymore. Even Mr. Gorbachev, the last president of the defunct Soviet Union confessed that their system did not work anymore and that it needed a major overhaul. He tried to renovate this system through "Perestroika" and "Glasnost" but these were not enough. Then, why could the system, which was once regarded as a worker's paradise and thereby attracted a large number of workers to join the communist revolution, not be sustained anymore? That is simply because the system could not produce enough goods for the people who lived in the country. Every political unit needs some kind of a system to solve two major economic problems in order to feed their own people-: **how to produce** and **how to distribute**.

The communist system adopted two economic doctrines to solve these two major economic problems; **joint production** and **equal distribution**. Unfortunately one of the major communist economic doctrines, "equal distribution" started to cause a serious problem in their production. **The equal distribution doctrine failed to provide work motivation because the system ignored basic human psychology**. When workers realized that everybody would get an equal share regardless of their performance, it was quite clear that nobody would work very hard. It is the major fallacy of the system. The irony here is that the very basic doctrine (equal distribution) that attracted so many workers to join the communist revolution to create a worker's paradise failed to provide work motivation and became the major cause of the collapse of the communist system.

Today, the more relevant question is whether the world is a more peaceful place because the communist system and Soviet Union collapsed? The answer is, unfortunately "No." There are even more problems than before. When the Soviet Union and the communist system failed, it left a huge vacuum in the world's political system. Many countries, which used to be under a strong influence of the Soviet Union, restored their political autonomy and became very independent in implementing their own foreign policies without having any intervention from the Soviet Union. This makes it more difficult for U.S. policy makers to develop workable foreign policies because they now have to deal with so many different enemies rather than one big enemy like the Old Soviet Union. On the other side, the alliance between the U.S. and the Western countries weakened significantly after the loss of their common enemy; the Soviet Union. In the absence of a mighty military threat from the Soviet Union, the degree of cohesion among the western allies became very loose. Therefore, after the collapse of the Soviet Union, the world's political system became very shaky and instable. The old "bipolar system" is gone but a new system is yet to arrive. We are now living in a transitory period from one system to another. In the wake of the vacuum created in the world's political system as a result of Soviet Union collapse, Nationalism, which has been suppressed for a long time by ideology, is now coming back very strongly in those regions. The ghost of Nationalism, which is the ultimate and fundamental source of international contention for thousands of years, is resurging. Thus, a new system is needed to deal with this new political environment, which will bring back stability in the world's political system. The United States may want to have a uni-polar system, in which it becomes the global police country. However, this option might be very expensive and risky. U.S. taxpayers may not want to bear the cost of this strategy. The world and the U.S. are not ready for a multi-polar system where several countries share the power. Unfortunately, there is no clear system and direction to support world peace as of today. The world's instability and uncertainty, recently brewed by the dramatic changes in the political environment, significantly influences the business activities across national boundaries through its impact on the level of political risk that Multinational Companies (MNCs) have to deal with.

Globalization

Socio-cultural and economic environment for the past several decades has been changed dramatically under the name of Globalization. The word "globalization" has been a buzz word everywhere now. Then, what is globalization?

Multi-facetedness of Globalization

Globalization is a multi-facet social phenomenon. Thus, it is very hard to define even if it is a multi-purpose buzz word these days. The definition and interpretation of Globalization depends on who you are and what kind of disciplines you have.

Sociologists view Globalization as a **process of growing consciousness of global village**. People start to think of themselves as citizens of one big global village. Some researchers describe it as global **"unicity"** or global one-ness. People start to lose the sense of territorialism which was based on national boundary or ethnic boundary. **"Deterritorialization"** is another way to describe this phenomenon.

Anthropologists look at the process as the spread of Western culture such as modernity on the rest of the world **"West on the Rest"** and emphasize the **cultural convergence** between East and West and North and South. This group focuses on the emergence of a global culture.

Political scientists believe, globalization is the **process of losing national sovereignty** and they view the process as the beginning of the collapse of nations and states because as the world becomes more globalize many nations and states start to lose their autonomy to control their own destiny. Besides, recent technology development empowers the ordinary people by giving them ability to access all the information which used to be monopolized and controlled by the government. The same technology also makes it easy for the people to organize a powerful network against the traditional government run public organizations.

Many **economists** view the process as the rapid **expansion of free market capitalism** among the nations and states and **acceleration of cross border transaction** facilitated by the recent technology development.

Even if each discipline has its own interpretation of Globalization, most widely accepted definition of Globalization, which is provided by World Bank is:

Globalization is the growing socio/economic/cultural inter-dependence of countries abetted by the recent technological advances that facilitated cross-border transactions.

The Evolution of Economic Globalization

First stage- Globalization of Markets

The globalization of the markets refers to the merging of traditionally distinct and separate national markets protected by the national barriers into one huge global marketplace. Elimination of visible and invisible barriers to cross-border trade has made it easier to trade internationally. It has been argued for some time that the preferences of consumers in different nations are beginning to converge on some global norm, thereby helping to create a global brand and global market. Coca-Cola soft drinks and McDonald's hamburgers are the typical examples of this trend. By offering a standardized product globally, they help to create a global market by developing a global brand.

The second stage- Globalization of resources and Production

In this second stage, firms start to build their production facilities wherever they can produce the goods most efficiently. The globalization of production refers to the sourcing of goods and services from locations around the world to take advantage of cheap resources (such as labor, energy, land, and capital). This is done because firms want to reduce their overall cost and/or improve the efficiency of their production in an attempt to improve their global competitiveness.

Robert Reich has argued that as a result of globalization of production and sourcing, in many industries it is becoming irrelevant to talk about American products, Japanese products, German products, or Korean products. The meaning of country of origins starts to wane significantly as the result of globalization. Increasingly, according to Reich, the outsourcing of productive activities to different suppliers results in the creation of products that are global in nature; that is, "global products."

The third stage- Globalization of capital market

Under a globalized capital market, a country becomes more like a company whose stocks and bonds can be bought by any global investors in tier portfolio. Global investors are more like shareholders of these companies (countries). Leaders of the countries become more like managers of these companies (countries). The global investors (shareholders) will ask the leaders of the countries to manage their economy better than other countries. Their performance will be evaluated by the global investors through investing/divesting and by their citizens through election based on their economic performances. Thus, there is no more national boundary protection for sovereignty under the globalized capital market. Even the government of the nation states can not control in and out flow of the capital.

The fourth stage- Globalization of Technology

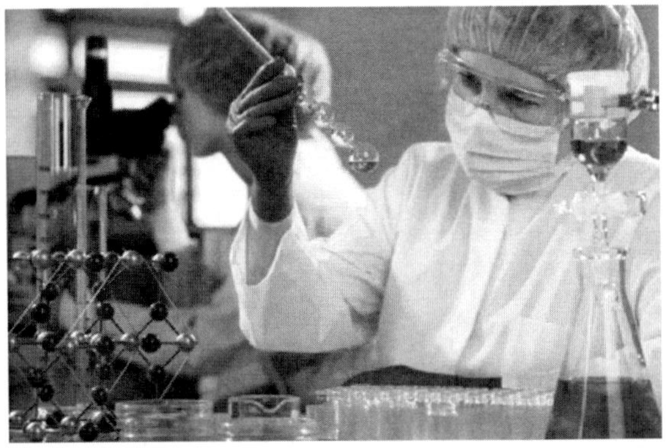

Recently so many MNCs start to search for the best technologies through global search or try to find a strategic partner who can jointly do research to develop a new product or new technology. Development of the new product of new technology normally takes long time and massive capital investment and yet there is a tremendous amount of risk involved with this process because in many cases the result may not be as desirable or practical as they may have originally predicted. Thus, in an attempt to reduce this type of risk and to pool all the possible resources together that may be needed to develop a new product or new techology, many MNCs started to establish a joint research center in the country where the cost of doing research is relatively cheap and abundant highly skilled technicians are available. A typical example of this type of operation is many US pharmaceutical firms' medical laboratory established in India where they can get abundant sample patient population and highly competent medical doctors and technicians at a relatively low cost.

The fifth stage- Globalization of Human Capital

In this stage, firms seek the best brains through global search. Recently many countries are supplying an increase share of the world's skilled human capital. Skill shortages in key economic sectors of the United States accelerated the requests from the business sectors for increases in the number of H-1 visas, which allows foreign workers to remain in the United States for up to six years. Despite recent increases in the numbers of H-1 visas issued demand still exceeds supply. Firms will either have to invest significant resources in training workers domestically or locate operations in areas where supply of the needed skills are in abundance such as India. For many American companies seeking to compete on a global scale, India is a magnet- especially for white-collar, service sector employees because of the lure of the lower wage, highly educated workers who are fluent in English.

Major Outcomes of Globalization

As the world's economy has become more and more globalized, the economic power has dramatically shifted from nations and states to Multinational Companies (MNCs). The nations and states rapidly lose their power to MNCs and they can easily override the ability of nations and state to control their own economy. The main reasons why MNCs becomes so powerful are:

1) Today, 500 MNCs with 200,000 subsidiaries control 70% of the world trade and 200 MNCs produce 30% of the world output. Of the 100 largest economies in the world, 51 are MNCs. Any regular size MNCs can easily influence one smaller medium size country's economy through their subsidiaries scattered all over the World.

2) Borderless Markets: Deregulation and technological advances make it easy to make a cross-border transaction and physical national boundaries become meaningless. The significant portion of Multinational companies' business is conducted outside of their countries. The capital and commodities can now easily fly from one country to another country with less government intervention. Accordingly, it is extremely difficult for nations and states to control the activities of MNCs.

3) Stateless Corporations: Under a globalized world economy, nationality of a company becomes very blurry through various forms of strategic alliances among the MNCs from different countries. A recent merger between Chrysler and Daimler Benz is one of the typical examples. These types of multinational firms do not have any allegiance to one particular country. Their only concern is their stockholders who are scattered all over the world. It is predicted that global mergers and strategic alliances will continue way into the future.

New Rule of the game under Globalized economy;

Globalization brought additional sources of competition into the business world. Companies have to compete with both efficient foreign firms and globalized domestic firms. Since there will be no more national boundary protection under a globalized world economy, **the new rule of the game is that if you are not globally competitive, you can not survive even in your own market.**

Factors contributing to a globalized world economy:

1. Technology in communication & transportation
   The rapid technological advances in communication, such as fax, internet, e-mail and cordless phone, significantly accelerated the globalization process. Massive high-speed transportation devices such as jumbo airplane, bullet train and effective container system also facilitate the free flow of goods from one country to another country.

2. Institutional arrangements
   Many international institutions that we established also made a significant impact on the globalization process.
   WTO: World Trade Organization tries to eliminate trade barriers
   IMF: International Monetary Fund works to rescue troubled countries and to stabilize foreign exchange market.
   OECD: Organization for Economic Cooperation & Development works constantly to coordinate among the member countries to develop policies to deal with various socio-economic problems.

3. Deregulation for easier cross border transportation.
   Each country works hard to ease or eliminate restrictions in order to induce more foreign capital and to facilitate the cross border transaction.

Janus face of globalization

Is the shift toward a more integrated and independent global economy a good thing? In summary, Globalization offers two very different perspectives- one very positive and the other one very negative. Some researchers call this double-faced nature of globalization, a Janus face of globalization. The positive and negative aspect of globalization can be summarized as below.

Positive vs. **Negative**

- Economic prosperity (Efficient use of resources) | **- Income disparity** (Inequitable distribution amplified)

They argue that falling barriers to international trade and investment are the twin engines driving the global economy toward greater prosperity. They say increased international trade and cross-border investment through global cooperation will improve productivity and result in lower prices for goods and services. They believe that globalization stimulates economic growth and raises the incomes of consumers. Unfortunately, research also suggests that the evidence of **growing income inequality** may be suspect. What they found out was the fact that not everybody will be beneficiaries of this increased efficiency and additional economic prosperity. As the globalization process has been accelerated, the rich get richer and the poor get poorer. In other words, income disparity between the have and the have-nots has been much more amplified than before.

- More interdependence | **- More insecurity**

As the world economy becomes more intertwined of each other, the countries can rely on each other more than ever. This makes it possible for more cooperation among the nations and can improve the productivity and the efficiency of the scarce resources. However, more dependence can cause a serious problem. When one part of the world economy is in trouble it can quickly spread to other countries without any insulation between the countries. For example, a large amount of capital has been invested in other countries since the globalization of the capital market. However, if a host country that holds a large amount of foreign capital is in trouble, it can cause a very negative chain reaction in the home country of the investors. The recent international currency crisis observed in Asia and many Latin American countries are the typical example.

- Cultural convergence (pressure for global culture)

- Cultural decay (cultural imperialism)

One important aspect of globalization is the rapid spread of Western culture to the rest of the world, particularly the American culture. It was possible because of U.S. MNCs aggressive marketing and emergence of global brand such as Coca-Cola and McDonald. Another example is the rise of the Internet. The American culture imbedded in the Internet has been quickly exported to many other parts of the world through the technology they export. However, many foreigners are very much concerned about this trend and they are intimidated by the invasion of American culture into their life and worried about the loss of their cultural identity.

- Pollution Halo (improved environmental condition)

- Pollution Haven (deteriorated environmental condition)

Environment: "Pollution Haven." Hypothesis suggests that MNCs tend to move their production facilities to the country where the environmental regulations are most lenient and the developing countries are willing to negotiate the environmental regulations in an attempt to induce more foreign production facilities. Consequently, MNCs significantly deteriorate the environmental condition in many developing countries through this undesirable business practice. Quite contrary to this hypothesis is the "Pollution halo"

Hypothesis suggests that MNCs can actually improve the local environment by bringing in higher environmental standards and enhancing the environmental consciousness of the local firms and people in developing countries.

- Cost saving to MNCS
(develop local economy)

- Job flight (loss)
(exploit cheap labor: "Race to the Bottom hypothesis")

Even if the globalization of production made it possible for the firms to reduce their manufacturing cost by building their production facilities in the country, they can use the cheap resources. One concern frequently voiced by opponents of globalization is that falling barriers to international trade destroy manufacturing jobs in wealthy advanced economies such as the United States and the United Kingdom. The critics argue that falling trade barriers allow firms to move their manufacturing activities to countries where wage rates are much lower. "Race to the Bottom" Hypothesis suggests that MNCs competitively move their production first to the country where the labor is the cheapest and thereby exploit the labor in the developing countries and this causes the job to shift from the industrialized countries to the developing countries.

What is International Business?

International Business can be defined as the study of any business activity conducted across national boundaries either by the private sector or the government. Any international business activity requires the transfer of goods and services. Some examples would be international trade (import and export), licensing, joint venture, wholly owned foreign subsidiary.

Law of One Price: The Law that governs the transfer of goods and services

The Law of one price states that in competitive markets, free of transportation costs and barriers such as tariffs, identical products sold in one place must sell for the same price in other places. In other words, this law states that we should have one price for the same product if there is no external constraint on the flow of the goods. If the price is different in two markets, then everybody will try to buy the goods from the low priced market and sell it in the high priced market. This will move the goods from a low priced market to a high priced market, where a profit can be made. This action, which is called "arbitrage" in the market, will eventually drive down the price in the high priced market because of the additional supply in the market and raise the price in the low priced market because of the additional demand in the market. Thus, the markets will be realigned and the end result will be the same one price for the same product in both markets.

There are two conventional ways to implement the Law of One Price:

1. **Arbitrage**: When price difference exists as a fact, you can do arbitrage by buying at low priced market and selling at the high priced market. If everybody tries to buy at the low priced market, the price there will go up. When everybody tries to sell at the high priced market, the price there will go down. The end result will be the equalization of the prices between the two markets. One very important thing to remember when you want to do arbitrages is quick action to "beat the market". The art of arbitrage requires an almost **simultaneous buying and selling** otherwise the market will be quickly re-aligned, equilibrium will be restored, and no more chances will be available for arbitrage.

2. **Speculation** is another way to implement the law of one price. When you expect that the price in the future will rise, you buy the goods with an expectation to sell it at the higher price in the future. However, when everybody tries to buy now, the price now will go up and when everybody tries to sell in the future, the price in the future will go down. The end result is the equalization of the price between now and the future. Thus, this is one way to equalize the price between two time periods.

International Economics vs. International Business

The ultimate goal of International Economics is how to maximize the efficient use of limited resources globally. The major objective of International Business, on the other hand, is how to maximize the shareholder's wealth of the international firms. Most of the economic theories are based on the assumptions that all human beings are equal and they are always rational. In International Business, however, rationality and equality of human beings are not the assumption that they make in developing a theory. Instead, the researchers in this field pay a greater deal of attention to the behavioral aspects of human beings. Since culture is the main spring to dictate human behavior, researchers heavily rely on culture to explain and understand the behaviors of people in many different countries.

International Business vs. Domestic Business

A fundamental difference between Domestic Business and International Business is the **environment** in which the business is conducted. Many factors contribute to this difference:

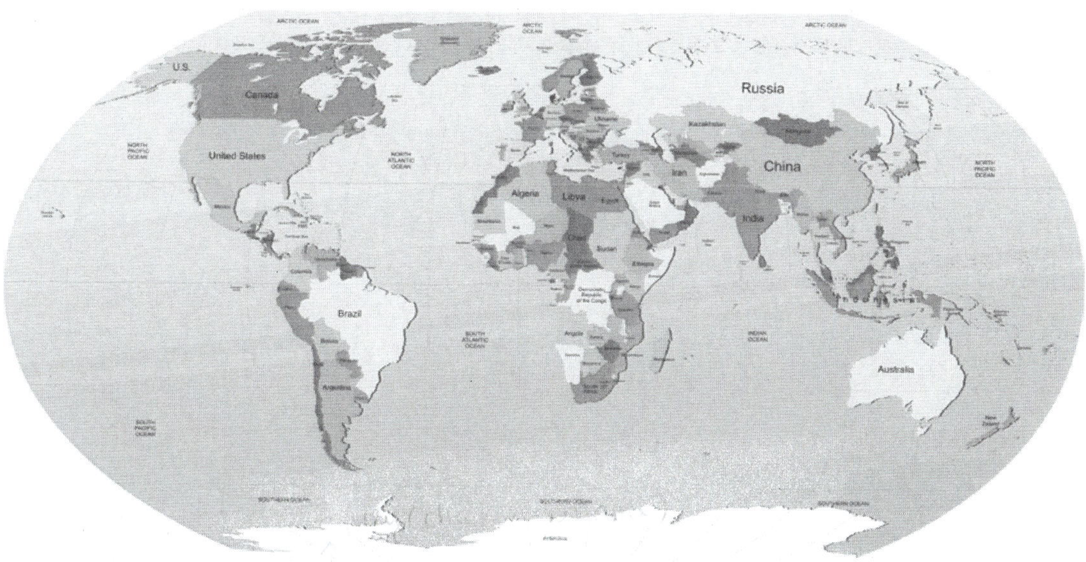

Geography (resources, weather) — History (internal, external) — Legal System (common, civil) — Political System — Economic System — Culture

International Marketing — International Management — International Finance — International Accounting — International Taxation

Each business function should be carried out under very different business environments that are influenced by the various factors identified above.

Patterns of Major International

World Trade and total output

After World War II, the United States became the world's dominant industrial power in terms of output and trade. However, the dominance of the U.S. economic power started to diminish significantly since the 1960's. Most of the other western industrial countries such as France, the United Kingdom and Germany followed the same trail. This decline in the U.S. and western industrialized countries' position in the world economy does not necessarily mean those countries actually had a negative growth during the period. This decline in economic prominence of those countries can rather be attributed to the relatively fast economic growth of several other economies such as Japan and other Asian countries during the same period. The countries that noticeably increased their share of world output included Taiwan, South Korea, Thailand, Singapore, and Malaysia. More recently, China is emerging as a potential economic giant because of its speed of industrialization and the size of its economy.

The Changing Pattern of World Output and Trade

Country	Share of World GDP, 2008	Share of World Exports, 2008
United States	20.70%	9.30%
Germany	4.2	8.7
France	3.1	3.8
Italy	2.6	3.4
United Kingdom	3.2	3.9
Canada	1.9	2.7
Japan	6.4	4.5
China	11.4	8.4

Sources; IMF, World Economic Outlook, April 2009.

For the last several decades, the dominance of the U.S. as an exporter started to decline while the share of world trade of some other countries such as Japan, Germany, and a number of newly industrialized countries such as South Korea and China have increased dramatically.

The World Bank has recently predicted that if current trends continue, the Chinese economy could be larger than that of the United States and the economy of India will approach that of Germany by 2020. Forecasts are not always accurate, but these strongly indicate that the gravity of the world economy is rapidly shifting. The implications of this changing economic environment for international Businessmen are quite clear: This new changing environment present a tremendous amount of threat to us but also will provide a great deal of opportunities.

Foreign Direct Investment

As in the case of world output and trade, the U.S. maintains its dominance in foreign direct investment. U.S. firms accounted for almost two thirds of worldwide foreign direct investment flows in the 1960's. Many European countries were very much threatened by the U.S. dominance in foreign direct investment in European continent and initiated some control on inflow of US investment in the continent.

However, many non-U.S. firms began to increase their investment across national borders for last several decades. They did have a variety of motivation for this move. One of them is to get closer to their major foreign markets. Some of them tried to avoid the possible imposition of trade barriers. For example, Toyota and Hyundai, Asian automobile company, rapidly increased their investment in automobile production facilities in the U.S. lately to avoid the potential tariff that might be imposed on their products if they are imported into this country. Some of them tried to take advantage of being an insider by making FDI inside of the target market. Some of them tried to aggressively exploit the opportunities available in the "emerging markets".

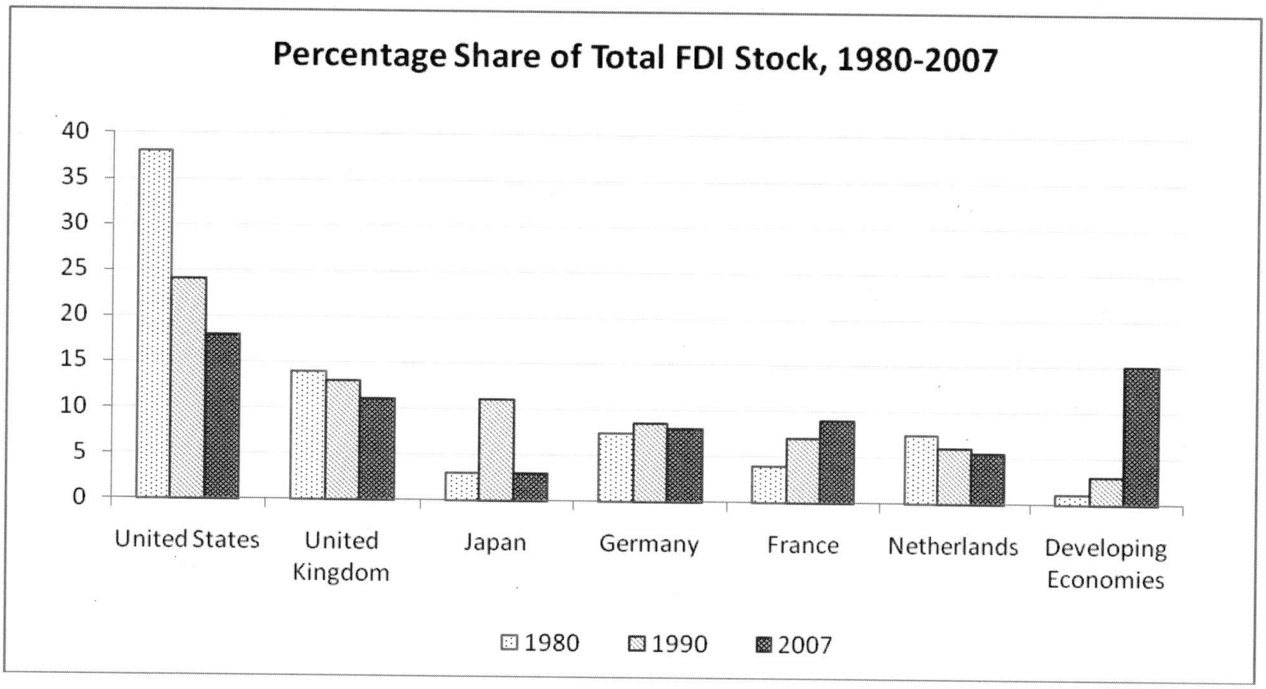

Source: UNCTAD, World Investment Report, 2008.

We can observe two other important trends in the following illustration. First – the cross-border flows of foreign direct investment have been continuously growing. Secondly, the flow of FDI into the developing countries has been increasing dramatically. Despite the slump caused by the 1997-1998 Asian currency crises, the total amount of FDI inflow to the region has been steadily increasing and China continued to be the major recipient of foreign direct investment among developing economies since the mid-1990s. The trend may be able to improve the efficiency of scarce resource globally and present more opportunity to all the parties involved if all the disputes and concerns are addressed correctly.

Review Questions

What was the major reason why the world political environment changed so dramatically for last couple of decades?

How can we characterize the current international political system?

What are the major causes of the failure of the communist system?

What is globalization?

Discuss the different interpretations of Globalization.

What are the factors that contributed to the globalization of the world economy?

What is the major economic impact of globalization?

What are the positive and negative aspects of globalization?

What is the new rule of game under Globalized World Economy?

How can we define International Business?

What is the major implication of the Law of One Price?

What is the difference between Speculation and Arbitrage?

What is the major difference between domestic business and international business?

Identify some of the major patterns in recent world trade and foreign direct Investment.

CHAPTER 2. BALANCE OF PAYMENT

Definition of Balance of Payment

A Balance of Payment is a summary of international business activities of one country, which uses the *double entry (debit/credit)* accounting system to reflect the country's *external liquidity* position. **External liquidity** is a country's ability to meet foreign claims (debt) and to buy foreign goods and services. If a country's external liquidity has a serious problem, the value of the country's currency will decline. On the Balance of Payment, the debits and credits simply reflect which way money flows. Balance of payment is neither an income statement nor a balance sheet. Balance of Payment is a sources-and-uses-of-statement. Any transaction that can contribute to inflow of money is called Credit Transaction and any transaction that can cause outflow of money is called Debit Transaction. **An inflow of money is posted as a credit, while an outflow of money is posted as a debit.**

Accounts on Balance of Payment

There are three major accounts on Balance of Payment; Current Account, Capital account and Official Reserve Account. Each major account has several sub-accounts as shown below:

Balance of Payment

	Credit	Debit	Balance
1. Current account			
a. Merchandise	export	import	**Merchandise balance**
b. Services			
Travel and transportation			
Fees			
Income earned abroad			**Trade balance**
c. Unilateral Transfer			**Current Account Balance**
2. Capital Account			
a. Long term capital account			**Basic balance**
b. Short term capital account			
3. Official Reserve Account			
a. Gold			
b. Foreign exchange			
c. SDR (Special Drawing Rights)			**Overall Balance**

1. The **Current Account** consists of:

   a. Merchandise – Any export of merchandise would result in money coming into a country, thereby it must be recorded on the credit side and any import would result in money flowing out of the country, thereby it must be recorded on the debit side. The difference between the debits and credits is called **Merchandise Balance**
   b. Services –Services represent the items, such as, travel and transportation, various fees, and income earned abroad.

   Travel and Transportation: if a Chinese tourist flies on Delta Airlines and spends money in the US, it would represent a credit (inflow) for the US balance of payment.

   Various Fees: If an American firm sells technology to foreign firms and collects licensing fee, then this transaction should be recorded on the credit side (cash inflow).

   Income earned abroad: if an American company is doing business in a foreign country and sends the profit back to its parent company in the U.S., the transaction will be recorded on the credit side of the US balance of payment (cash inflow).

   The total difference between all the debits and credits in services and merchandise is called the **Trade Balance.**

   c. Unilateral Transfer – This is a one-way flow of money, where there is no matching transaction. Examples of this would be foreign aid or an immigrant sending money back to his relatives.

   The total of Section 1 is called the **Current Account Balance.**

2. The **Capital Account** of a country is divided into:

   a. Long-term Capital Account – This includes FDI and long term loan with more than one year maturity or no maturity, such as stock. What is important to notice is that an initial FDI in a foreign country should be recorded as a debit under long-term capital account but when this FDI produce profit and send the profit back to the parent companies in the U.S., it must be recorded as a credit under an income-earned abroad. The total of the Long-term Capital Account along with the total of the Section 1, Current Account Balance, is called a country's **Basic Balance. This is the most important balance since it is this balance that indicates external liquidity position** (i.e.; ability to pay foreign debt or ability to buy foreign goods and services) **of one country**.

b. Short-term Capital Account – This account represents very short term capital accounts such as Money Market Instrument such a short term Certificate of Deposit (CD) or a loan with less than one year maturity. This account is deliberately excluded from the Basic Balance, as it is so volatile and easily reversed depending on the short-term interest of one country.

At this point you can draw an imaginary line to signify that all transactions above this line are autonomous, or self-governing, transactions. The next section (#3) is a net result of what happens above this line.

3. The **Official Reserve Account** is how much change happened in the holding of the internationally acceptable currencies. The most widely accepted international currencies are Gold, US dollar, Euro, British Pound and Japanese Yen. Another acceptable international currency is Special Drawing Rights (SDR), which are also known as "paper gold". The SDR is artificially created international money by the IMF and used to settle for foreign debts.

Another aspect of double entry system is that any transaction is conceptually divided into two analytical categories, sum of which is zero. Thus, one transaction is posted twice –one time under credit and the same amount under debit. Because of this nature of double entry system, the overall balance on the balance of payment, which is the summation of all the accounts, is supposed to be balanced (zero) all the time. The **Overall Balance** has therefore little meaning.

Major Implication of Balance of Payment Deficit

A Balance of Payment (BOP) deficit means that the Basic Balance of the country is negative. The country, which has a large amount of balance of payment deficit, does not have enough amount of international currency to pay foreign debt or to buy foreign goods. **Therefore, if a country has a huge balance of payment deficit, its currency will actually devaluate if the country has a floating exchange system. If it has a fixed exchange system, the country will at least be under pressure to devaluate its currency.**

Several Economic variables constantly influence the BOP condition of a country. In inflationary time, overall prices in the country increase, causing exports to decrease which will have a negative impact on the BOP deficit (Trade deficit). If the *interest rates* go up, foreign investors try to take advantage of high interest rates available in the country increasing foreign portfolio investment (indirect investment) and thereby causing inflow of capital and making a positive impact. If *national income* increases, there is the propensity to buy more foreign goods. This will have a negative impact and creates a Trade deficit. However, in reality, those three economic variables can work simultaneously. Thus, it is very difficult to understand the sole effect of one variable on a country's balance of payment condition.

As discussed earlier, the Basic Balance is a very important balance for most of the countries. For them, a balance of payment deficit means they do not have enough amount of internationally acceptable currency. Practically this means they do not have enough amount of U.S. dollar because the U.S. dollar is the most widely accepted international currency. However, the U.S. does not have to worry about Basic Balance much because the U.S. dollar is not only the major international currency but it is also the domestic currency of the U.S. Instead, the U.S. worries more about their Merchandise Balance and Trade Balance because of the large amount of chronic trade deficit (merchandise balance). Originally the definition of trade balance was the difference between the exports and the imports, which is now called merchandise balance. Even if we have been trying everything possible to reduce the original definition of trade, we miserably failed to do so. Thus, the U.S. government decided to change the definition of trade balance to include the service sector, in which the U.S. has a relatively strong position.

Various reasons for a chronic U.S. Merchandise deficit

External reasons

1) The **lack of reciprocity**. Foreign countries refuse to open their markets to the extent that U.S. opened its market for their products. They established very high tariff and non-tariff, visible and invisible barrier to block U.S. products from their markets.

2) **Foreign government subsidies**. Many foreign governments provide various forms of subsidies to their local firms to build artificial competitiveness. The government subsidies normally take the forms of lower interest loan, tax exemption for export industries, R&D support and duty drawback system (refund of tariff when the product is exported). These foreign government subsidies distort seriously the international trade picture and international trade becomes a managed trade (by the government) rather than a fair trade based on comparative advantage.

Internal reasons

1) **Inefficient management of technology**. The U.S. R&D is known as innovative R&D. This type of R&D requires large sums of money and efforts with ingenuity. However, after many U.S. firms develop a new technology spending large amount of money and time, they quickly sell out all those technologies to foreign firms.
2) This allows other countries to do a different kind of R&D called "adaptive R&D", which makes it possible for them to buy some basic technology and extend it. This kind of R&D is much less expensive and often gives them a competitive edge with minimal efforts and expenses.

3) **Too stringent domestic regulations** (environmental & safety) often results in increasing the manufacturing costs of the American firms and thereby undermines the competitiveness of the U.S. firms in international market.

4) **Cultural insensitivity** is another serious problem because many U.S. firms naively assume that they can sell their products anywhere if they can sell domestically. However, tastes and preferences across cultures can be significantly different and make it very difficult to sell standardized American products abroad.

5) In many cases, the U.S. government does not allow U.S. firms to sell many products for **National Security** reason. For example, exportation of military sensitive equipment and technology for space industry can jeopardize the national security of this country.

6) **Political objective** is often mixed up with trade issues. For example, the U.S. simply wants to help other countries by buying their products or to punish other countries by not buying their products. For example, the U.S. agreed to buy a large amount of Turkish textiles in return for Turkish cooperation in shutting off the Iraq pipeline during the Gulf War. Another recent example, the U.S. agreed to buy more of Pakistani textile products since they helped the U.S. a lot to crack down Al-Qaeda terrorist network inside of their territory.

7) **A lack of government support** for the export industry can be another reason for a chronic trade deficit. Unlike many other foreign governments, the U.S. government has not been cordial to the export industry and refused to give them any special help. This lack of government support undermines U.S. firms' global competitiveness in the presence of foreign government subsidies to their domestic industries.

8) Another reason why the US started to have a large amount of merchandise deficit is because a significant portion of traditional **export has been replaced by FDI.** Many U.S. firms actually started to build their plants in foreign countries, producing and selling their products directly from that plant to local markets rather than producing the goods here and selling through export.

Correcting Balance of Trade

The J-Curve

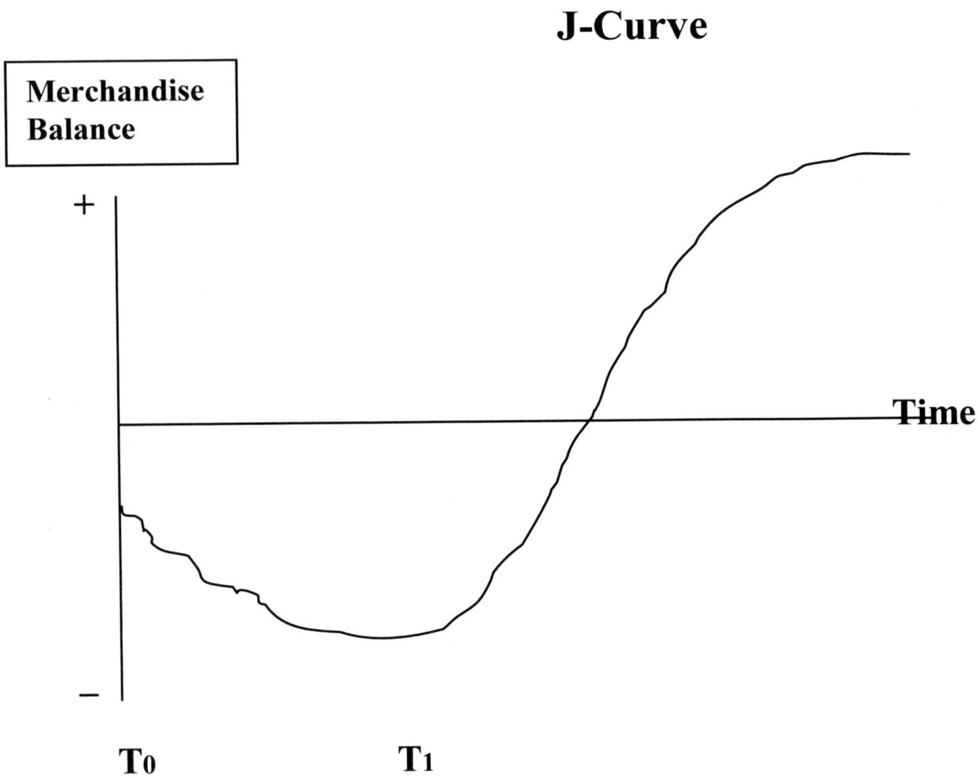

To = Time of Initial currency depreciation
T1 = Time at which net merchandise balance begins to improve

When a country develops a large amount of trade (merchandise) deficit, they may consider various options to reduce it. One way to reduce the undesirable merchandise trade deficit is by deliberately devaluating their currency. This will make their product cheaper in international markets and at the same time it will make imported foreign products expensive. However, when a country actually devalues their currency, the effect of devaluation on Balance of Trade will not be readily materialized. Rather, it will take time to get the full effect of devaluation on the balance of trade. The effect of devaluation on the improvement of balance of trade display follows the J-curve shape. The J-curve is a fashionably way of sketching the evolution of the nominal trade balance after a depreciation or devaluation of a currency. As its name implies, the J-curve represents a balance that initially falls sharply, remains temporarily low, gradually begins to improve, and ultimately rises above its previous level as time passes. To identify the time path of changes underlying the J-curve, we can divide the trade balance into four parts, which are related in the following equation:

TB = (Px * X) – (Pm * M),

where TB is net merchandise exports (that is, the balance of trade) in current prices; Px and Pm are, respectively, the average price indexes of exports and imports; and X and M are, respectively, the total volume of exports and imports. The term enclosed in the equation's first parenthesis (Px * X) represents *nominal exports*; the term in the second parenthesis (Pm * M) is *nominal imports*. When TB is negative, the balance of trade in the United States is at a deficit.

In standard J-curve theory, each of the four elements of the balance of trade responds over its own time path to exchange rate fluctuations. Together these changes produce the overall trade balance's reaction to the exchange rate. The standard J-curve explanation argues that – initially – only Pm, import prices, will change early as lower dollar exchange rates directly increase import prices; hence, in the absence of changes in import and export volumes, total payout for imports will increase and the trade balance will deteriorate. Export prices in dollar terms would not be expected to change in the short run but might slightly in the longer run either as U.S. producers pass on the increased costs of imported intermediate inputs, by raising their prices or as rising export demand pushes U.S. producers toward capacity constraints. Generally, however, dollar export prices are expected to remain more or less stable.

Changes in import and export volumes, M and X, are expected to occur later, as purchasers react to the dollar's depreciation, by eventually finding new sources of products. In response to rising import prices, import volumes, M, would be expected to decline eventually. This reaction would help to counteract the early impact of import price increases and push the balance of trade toward improvement. Export volumes, X, would be expected to increase as foreigners face lower prices in their own currencies for dollar-priced goods from the United States. The effect, too, would tend to improve the U.S. balance of trade.

Combined, these four sets of reactions suggest the J-curve shape. The trade balance's short-run decline is accounted for by a quick rise in import prices, but with little change. The trade balances later improvement occurs when falling import volume and rising export volume offset higher import prices. If the responses of trade volumes are sufficient, the rising section of the J-curve will move above its level, at the time of ~~the~~ currency depreciation. That is, the trade balance will recover and surpass its level when the currency begins depreciating.

In summary,

TB = (Px * X) – (Pm * M)

Short term: only Pm up & Px down as the result of devaluation and we don't have enough time to change the quantity of M and X. Thus, TB deteriorates.

Long term: we have enough time to adjust the contract quality for import and export Pm up so M down. Thus, nominal import goes down, Px down and so X up. Thus, nominal export goes up. Accordingly, TB improves.

Review Questions

What is Balance of Payment?

What is the meaning of external liquidity?

What are the meanings of each item on Balance of payment?

What are the meanings of each balance on Balance of payment?

What kinds of items are included in each balance?

What is the major implication of the balance of payment deficit?

How can some major economic variables influence balance of payment condition of one country?

What are the reasons for the chronic US merchandise balance deficit?

What is J-curve effect and why is there a lagged effect of devaluation on balance of trade?

CHAPTER 3. INTERNATIONAL TRADE THEORIES

Mercantilistic Theory (Hume and Colbert)

The oldest theory of international trade emerged in England in the mid 16^{th}century with the modernization of the state and it was a little more elaborated and developed later by Jean Baptiste Colbert in France and David Hume in England in the 17th- 18th Century. However, it was still a loosely defined theory and was more like an economic philosophy of colonial power rather than a well defined theory. Most of the old International trade theories start with the definition of a nation's wealth. **The Mercantilistic Theory defines a nation's wealth as the accumulation of precious metal or the holding of treasure, particularly in terms of gold.** Gold was vital to consolidate the power of the government and to solidify the people's allegiance to the government. The theory recognizes international trade as a way to maximize the nation's wealth such defined. Countries want to increase their nation's wealth through international trade because gold was used not only as a form of domestic money but also used as an instrument to settle international trade. So, when they sold their products to other countries, they were paid in terms of gold. That is how they could increase their nation's wealth when they exported. However, when they were buying something from foreign countries, they had to pay in terms of gold. Thus, their nation's wealth (defined as the amount of gold holding) would drain. Based on this thought, the theory developed a simple formula to maximize nation's wealth:

Export ↑ - Import ↓ = Nation's Wealth ↑

This equation shows that if you increase exports and decrease imports, the result would be an increased nation's wealth. In other words, to mercantilist countries, export is a blessing and import is a curse for their nation's wealth. Thus, under the Mercantilistic trade policy, the countries always relentlessly try to maximize their exports and to minimize their importations from other countries in an attempt to maximize their nation's wealth.

Economic Doctrines under Mercantilism

The first economic doctrine developed to maximize a nation's wealth under this theory dictated that the country should have a self-sustaining economy and should produce everything the country would need since any importation from other countries will drain the nation's wealth. Second, the government prohibited the colonies from manufacturing in an attempt to sell more of the mother country's products to the colonies. Lastly, the government monopolized international trade. Private citizens were not allowed to import or export. Only royal families were allowed participate in international trade. Under Mercantilistic theory for international trade, particularly under this third doctrine, which prohibited the individual citizens to do international trade, it became very clear whose wealth the countries tried to maximize. The wealth that they want to maximize was not the citizens' wealth but the monarch's wealth. They simply used this theory to maximize the monarch's wealth at the sacrifice of their citizens well being.

Problems under the Merchantilistic theory

First of all, under this Mercantilistic trade policy prohibiting citizens to get involved with any types of international trade, **the citizens would have to buy expensive domestic goods even if cheap foreign goods were available** because any importation from foreign countries were considered drainage of a nation's wealth and prohibited by the government. **Externally, Mercantilistic attitudes in international trade always create conflict with trading partners**. When one country wants to sell everything and does not want to buy anything from others, nobody would want to trade with this nation because this nation would indefinitely push their trading partners to have more trade deficit. This situation can easily escalate to a conflict in international trade and international trade can easily become a zero-sum game rather than a positive sum game.

Neo-mercantilism

Some countries today still maintain this kind of Mercantilistic attitudes even under the current globalized world economy. We often observe that a country relentlessly tries to maximize its trade surplus even at the sacrifice of its trade partner's economic well-being. Even if they have a trade surplus, they still want to have more surplus and they constantly push other nations to have greater trade deficits. Those countries are collectively called Neo-Mercantilistic countries.

Absolute Advantage Theory (Adam Smith)

The question Adam Smith raised was why should the citizens buy expensive domestic goods when cheap foreign goods were available? He believed the reason for this erroneous economic doctrine is the result of the wrong definition of nation's wealth. Accordingly, he redefined **nation's wealth as the amount of goods and services available to the citizens** not the amount of gold holding as Mercantilistic theories defined.

In his 1776 book *The Wealth of Nations,* Adam Smith argued that countries differ in their ability to produce goods efficiently. In his time, the English were the world's most efficient textile manufacturers due to their superior manufacturing process and the French were the world's most efficient wine producers due to their favorable climate and good soils. The English had an absolute advantage in the production of textiles, while the French had an absolute advantage in the production of wine. Absolute advantage in this context indicates an ability to produce goods more efficiently, which means ability to produce with a less actual cost (less input). Thus, a country has an absolute advantage in the production of goods when it can produce the same amount of goods with a less actual cost (less input) than other countries.

According to Smith, **countries should specialize in the production of goods that they have an absolute advantage in (ability to produce goods with a less amount of actual cost/input) and then trade these for goods produced by other countries.** In Smith's time, this suggested that the English should specialize in the production of textiles while the French should specialize in the production of wine. England could get all the wine it needed by selling its textiles to France and buying wine in exchange. Similarly, France could get all the textiles it needed by selling wine to England and buying textiles in exchange. Smith's basic argument, therefore, is that a country should never produce goods at home it can buy at a lower price from other countries. Smith demonstrates that by specializing in the production of goods in which each has an absolute advantage, both countries benefit by engaging in trade.

Basically, his proposition under the Absolute Advantage was that countries should specialize in the commodity they have an absolute advantage in, and then trade with each other. This theory emphasizes the division of labor and the need to specialize for maximum output. He believed the specialization based on division of labor would increase his new definition of nation's wealth—the amount of goods available to the citizens.

To prove his proposition, we will use the **Labor Theory of Value** where we assume that labor is only one factor to produce the goods to simplify the situation.
We will use the following example using the U.S. and the U.K. where each country has only 100 units of labor available. The U.S. needs 10 units of labor to produce 1 yard of textile while the U.K. needs 5 units of labor to produce same 1 yard of textile. For wheat production, the U.S. needs 4 units of labor to produce 1 bushel of wheat while the U.K. needs 10 units of labor to produce same 1 bushel of wheat.

	US	**UK**	**World Output**
Textile	10 labor/1 yd	5 labor/1 yard	
Agri (Wheat)	4 labor/1 bushel	10 labor/1 bushel	
assuming 100 units of labor:			
1st Case Mercantilistic (no imports)			
(1/2) 50 labor	5 yds.	10 yds.	15yds
(1/2) 50 labor	12.5 bushels	5 bushels	17.5 bushels
2nd Case Absolute Advantage			
Textile	0 yds.	20 yds.	20yds (+5yds)
Wheat	25 bushels	0 yds.	25bushels(+7.5 bsl)

In the first case (Mercantilistic case), both countries do not want to buy anything from other countries. Accordingly, they have to produce both goods—textile and wheat. Assuming that each country uses half of its total labor (50 units of labor) for textile production and remaining half for wheat production, then the U.S. will produce 5 yards of textile and 12.5 bushels of wheat and the U.K. will produce 10 yards of textile and 5 bushels of wheat. In this case, total world output (U.S. and U.K.) is 15 yards of textile and 17.5 bushels of wheat.

When you look at the second case (Absolute Advantage case), each country is supposed to specialize in the goods they have an absolute advantage in. To decide which country should specialize in what product, we have to compare actual cost of producing each commodity between the two countries. When we compare actual cost of producing 1 yard of textile between the two countries, you will find the cost of producing 1 yard in U.S. to be 10 units of labor and the cost of producing same 1 yard of textile in U.K. is only 5 units of Labor. Thus, since the actual cost of producing 1 yard of textile in U.K. (5 units of labor) is a lot less than that of U.S. (10 units of labor), the U.K. will have absolute advantage in Textile production and thereby U.K. will specialize in Textile production. If you compare the actual cost of wheat production between the two countries, you will find the actual cost of producing 1 bushel of wheat in U.S. (4 units of labor) is a lot less than that in U.K. (10 units of labor). That's why The U.S. has an absolute advantage in wheat production and thereby the U.S. will specialize in wheat production.

As discussed earlier, Absolute Advantage theory proposes that each country should specialize in the commodity that it has an absolute advantage in (lower actual cost). Thus, according to the Absolute Advantage theory, the U.S. will specialize in wheat production since it has an absolute advantage in wheat, and the U.K. will specialize in textile production since they have an absolute advantage in textile production. If each country specializes in the commodity in which it has an absolute advantage in, the U.S. will produce 25 bushels of wheat and the U.K. will produce 20 yards of textile. If we compare this level of world output with that of previous Mercantilistic case (17.5 bushel of wheat and 15 yards of textile), you will see a significant incremental change in the output of both textile and wheat. What the two countries have to do is to share this additional output produced as the result of specialization. This will undoubtedly increase the amount of goods available to both countries (nation's wealth). This mathematical illustration actually proves Adam Smith's points and demonstrates how a nation's wealth (amount of goods and services available to the citizens) can increase if each country specializes in the commodity in which it has an absolute advantage in.

Comparative Advantage Theory (Ricardo & Torrens)

As discussed above, the Absolute Advantage theory proves how world output can increase if both countries specialize in the commodity in which they have an absolute advantage in. However, unfortunately, the theory cannot give us definite answers for all the cases.

Ricardo and Torrens raised a very intriguing question: what if a country has an absolute advantage in both goods? In this case, the question in point is who should produce what or what products should a country specialize in when one country has an absolute advantage in both and the other country does not have an absolute advantage in any commodities? In the previous absolute advantage case, to decide who should produce what, all we had to do was **to compare actual cost** between the two countries. However, as you can see in following case, now actual cost of producing both commodities in the U.S. is lower than those of U.K. In other words, the U.S. has an absolute advantage in both commodities. In this case, it is very difficult to tell who should produce what because the U.S. has an absolute advantage in both commodity and the U.K. does not have any absolute advantages in any commodity. According to the previously discussed Absolute Advantage theory, the U.S. should produce both because it has an absolute advantage in both commodities and the U.K. should not produce anything because they do not have an absolute advantage in any commodity. However, we know intuitively this is not correct. Even if the U.K. does not have any absolute advantages at all, we know that they have to produce something. Even if the U.S. has an absolute advantage in both, the country cannot produce them all.

The following case will illustrate the point. Suppose we have a very competent manager who is also a good typewriter. Even if he is very good at typewriting, he still needs a typist so that he can concentrate in the job for which he has more talent. Even if the typist may be inferior to the manager both in typing and managing the company, the typist can still make a contribution to the company by helping the manager and relieving his precious time to concentrate more on management side.

Going back to the question of who should produce what when one country has an absolute advantage in both commodities and the other country does not have any absolute advantages at all, Ricardo and Torrens realized that they could not solve the question simply by comparing actual cost alone. Here is where the concept of opportunity cost comes in handy and helps greatly solve this very intriguing question. Then, what is opportunity cost?

Opportunity cost, in general, is the amount of sacrifices (costs) that you have to make when limited resources are used for alternatives.

In the present case, opportunity cost is the possible output of one product (either textile or wheat) that you have to give up when you produce another product; using limited resources (labor in this case). Since we only have limited amount of resources available, (i.e. 100 units of labor given to each country), if we produce one product, then, we have to give up another product. Opportunity cost inevitably incurs because we always have a limited amount of resources (money, time, etc). Ricardo and Torrens argued that we should produce a commodity that we have a comparative advantage and then trade each other. **A comparative advantage in this context means an ability to produce goods with a less amount of sacrifice**. Thus, in order to know who has comparative advantage in what commodity and who should produce what commodity, we should compare the opportunity cost (amount of sacrifices that we have to make when we produce the same amount of product) rather than comparing actual cost.

Continuing with the previous example, in order to find the answer for the question who should produce what, we have to calculate and compare opportunity cost of two countries. In order to calculate opportunity cost for comparison between the two countries, we need to elaborate on it more clearly.

In generic term, opportunity cost of A in terms of B indicates how much amount of B we have to sacrifice to produce 1 unit of A. Thus, **the opportunity cost of wheat in terms of textile in this case, means how many yards of textile that we have to sacrifice to produce 1 bushel of wheat**.

Now, from the following information, what would be the opportunity cost of wheat in terms of textile in both countries? Whose sacrifice (in terms of textile) will be less when both countries try to produce 1 bushel of wheat? Suppose the U.S. produced 1 bushel of wheat. This means, the U.S. already used up 4 units of labor out of 5 units, which are needed to produce 1 yard of textile. This means the U.S. has to sacrifice 4/5 yard of textile. When the U.K. produces the same 1 bushel of wheat, they have to sacrifice 1/1 yard of textile. This indicates that when both countries try to produce 1 bushel of wheat, the U.S.'s sacrifice (4/5 unit of textile) is less than that of the U.K. (1/1 yard of textile). In other words, the **U.S. has less opportunity cost of wheat than that of the U.K. This indicates that the U.S. has a comparative advantage in wheat production**. This is why the U.S. should specialize in wheat production. If the U.S. specializes in wheat production, it can minimize the amount of sacrifice in textile production.

Now, in order to find out the answer for the question: who has a comparative advantage in textile, you have to calculate the opportunity cost of textile in terms of wheat (amount of wheat that we have to sacrifice when we produce 1 yard of textile) and compare those between the two countries. You will find that this time the opportunity cost of textile in the U.K. (amount of wheat that U.K. has to sacrifice to produce 1 yard of textile) is less (1/1 bushel) than that in the U.S. (5/4 bushel). Accordingly, the U.K. has less opportunity cost in textile production thereby they have a comparative advantage in textile production.

Thus, the Comparative Advantage theory suggests that the U.S. should specialize in wheat production not because the U.S. has an absolute advantage there but because it has a comparative advantage in wheat production. The U.K. should specialize in textile production because they do have a comparative advantage at least in textile industry even if they do not have any absolute advantages at all in any industry. Even if both U.K. industries are absolutely inferior to the two U.S. industries, still the U.K. textile industry is less inferior compared to the wheat industry when their industries are compared to the two U.S. industries. Here is where their comparative advantage lies.

However, as you can see in the second comparative advantage case, if each country specializes in the commodity in which they have a comparative advantage in, we cannot see the clear benefits. This because even if total world wheat production increases from 17.5 bushels to 25 bushels, the total world textile output decreases from 15 yards to 10 yards. In order to show the clear benefits of the comparative advantage theory, we need a little adjustment. We want to see what will happen to the total world textile output if the U.S. produces the same level of wheat under the Mercantilistic case. This will be presented in case 3 below. If the U.S. produces the previous level of world wheat production under Mercantilistic approach, we will need 70 units of labor (17.5 bushel X 4 labor = 70 labor). If we use the remaining 30 units of labor to produce textile, we can produce 6 yards of textile (30 labor /5 labor = 6 yards). In this case total world textile turns out to be 16 yards of textile and total world wheat production will be 17.5 bushels. We can definitely say that this level of total world output is absolutely better than the total world output under Mercantilistic approach (15 yards of textile and 17.5 bushels of wheat). This proves Ricardo and Torrens point that world output can actually increase if countries specialize based on Comparative Advantage. They prove that we really do not need an absolute advantage to produce the goods. Every country needs to produce a certain product in order to have a comparative advantage. Any country can have a comparative advantage because if they compare domestic industries to foreign industries, they may all be inferior to foreign industries, but at least, a certain industry will be less inferior to the other. That industry will have a comparative advantage. The Comparative Advantage theory proves that even the poorest or least technological developed country can still make a contribution to world output if it specializes in the industry in which it is less inferior. For this reason, this theory is the most powerful theory to advocate and support free world trade.

	US	UK	US	UK	Output
1. Mercantilistic:					
Textile	5/yd	10/yd	10 yds	5 yds	15 yds
Wheat	4/yd	10/bushel	12.5 bush.	5 bush.	17.5 bush.
2. Comparative Advantage:					
Textile			0 yds	10 yds	10 yds
Wheat			25 bush.	0 bush.	25 bush.
3. Comparative Advantage: adjusted case					
Textile	30 labor		6 yds	10 yds	16 yds
Wheat	70 labor		17.5 bush.	0 bush.	17.5 bush.

Factor Proportion Theory (Heckscher-Ohlin Theorem)

Even if the Comparative Advantage theory by Ricardo and Torrens can prove that the world output can increase if countries specialize based on comparative advantage, the theory itself could not provide much information about what commodity a country is likely to have a comparative advantage in.

Two Swedish economists Eli Heckscher and Bertil Ohlin put forward a different explanation of comparative advantage and tried to find an answer to the question. They argued that comparative advantage arises from differences in national factor endowments. By factor endowments they meant the extent to which a country is endowed with such resources as land, labor and capital. Nations have varying factor endowments, and these different factor endowments explain differences in factor costs. It is conceivable that the more abundant a factor, the lower its cost.

Based on this, they developed the Heckscher-Ohlin Theorem, which states that a country will have a comparative advantage in the commodity for which they can use more abundant factors more intensively. For example, in Mexico labor is abundant, so they would have a comparative advantage in the commodity for which they can use more labor more intensively (a labor-intensive commodity). The U.S. is capital abundant so the U.S. is likely to have a comparative advantage in capital intensive products. Therefore each country should specialize in the commodity in which it has a comparative advantage and export the products for which it has a comparative advantage. The Heckscher-Ohlin theorem predicts that countries will export those goods that make intensive use of factors that are locally abundant, while importing goods that make intensive use of factors that are locally scarce. Thus, the Heckscher-Ohlin theorem argues that free trade is beneficial. Unlike Ricardo's theory, the Heckscher-Ohlin theorem argues that the pattern of international trade is determined by differences in factor endowments, rather than differences in productivity.

Leontieff Paradox

Most economists favor the Heckscher-Ohlin theorem more than Ricardo and Torren's comparative advantage theory because it has more simplistic and realistic assumptions. As a result of these merits influence, many empirical tests have been conducted for the Heckscher-Ohlin theorem. One of the most famous studies was the research conducted by Wassily Leontieff (winner of the Nobel Prize) in 1953. Using the Heckscher-Ohlin theorem, Leontieff predicted that since the United States was relatively abundant in capital compared to other nations, the United States would be an exporter of capital-intensive goods and an importer of labor-intensive goods. Quite contrary to his initial prediction, however, he found that the U.S. exports were less capital-intensive than U.S. imports. Since this result was contradictory to the predictions of the theory, it has become known as the Leontieff paradox.

One possible explanation is that the United States has a special advantage in producing new products made with innovative technologies. Such newly introduced products may be less capital intensive than the products that are mature enough for mass production which will require a large amount of capital. Thus, the U.S. may be exporting new innovative products that still require skilled labor intensively and innovative entrepreneurship, such as computer software, while importing mass produced goods that require large amounts of capital. Several recent empirical tests of the Heckscher-Ohlin theorem using data for a large number of countries tend to confirm, the existence of the Leontieff paradox.

Even if classical theories for international trade, such as the Absolute and Comparative Advantage theories, can provide us with some understanding of the international trade patterns, those theories have some limitations when trying to explain the relatively recent international trade patterns as the world economy becomes more globalized. More recently, various production factors such as labor and capital can freely flow from one country to another and technology plays a major role in international trade patterns. Consequently, we have a necessity for the development of a new theory that can explain more recent international trade patterns.

International Product Life Cycle Theory

Raymond Vernon's international product life cycle (PLC) theory of trade proposes that certain types of products go through a cycle that consists of four stages – introduction, growth, maturity, and decline. He also investigates each stage of the product life cycle from four different perspectives; overall demand, technology, production location and US export.

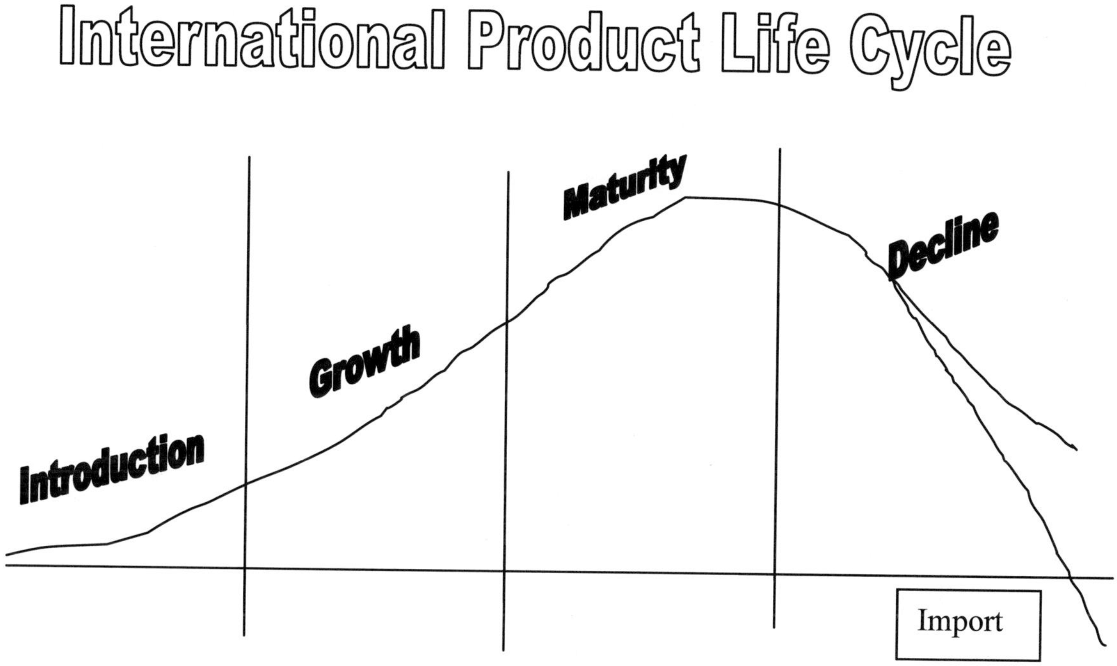

Stage 1: Introduction

Most new products are produced in and exported from the high-income industrial countries such as the U.S. This is the case because of their combined demand conditions, high level of national income, their culture and the level of technology.

Companies develop new products because there is a market for them. This means that a U.S company is most apt to develop a new product for the U.S market. There are two major reasons why most of the innovations happen in the US. First, high level of national income in the U.S. makes it possible for the customers to afford the newly introduced and highly priced products. Another element is the American culture, which receives the new idea relatively well compared to the traditional society. Once a company has created a new product, theoretically it can manufacture that product anywhere in the world. In practice, however, the early production generally occurs in a domestic location so the company can obtain rapid market feedback, as well as save costs on transport.

At the later part of the introduction stage of a product's life cycle, companies may sell a small part of their production to customers in foreign markets who have heard about the new product and actively seek to obtain it. These foreign customers are mostly found in other industrial countries because they have the income to spend on newer products.
The production process is apt to be more labor-intensive in this stage than in later stages. Market feedback dictates that production process must permit rapid changes in product characteristics because the product is not yet standardized. This implies high labor input as opposed to automated production, which is more capital intensive. Furthermore, the capital machinery that is necessary to produce a product on a large scale usually develops later than product technology. It does only when sales begin to expand rapidly enough (stage 2)

to warrant the high development costs of the machines for the new process. The early production is most apt to occur in industrial countries, which have high labor rates.

Stage 2: Growth

As sales of the new product starts growing and the idea of this new product disseminate from the innovating country to other industrialized countries, export from the innovating country increases dramatically during the growth stage. However, at the same time, demand is likely to grow substantially in foreign markets, particularly in other industrial countries. In fact, demand may be sufficient to justify producing in some foreign markets, particularly other industrialized countries, to reduce or eliminate transport charges.

The original producing country will increase its exports in this stage but lose certain key export markets in which competitors commence local production.

Stage 3: Maturity

In Stage 3, maturity, worldwide demand begins to level off, although it may be growing in some countries (developing and less developed countries) and declining in others (industrialized countries). There often is a shakeout of producers such that product models become highly standardize, making cost an important competitive weapon. Longer production runs become possible for foreign plants, which in turn reduce per unit cost for their output. The lower per unit cost creates demand in emerging markets.

The innovating country no longer has a production advantage, because markets and technologies are widespread, There are incentives to begin moving plants to emerging markets and Newly Industrialized Countries (NICS) where unskilled, inexpensive labor is efficient for standardized processes. Exports decrease from the innovating country as foreign production displaces it.

Stage 4: Decline

As a product moves to the decline stage, those factors occurring during the mature stage continue to evolve. The markets in industrial countries decline more rapidly than those in emerging markets, as affluent customers demand ever-newer products. By this time, the product technology (how to produce) and the process technology (how to build the plant) become completely standardized. Thus, cost factors have dictated that almost all production is made in Less Developed Countries where the wage is the cheapest. At this stage, those LDC will export to the declining or small-niche markets in industrial countries. In other words, the country in which the innovation first emerged – and exported from – then becomes the importer.

Limitations of PLC Theory

International product life cycle theory is very powerful and comprehensive theory to explain the relatively recent international trade and FDI patterns simultaneously. However, it also suffers from some criticism. For example, there are many products that never ride product life cycle such as agricultural products. There are many types of products for which shifts in production location do not usually take place.

More recently, regardless of the product type, there has been an increased tendency on the part of MNCs to introduce new products at home and abroad simultaneously as they move from multi domestic to global strategies. Further, MNCs sometimes produce abroad simply to take advantage of cheap production factors such as cheap labor rather than in response to growing foreign markets.

Summary of International Product Life Cycle

	Introduction	Growth	Maturity	Decline
Overall demand	Demand for new products & innovation in the U.S. due to high Income /culture.	Rapid increase in industrial countries	Levels off because of growth in developing countries but decrease in the U.S. & industrial countries	Rapid decline
Technology & labor	U.S. near Monopoly High labor Skills needed	Slightly diffused More capital Input needed	Product technology Standardized Less labor skills needed	Process techn-ology diffused & standardized unskilled labor needed
Production Location	U.S. Innovating Country	Industrialized or developed countries	Lead Developing or Newly Industrialized countries (NICs)	Less developed countries (LDCs)
How U.S. export changes	Start at later half to export	Dramatically increase	Decline at later half	Negative export (import)
Examples	Space, defense, fiber optics	Cars, color TV Computers,	Minor electronics, Simple equipment	Textile, shoes

The Theory of Competitive Advantage (Porter)

Porter, a Harvard researcher through his extensive research collecting data from many industries in many countries, identifies four broad attributes of a nation that can significantly influence the global competitiveness of the firms and constitute the *diamond as below.*

He argues that firms are most likely to succeed in industries or industry segments where the diamond is most favorable. He also argues that the diamond is a mutually reinforcing system. The effect of one attribute is contingent on the state of others.

Those four attributes constituting the famous "Porter's diamond" are shown below.

Four conditions for Global competitiveness
Porter's Diamond

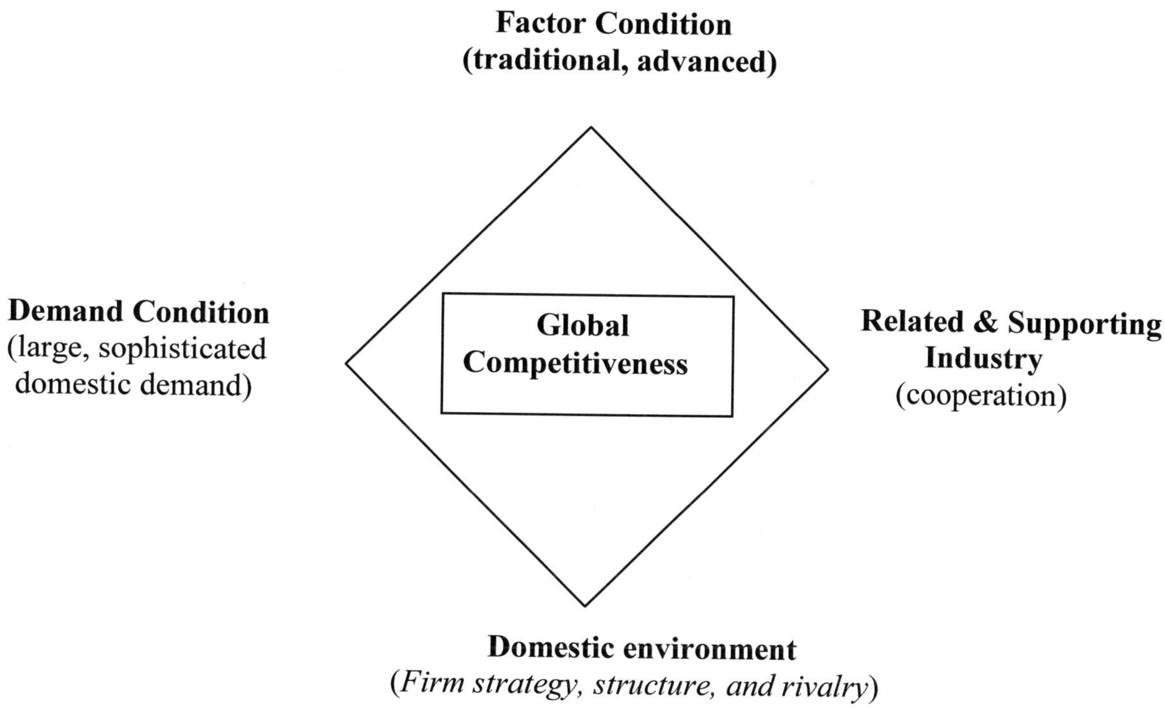

Factor Endowments

As Heckscher-Ohlin theory argues, Porter also believes that factor endowments (how much amount of factor is given to a country) will play a significant role in deciding who is likely have a global competitiveness in what industry. However, Porter distinguishes between **basic factors**; natural factors such as natural resources, climate, location, land, labor and demographics and **advanced (man-made) factors** (e.g., infrastructure, sophisticated and skilled labor, research facilities, and technological know-how). He argues that advanced factors are the most significant for competitive advantage. Primarily because advanced factors can be result of investment by individuals, companies, and government. Consequently, investments made either by the government or private sectors in higher education or infrastructure can improve a nation's global competitiveness.

Demand Conditions

Another factor that Porter emphasizes on is the role and nature of domestic demand. Firms tend to be more sensitive to the needs of their domestic customers than to the ones far away in other countries. Thus, the characteristics of domestic demand are particularly crucial in developing product design and policy formulation. Porter argues that a firm can develop global competitiveness if their domestic consumers are sophisticated and demanding because they will put pressure on local firms to meet high quality standards of product and to produce more attractive products. The example that Porter took to emphasize his point was that Japanese consumers' sophisticated and insatiable demand for better electronic products put a great amount of pressure and helped stimulate the Japanese electronic industry to improve product quality and to introduce more innovation. Another recent example may be found in the wireless cellular phone industry, where sophisticated and demanding local customers in Korea helped push Samsung and LG of Korea where more than 80% of the population possesses one of these equipments. As a result, Samsung and LG together with Motorola are the major players in the global cellular phone equipment industry.

Related and Supporting Industries

Another major attribute for global competitive advantage is the presence of strong and efficient suppliers or related industries that have international competitiveness. The strength of these related and supporting industries can spill over into the main industry, thereby helping it achieve a strong competitive position internationally. The main industry can also coordinate with this strong supporting industry to exchange the idea for new or better products. Technological competitiveness in the U.S. semiconductor industry provided the basis for the U.S. global competitiveness in personal computers and several other technically advanced electronic products. One of the most interesting findings of Porter's study is that successful industries within a country tend to be grouped into clusters of related industries. One such cluster found by Porter is the German textile and apparel sector, which include high quality cotton, wool, synthetic fibers, sewing machine needles, and a wide range of textile machinery. Another example may be Japanese automobile industries which includes top quality suppliers of audio equipment, and small air-conditioner. Such clusters are important, because valuable knowledge can flow between the firms within a geographic cluster, benefiting all the parties within that cluster.

Firm Strategy, Structure, and Rivalry (Domestic Environment)

The last attribute of global competitive advantage in Porter's diamond is what kind of domestic environment they have in terms of strategy, structure, and rivalry of firms within a nation. He argues that the management's orientation and ideology very much influences in what industry a nation is likely to have a global competitiveness. Porter insists that the predominance of engineers in top management at German and Japanese firms give them a more competitive edge in manufacturing processes and product design. In contrast, the predominance of people with finance backgrounds in typical American firms resulted in lack of attention to improving manufacturing processes and product design (e.g., the automobile industry).

Another important issue he raised is the possibility of a strong correlation between vigorous domestic rivalry and the level of global competitiveness in an industry. Fierce domestic rivalry will put more pressure to find better ways to improve efficiency, to reduce cost and to introduce innovation, which will eventually makes them all better international competitors. A typical example that Porter illustrates is the Japanese automobile industry. So many domestic rivals crowded in a small country put a tremendous amount of pressure on them to survive. Thus, they had no choice but to work so hard to survive this fierce domestic competition by developing more efficient small engine, better quality parts and better strategies.

Porter also argues that two external factors can influence his diamond: chance and government. Chance events, such as major breakthrough in innovations, can completely reshape the industry structure and provide the opportunity for one nation's firms to dominate over the firms in other countries. Government, by its way to allocate the resources in prioritizing the policies, can deteriorate or improve national advantage. For example, heavy investments in education or infrastructure can change the quality of advanced factors in a nation and significantly influence the global competitiveness of the country. Another example can be that domestic regulation such as antitrust laws can influence the intensity of rivalry within an industry, hamper the cross sectional cooperation and impede the development of the cluster that can provide a benefit to all the parties involved.

Review Questions

(Mercantilism)
What is the definition of Nation's Wealth under Mercantilism?

What are the major economic doctrines under mercantilism?

What are the potential problems under Mercantilistic approach for international trade?

What is Neo-Mercantilism?

(Absolute Advantage Theory)

What is the definition of a nation's wealth by Adam Smith?

What is the major proposition of Absolute Advantage theory?

What kind of cost should be compared in order to know who has absolute advantage?

(Comparative Advantage Theory)
What kind of cost should be compared in order to know who has comparative advantage?

What is the definition of Opportunity Cost in general?

What does the "opportunity cost of A in terms of B" mean?

How can you calculate the opportunity cost of A in terms of B?

What is Heckscher–Ohlin Theorem and its implication?

What is Leontieff Paradox?

(International Product Life Cycle Theory)

Identify four different phases in IPLC.

What are the four perspectives from which each phase of IPLC is scrutinized?

What are the major characteristics of each phase in IPLC?

What are the major drawbacks and limitations of this theory?

(Theory of Competitive Advantage)
What are the examples of traditional and advanced factors?

What are the four conditions needed to have a global competitiveness?

Practice Questions

Assuming that two countries have same amount of labor to produce steel(unit; MT) and wheat(unit: BS) and each country needs following amount of labor to produce both products ;

	US	FRANCE
Steel	4 labor/MT	5 labor/MT
Wheat	3 labor/BS	5 labor/BS

1. What kind of product France should produce under Absolute Advantage theory?

2. What is the meaning of opportunity cost of wheat in terms of steel ?

3. What is opportunity cost of wheat in terms of steel in US?

4. What is opportunity cost of wheat in terms of steel in UK?

5. Who has comparative advantage in wheat and why?

Answers;

1. None.

2. How much amount of steel we need to sacrifice to produce one bushel of wheat.

3. ¾ MT of steel.

4. 1 MT of steel.

5. US because US can produce wheat with less amount of sacrifice in steel products. (While UK needs to sacrifice 1 MT of steel to produce 1 bushel of wheat, US needs to sacrifice only 3/4MT of steel to produce same 1 bushel of wheat).

CHAPTER 4. FOREIGN DIRECT INVESTMENT THEORIES

The Growth of FDI

For the last couple of decades, there has been a dramatic increase both in the number and volume of FDI in the world economy. The total number and volume of FDI not only increased over the last quarter century, but it also accelerated faster than any other economic activity including the world GDP and International trade.

There are several reasons for this trend. **First**, political environment changes in previous socialistic countries, which allows foreign direct investment in those regions mostly in the form of privatizing their existing facilities to outside investors. The general shift towards democratic political institutions and free market economies has encouraged FDI in the regions such as Eastern Europe, Asia and Latin America.

Secondly, economic growth in so called "emerging markets" in many Asian and Latin countries provided additional business opportunities for many MNCs in those countries and economic integration provided a favorable environment for the member countries' FDI. Besides, during the same period, so many countries created their own forms of mutually exclusive economic integrations such as E.U. and N.A.F.T.A. MNCs have been afraid that the creations of these mutually exclusive economic blocs might establish even higher tariff barriers against the non-member countries. Thus, FDI is viewed by MNCs as a way of avoiding existing and future trade barriers.

Finally, economic deregulation to induce more FDI by the many country's governments and the removal of many restrictions on FDI have all made these countries more attractive to foreign investors. Most of the governments want to induce more FDI because of its positive impact on their balance of payment and job creation. Many developing countries attitudes towards FDI have changed dramatically from negative to positive as they observed successful transformation of several developing countries to newly industrialized countries such as South Korea and Taiwan, who efficiently utilize FDI as an instrument to improve and develop their economies.

Even if FDI is one of the most popular forms of international business lately, FDI is still a relatively new form of International Business. Thus, we are in the process of building a theory for FDI. The practice runs way ahead of the theory in this field and each theory carries a grain of truth and not a single theory is powerful enough to explain the various aspects of Foreign Direct Investment.

The Pattern of FDI inflow (1988- 2008)

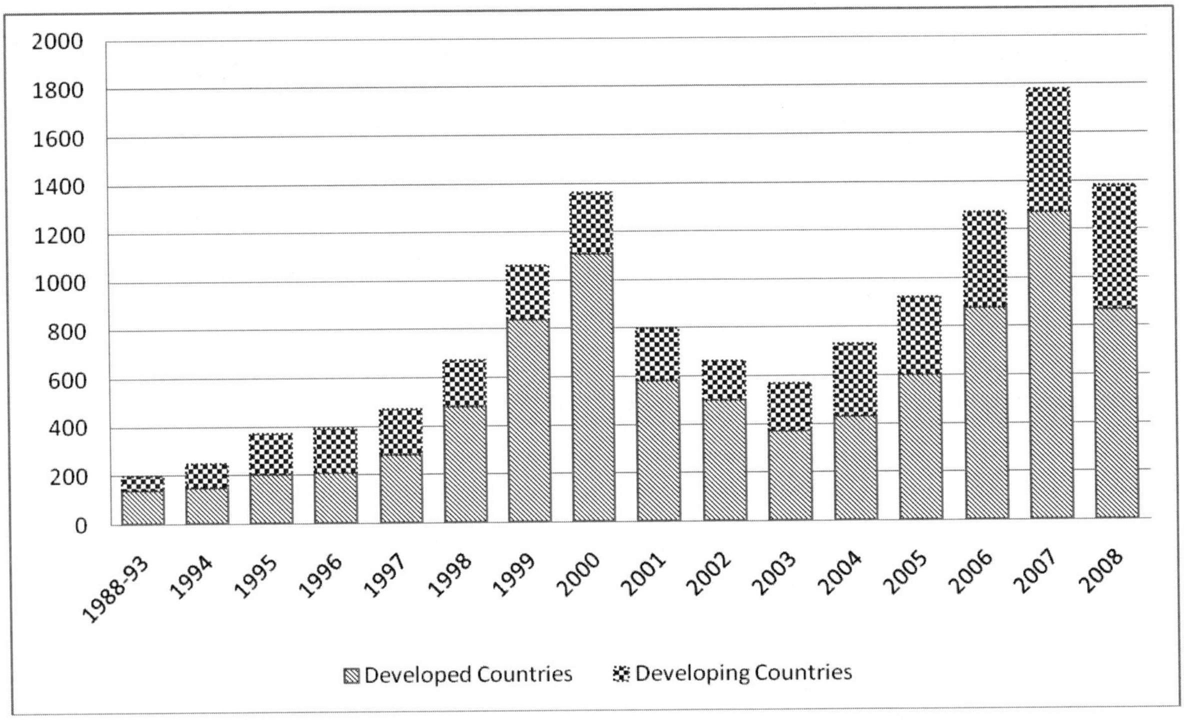

Source: UNCTAD, World Investment Report, 2008.UNCTAD Press release, Global Foreign Investment now in decline, January 2009.

Monopolistic Advantage Theory (Hymer)

Hymer found out, through his empirical study, that the majority of FDI has been made by large size, monopolistic firms rather than small firms under perfect competition. He believes that the reason for this phenomenon is because of the Liability of Foreign investors. **"Liability of foreignness"** means **additional cost or disadvantage of doing business in foreign countries**. When a company makes a FDI in other countries, as a foreign investor who is not familiar with local business environment, it has a definite disadvantage (additional liability as a foreign firm) compared to local firms. In order to overcome this liability/disadvantage and to survive in the local market, the foreign investor must have a special advantage that will enable him to overcome already built-in disadvantages (liability of foreignness). According to Hymer, only the big size monopolistic firms who have special advantages, known as a **monopolistic advantage** (such as economy of scale, superior technology, efficient manufacturing and excellent marketing and managerial skills) can overcome this liability (built-in disadvantage as foreign investor) and survive in foreign markets. This is the reason why the majority of the FDI has been made by large size monopolistic firms rather than small firms under perfect competition.

Imperfect Market Theory (Caves)

Caves, a Harvard economist, focused more on the technology side of MNCs and their ability to produce superior products compared to local firms. He expanded on Hymer's work to show that superior knowledge that MNCs have actually allowed them to produce differentiated products that consumers would prefer to similar locally made goods. This superior technology that enables them to produce differentiated products over the locally made ones would give the MNCs some control over the selling price/market share and give them some advantages over indigenous firms. To support these contentions, he noted that the companies investing overseas were in industries that typically engaged in heavy product research and marketing efforts.

Oligopolistic Theory (Knickerbocker)

Knickerbocker observed that a significant portion of U.S. FDI has been made by Oligopolistic companies such as petrochemical and pharmaceutical companies in a very short period of time in the late 1960's. He recognized this **FDI pattern as a typical oligopolistic reaction**. As we know, some of the major characteristics of Oligopoly (such as automobile and petrochemical industry) are, first, few suppliers control the market, second, they prefer non-price competition than price competition and finally they are very sensitive and defensive of each other. When one firm in the oligopolistic industry starts to do something, everybody will follow because they do not want to lose their competitiveness by not doing what their competitors do. Knickerbocker believes it is the nature of an Oligopoly that triggered intensive FDI by companies in oligopolistic industries for such a short period of time in the late 1960's. For instance, one firm in an oligopolistic industry starts to make a FDI in another country trying to take advantage of growing local market or incentives offered by local government. Then, all other firms in the same oligopolistic industry follow the leader to defend their competitive edge and start to make a FDI in other countries. In *oligopolistic industries* (those with few suppliers), several companies often establish facilities in a given country almost simultaneously within a very short period of time. A more recent example may be the case when eleven different automobile companies decided to make investment in Vietnam between 1991 and 1995. One potential drawback to this theory may be the fact that even if this theory can explain the motivation of the firms in the oligopolistic industries who make FDI in a country following the leader, it cannot explain the motivation of the first investor.

Cross Investment Theory (Graham)

Like Knickerbocker, Graham found out that massive FDI was made by U.S. firms in the late 1960's. However, he also noticed that most of this U.S. FDI actually went to Europe. He later found out that many European MNCs started to make extensive FDI in the U.S. in the early 1970's. He believes that these European MNCs' FDI in the U.S. in the early 1970's was actually their retaliation against the U.S.' initial FDI made in Europe in the late 1960's. Thus, he recognizes that the FDI is a part of retaliatory behaviors among the MNCs with different nationalities. According to Graham, **FDI is viewed by MNCs as an invasion into another country's market**. If they view FDI as a foreign firm's invasion into their home market, they feel threatened by this and try to retaliate by making counter FDI in the country who initiated this investment war. In his view, FDI is a war among the MNCs with different nationalities to protect their own territory.

Capital Market Theory (Aliber)

Capital market theory is an extension of the Imperfect market theory because this theory is developed based on imperfection in foreign exchange market.
If we had a perfect foreign exchange market, we would have purchasing power parity.

Purchasing power parity exists when we can buy exactly the same amount of goods in another country when we convert our currency to their currency.
Imparity condition exists when we can buy more or less amount of goods when we convert one currency to another currency. In reality imparity condition exists most of the time. These theorists propose that the FDI should flow from overvalued currency countries to undervalued currency countries. For your further understanding of the issue, the following illustration is presented:

Time	US	Exchange	UK	
T0	$ 4/Mc	$4 /£1	£1/Mc	Purchasing Power Parity
T1	$4/Mc	$2 /£1	£1/Mc	Purchasing Power Imparity

At the time period T0, the price of one Big Mac in the U.S. is $4 and the price of the same Big Mac in the U.K. is £1. Suppose the exchange rate between dollars ($) and pounds (£) was $4 for £1 at T0. In this case, with $4, we can buy one Big Mac in the U.S. and if we convert $4 to U.K. £ at current rate ($4/£1), you can buy the same Big Mac with £1 in the U.K. Thus, we have purchasing power parity condition at time period T0. However, if the exchange rate changes from $4/£1 to $2/£1, we will lose purchasing power parity because we can buy only one Big Mac with $4 in the U.S. but if it is converted to £ at the rate of $2/£1, you can buy two Big Mac with two £. In this case, we have purchasing power imparity condition between the two currencies and the U.S. dollar ($) is overvalued and the U.K. pound (£) is undervalued. This theory suggests that if we have imparity condition like this due to imperfection in foreign exchange market, MNCs should make a FDI in the U.K. (undervalued currency country) because they can build much bigger plant with same amount of money or they build the same size plant with much less money.

Diversification Theory (Lessard)

Many researchers found out that one of the prime motivations for FDI by MNCs is diversification of the risk, not necessarily maximization of profit.

The risk that they want to diversify by making FDI is the risk of earning fluctuation. If a firm invests solely in one country, if that country's economy is in trouble, the firm will be in trouble also as their earning streams would totally depend on this one country's economy. If you invest all of your money in domestic market, your income stream will totally depend on the performance of the domestic economy. This indicates that your income stream will follow domestic business cycle as you can see below.

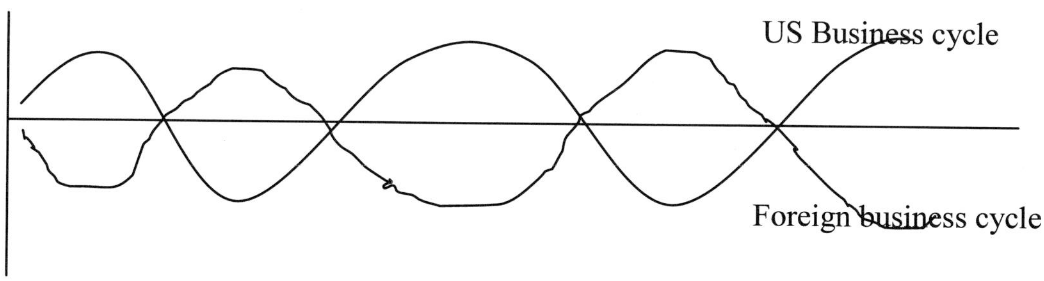

If the domestic economy is booming, your investment will generate a considerable amount of profit. However, if the domestic economy is in trouble, your income from domestic investments will significantly decrease and in case of a firm, it may face a serious cash flow problem during this economic downturn. If a company has a serious cash flow or liquidity problem, then even if it has a large amount of fixed assets or inventory, it can easily go bankrupt by failing to meet the short term debts due date. Most of the firms hate this situation and want to develop a strategy to deal with these types of problems. Thus, the strategy is not to lay all the eggs in one basket. To avoid the potential risk of earning fluctuation, MNCs want to make FDI in other countries where overall business environment such as business cycle, inflation, interest rates and growth rates are very different from domestic market. The benefits of international diversification can also be illustrated by the following graph. The modern portfolio suggests that earning variance from an investment can be significantly reduced if 30 different stocks are added to the portfolio. This type of risk is known as unsystematic risk. **However, even if you add 30 different stocks to the portfolio, there is a type of risk that you cannot diversify, which is known as "systematic risk" or market risk.** We cannot eliminate this type of risk in the domestic market because all the firms in the same country will be exposed to the same business environment and the same business cycle. However, if we expand our investment horizon by making FDI in other countries, where overall business environment is very different, **we can even reduce this systematic risk**.

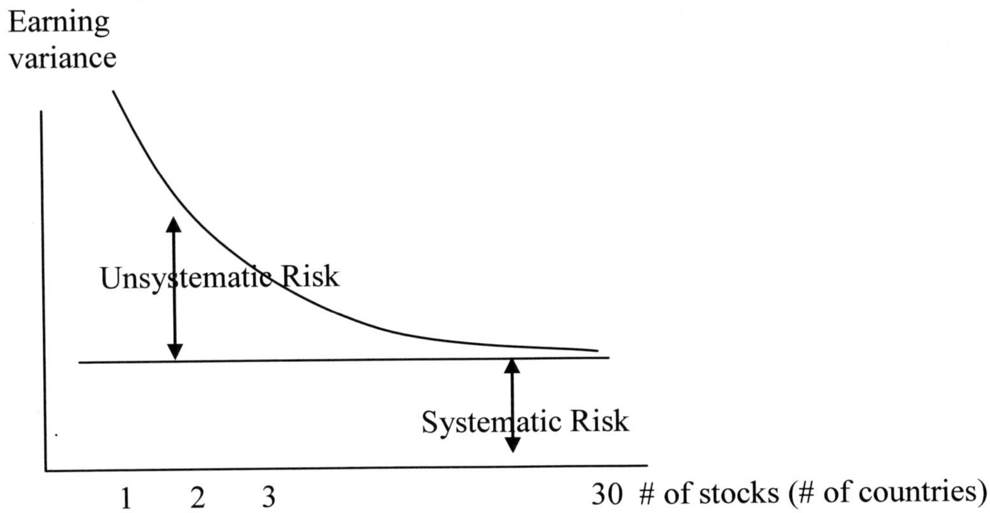

Internalization Theory (Buckely, Casson)

This theory focuses more on the potential problems that MNCs may have when they produce the goods in foreign countries without having their own production facilities.

Internalization theorists believe that imperfection alone is not good enough to justify FDI. Imperfection can provide an opportunity for foreign direct investment but it can still be exploited without having foreign direct investment. As in the case of Nike, MNCs can take advantage of cheap labor in other countries simply by producing their products based on the contract with foreign companies. Then, why do some MNCs still need physical presence such as FDI while there are some other ways available to exploit the cheap labor or other incentives. The reason for that is when you want to produce the goods in foreign countries without having your own production facilities; you will face a series of problems called "Transaction costs". **Transaction cost is a potential problem or difficulty that you may have if you don't have your own production facility in a foreign country.**

If you don't have your own production facility, you have to make a contract with a third party to produce your goods. In this case, you may encounter a variety of problems. For example, when you want to sell through a third party agent or produce your goods based on the contract with a third party, there will be a considerable amount of uncertainties in implementing the contract. Another potential source of problem is how to ensure the quality of the product produced by a third party. Besides, there is a great deal of risk of technology diffusion when contract expires because when you ask a third party to produce your goods, you have to provide detailed specifications. Thus, Internalization theorists believe that one of the prime motivations for FDI by MNCs is to reduce this "transaction cost" (potential source of problems when you hire a third party agent). In order to reduce this transaction cost, MNCs try to **"internalize"** the foreign market, which means **MNCs treat the foreign market (even if it is physically located in foreign country) just like a domestic market by handling everything from production to selling of their products by themselves without hiring a third party agent**.

That is why they need a physical presence in the foreign country in terms of FDI, even if there are several other options to take advantage of in an imperfect market.

Eclectic Theory (Dunning)

John Dunning believes that even if we have many different theories developed for FDI, none of them is powerful and comprehensive enough to explain the various aspects of FDI. He maintains that if a firm wants to invest in foreign countries, it must have three kinds of advantages;

1. Firm (owner) specific advantage– This is the extent to which a firm has or can have tangible and intangible assets not available to other firms such as monopolistic advantages or superior technology that will give competitive edge over the indigenous local firms.

2. Location (country) specific advantage - The host country must be able to offer special advantage over other countries including MNCs home country to invite FDI such as cheap labor or cheap raw material cost or any other incentives that other countries can not offer.

3. Internalization Advantage; MNCs must have strong motivation to be physically present in the target country (in terms of FDI) to minimize transaction cost by internalizing the foreign market rather than producing the goods based on the contract or licensing with the third party (externalizing).

Thus, he decided to synthesize several theories to explain the various aspects of FDI simultaneously. He insists that, **first of all**, the FDI theory must be able to explain the ability of foreign investors to make FDI and to survive when making FDI in other countries. For this end, the firms who want to make FDI must have some **firm specific advantages** (such as monopolistic advantage) which will enable them to overcome the liability of foreignness. For example, Monopolistic advantage theory proposes that only the large monopolistic firms have the ability to survive in foreign countries due to monopolistic advantages that they can enjoy. **Secondly**, if a firm wants to make an investment in a specific country, that country must be able to offer certain country-specific advantages over the other countries. Some countries can offer cheap production factors such as cheap labor or cheaper raw materials. Some countries can offer better business environment such as low tax or simply offer better politically stable environment. **Finally**, to explain the motivation for FDI, Internalization theory was adopted. Under internalization theory, the strongest motivation for MNCs to have FDI is to minimize **"transaction cost"**, which is the potential source of problems and difficulties that you may have when you produce your products through a third party agent without having your own production facilities. By having your own production facilities in the target market through FDI, you can eliminate or at least minimize these potential sources of troubles in the future.

Other strategic motivations for FDI

MNCs can make FDI for many reasons other than the ones described above. Below we discuss how other factors can influence MNCs' decision for FDI.

Trade Restrictions Avoidance

Governments impose restrictions on the goods imported from other countries for many reasons as discussed later in this book. Thus, many companies believe that it may help them to avoid these trade restrictions if they produce their goods inside of the target countries and sell them directly from that plant rather than exporting from here. Many U.S. MNCs have made direct investments in China because Chinese import restrictions prevent their serving that market by exporting to it. Recently, Hyundai is increasing its FDI in the U.S. because of possible import restrictions on its automobile export to this country. Recent creation of mutually exclusive economic blocs such as E.U. and N.A.F.T.A. also accelerates this trend because it is quite obvious that once they establish their own economic bloc, they will discriminate non member countries over member countries by imposing higher tariffs.

Dealing with Nationalistic Attitudes

In many countries, companies have promoted campaigns to persuade the citizens to buy locally produced goods. For example, in the United States, some manufacturers have promoted "Made in the USA" to appeal to consumers by appealing to American patriotism. A recent attempt by Toyota to promote the company's image as a job creator for this country and emphasize on corporate responsibility is a typical example on how to dodge the negative aspects of American nationalism. Many countries also implement a buy local policy by the law which makes it extremely difficult to export the products to those countries. Because of these reasons, many MNCs want to have their own production facilities inside of their target market rather than selling through exportation.

Utilizing Country of Origin Effect

Even if the quality of the products may be identical, consumers often have different quality perception based on the country of origin. Typically, the consumers tend to believe all Japanese electronics have top quality or all Colombian coffees have the best quality. This special effect is often called "country of origin effect" or "made in effect". In some cases, this effect on quality perception is so dramatically different that MNCs want to aggressively take advantage of these perceptual differences by building their own production facilities in the country which is viewed favorably by the consumers.

Reduction of Delivery Risk

Another potential reason for FDI in another country is the fact that many consumers fear that the delivery of foreign made products may be interrupted. For some industries, timely delivery of products, services and replacement parts may be crucial for the successful operation and consumer satisfaction. Particularly, many industrial consumers are often more willing to pay a higher price to a nearby local producer rather than to import from the producer located in other countries. This happens because they are so much concerned about the risk of non-delivery or late delivery due to possible sources of troubles associated with international transportation. Thus, in order to ensure an uninterrupted delivery and to improve the consumer satisfaction, many MNCs actually move their production facilities into the country where their customer is located.

Political Environment for FDI

Host government attitudes toward Foreign Direct investment

How FDI is viewed by the government is very important issue because it can significantly influence the way MNCs operate in the host country. This is true particularly through its impact on host government policy for FDI and how their properties are protected. Political ideology toward FDI has ranged from a very negative and hostile to very positive or laissez-faire approach based on their philosophy about the foreign ownership in the country.

The Nationalistic (Marxist) view

Traditionally, many previous socialist countries and several Latin and Middle Eastern countries used to share this view. Those who share this view believe that FDI by the MNCs is only a tool for exploiting host countries to the exclusive benefit of their capitalist-imperialist home countries. They insist that MNCS exploit the host country and take the profits back to their home country, making no contribution to the host country. Thus, according to this radical thought, no FDI should be permitted, since they can never be instruments of economic development of the host country. Consequently, when a new government steps in with this kind of view, they try to nationalize or confiscate the existing production facilities owned by MNCs and thereby seriously deteriorate the political relationship between the MNCs and host country. Recently, the emergence of several leftist governments in Latin America increases the risk of potential take over of MNCs' production facilities by the government since some of those countries new governments seem to share this view.

The Laissez-faire (Free market) View

The market view argues that the limited resources must be allocated to maximize its efficiency and FDI is the best way to maximize the efficiency of scarce resources globally by combining abundant resources in one country with deficient resources in another

country. For example, FDI by U.S. MNCs in Mexico is the best way to combine the abundant capital of the U.S. and abundant labor of Mexico. By combining these two critical resources of the two countries through FDI, we can maximize the efficiency of the resources globally regardless of national borders. Besides, MNCs can reduce their manufacturing cost significantly and the consumers will be the major beneficiary of FDI.
In addition, the FDI recipient country will have a positive impact on their balance of payment, gain technology, skills, and capital that the MNC will bring in together with FDI. Contrary to the radical view, the free market view argue that FDI is beneficial to both parties; host country and the investor. Most of typical democratic capitalist countries take this view. Probably the most extreme case may be Canada. As the result of their almost non-intervention policy on FDI, almost 80 % of Canadian firms are now own by foreigners.

Practical View

More recently, many countries started to ease the restrictions on FDI and created a more favorable environment for FDI after they witnessed the dramatic economic performance of several countries for the last couple of decades who utilize FDI as an effective instrument to improve their economic condition such as South Korea, Taiwan and Singapore. The desire of governments to facilitate FDI has also been reflected in a dramatic increase in the number of bilateral investment treaties designed to protect and promote investments between two countries. Many countries that previously held radical views started to understand the positive aspect of FDI on their economy through its impact on employment and technology transfer. Accordingly, the radical position starts to wane for the last couple of decades dramatically and yet they are still concerned about possible negative impact of too laissez-faire approach such as losing control of their own economy to foreigners or possible exploitation by MNCs. Because of these reasons, many developing countries started to accept this new hybrid pragmatic approach. They understand the negative and positive aspects of FDI on their economy and try to control FDI in order to maximize their economic well-being and to serve their best national interest. They carefully analyze the costs and benefits of FDI on a case by case basis and only when they believe the benefits exceed the costs, will they permit FDI.

Summary

Ideology	Attitudes about FDI	Host Government Policy
Nationalistic Marxist view	FDI is viewed as an instrument for imperialist to exploit the host country (negative against FDI).	Prohibit FDI Nationalize MNCs facilities in the host country
Laissez-Faire Free market view	FDI is viewed as an important tool to allocate the resources more efficiently. (positive about FDI)	No intervention on FDI

Practical Hybrid view	FDI is viewed as a necessary evil to improve their economy (They see both positive and negative aspects of FDI)	Only when the benefits exceeds the cost, FDI will be permitted.

Calvo Doctrine

The **Calvo Doctrine** is a foreign policy doctrine which holds that jurisdiction in international investment disputes lies with the country in which the investment is located. The Calvo Doctrine thus proposed to prohibit diplomatic (or armed) intervention before local resources were exhausted. An investor, under this doctrine, has no recourse but to use the local courts, rather than those of their home country. The principle, named after Carolos Calvo, an Argentine jurist, has been applied throughout Latin America and other areas of the world.

The doctrine arose from Calvos's ideas, expressed in his *Derecho internacional teórico y práctico de Europa y América* (Paris, 1868; greatly expanded in subsequent editions, which were published in French). Calvo justified his doctrine as necessary to prevent the abuse of the jurisdiction of weak nations by more powerful nations. It has since been incorporated as a part of several Latin American constitutions, as well as many other treaties, statutes, and contracts. The doctrine is used chiefly in concession contracts, the clause attempting to give local courts final jurisdiction and to obviate any appeal to diplomatic intervention.

Investor- State Dispute Settlement

A provision that empowers investors to sue a host government in special tribunals (normally in the third country) to obtain cash compensation for the host government policies or actions that violate the investor's rights rendered under the original agreement (such as "concession agreement"). If the investor wins its case, it can be awarded from the treasury of the host country without the host country's legal intervention. The US government, whenever possible, tries to include this provision in its free trade agreement with other countries to protect the interests of US investors from "Calvo doctrine".

Positive aspects of FDI

Employment Effects

One of the greatest benefits of FDI is that it creates jobs to a host country that would otherwise not be available. This is particularly more true when MNCs make a green-field investment rather than in the case of mergers and acquisitions. When FDI takes the form of a merger or acquisition of an existing local firm in the host economy, the immediate effect may be minimal. However, even in such cases, research suggests that after an initial restructuring, acquired firms tend to hire more employees later. Furthermore, many researchers also found that the firms investing in other countries tend to pay more than their domestic rival firms.

Technology Transfer

A new technology that MNCs will bring into the host country can stimulate economic development and industrialization. Many countries can't afford the huge amount of research and development expenses whose return is not guaranteed anywhere and in many cases, they are not technically capable of developing their own skills and technology to produce a certain type of product. A relatively new technology will help them produce some goods more efficiently and help them reduce expensive importation from other countries or even help them export extra surplus to other countries. This will help them greatly in their economic growth.

Efficient Use of Capital market

FDI can make a positive impact on a host country's economic growth by transferring much needed capital. MNCs can utilize abundant capital internally available and they can also easily access international capital market where they can finance their project with less financing cost. This will enable them to lower their cost significantly.

Balance-of-Payments Effects

As we discussed on balance of payment accounting, incoming FDI will make a positive impact on FDI recipient country's balance of payment condition because this transaction is recorded on the credit side (inflow of money) of the recipient country's balance of payment. This is the reason why so many countries with a balance of payment deficit desperately try to induce more FDI to ease the pain.

Management skills

As Hymer suggested, most FDI is made by large size MNCs who have superior management skills than small indigenous local firms. These excellent managerial skills of the MNCs will be eventually spread to local managers and help local firms improve their efficiency in their operation. The local managers trained in the large foreign MNCs can often help to improve the efficiency of operations in the indigenous firms when these managers are transferred later. Similar benefits may be obtained if the superior management skills of a foreign MNC are transferred to other local suppliers, distributors, and competitors.

Competition effect

As the Monopolistic advantage theory suggests, MNCs can enjoy many special advantages such as economy of scale and superior technology over small indigenous local firms. When an efficient and large size MNC makes an FDI, small local indigenous firms will feel very much threatened by the arrival of this power foreign firms. In order to survive under this additional source of competition and pressure, domestic firms will strive much harder than before and this will eventually help them improve their organizational efficiency and quality of products and services.

The Costs of FDI to Host Countries

Even if FDI can provide a great deal of contribution and make positive impact on the parties involved, there are several problems associated with it.

Adverse Effects on the Balance of Payments

As discussed earlier, initially incoming FDI will make a positive impact on the balance of payment of the recipient country. However, when this investment starts to generate a significant amount of earning and the majority of this earning is repatriated back to the parent company, this will cause an outflow of money and will be recorded on the debit side of the balance of payment of the host country. This situation can deteriorate the balance of payment condition of the host country, which can be quite contrary to what they originally expected. In this sense, FDI can be considered a "Trojan Horse" because initial FDI can help the balance of payment condition of the receiving countries because foreign investors will bring the capital to the countries. However, later on when the foreign investors generate a profit and send the profit back to their parent company, it will result in an outflow of money and thereby generate a negative impact on their balance of payment.

Economic Sovereignty/Autonomy

Some countries' governments are still concerned about inflow of FDI because of possible loss of control and economic autonomy to foreign firms. This is particularly true for key industries such as defense industry, utility industry, energy industry and natural resource extracting industry. The major concern is the risk of important decisions made by foreign firms who do not have any allegiance to the host government or any concerns for the overall well-being of the general public of the host country. Most of the scholars rejects such concerns as groundless and attribute to failure to understand the growing interdependence of the globalized world economy.

Adverse effects on Competition

Even if FDI improves the competitiveness of the local firms as described above, presence and power of the strong foreign firms can stymie the development of small indigenous firms and threaten the survival of them in their own market. Using all the resources available at the parent company, their subsidiary can easily overpower and wipe out small firms in the host country.

Review Questions

Identify three reasons why FDI increased so dramatically for last couple of decades.

What is the "liability of foreignness"?

What are the examples of monopolistic advantages?

What is the major implication of imperfect market?

What are the major characteristics of Oligopolistic industry?

How FDI is viewed under Cross-investment Theory?

What is the definition of purchasing power parity and imparity?

What is the major implication of purchasing power imparity condition on FDI flow?

What kind of risk that MNCs try to diversify under Diversification Theory for FDI?

What is the major motivation for FDI under Internalization Theory?

What is the meaning of Transaction Cost under Internalization Theory?

What is the meaning of Internalization?

Discuss the three theories employed for Eclectic Theory for FDI.

Discuss three different views for FDI.

What are the major benefits and costs of FDI to the host countries?

CHAPTER 5. FOREIGN EXCHANGE SYSTEM

The Gold Standard System

Pegging the value of one country's currency to a certain amount of gold and guaranteeing **convertibility** is known as the gold standard. Gold convertibility means, in theory, citizens can demand their government to convert their currency to the corresponding amount of gold as stipulated by their government and the government has an obligation to do that upon the citizens' request. Even if there was no international agreement or official coordination among the nations, most of the world's major trading nations, including Great Britain, Germany, Japan, and the United States had adopted the gold standard by the late 19th century. For example, under the gold standard system, one U.S. dollar was pegged to 23.22 grains of pure gold and one British pound was pegged to 113 grains of fine gold. This system lasted all the way up to World War I primarily because there were no major political or economic events or turmoil during the period.

<u>Advantages of the Gold Standard System</u>

One of the greatest advantages of the gold standard system is the **stability** in foreign exchange system. Since, under this system, every country's currencies were pegged to a certain amount of gold by the government, the exchange rate was not supposed to fluctuate and thereby we could eliminate uncertainty and volatility in the foreign exchange market. Another great strength of the gold standard was that it could enjoy a **built-in adjusting mechanism** for achieving balance-of-trade equilibrium. For example if country A has a trade surplus, under the gold standard system, it means that there will be a net flow of gold from its trading partner. These gold flows automatically increase country A's money supply due to a strict linkage between money supply and gold stock (gold convertibility). This additional supply of money will eventually cause inflation due to a positive correlation between money supply and price. An increase in money supply will raise overall price level in country A, which will eventually decrease country A's export as their products become more expensive. This will wipe out the original trade surplus that country A had and restore a balance-of-trade equilibrium.

Freely Floating Exchange rate system

Under a pure and clean floating exchange rate system, exchange rates are supposed to be solely determined by market forces (supply and demand) without intervention by the governments.

Advantages of a Freely Floating Exchange Rate System

One of the biggest advantages of having a free floating system is the **flexibility** and **freedom** that a monetary authority can have in their monetary policy. Since there is no stricter and direct linkage between money supply and gold holding, the monetary authority of a country can freely infuse more money whenever their economy needs it. An additional advantage of a freely floating system is that there is **no burden for managing exchange rate**. Under this system, a central bank is not required to constantly maintain exchange rates within specified boundaries. This means that the government does not have to reserve a large amount of foreign currency to defend their exchange rate at a stipulated level. Unlike a fixed exchange system, under a floating exchange system, countries do not have any obligation to maintain their rate at the stipulated level. Under this system, you can let the market decide the rate depending on the supply and demand conditions in the market. Thus, you don't have to spend a large amount of precious foreign currencies simply to keep your exchange rate within a certain boundary. When you have pressure to devaluate your currency for some reason, such as balance of payment deficit, the market will take care of this pressure and your exchange rate will be automatically adjusted (depreciated or appreciated) reflecting the market conditions.

Disadvantages of Freely Floating Exchange Rate System

One of the potential problems under free floating exchange rate system is the fact that the system is **inherently inflationary**. The reason for that is, under floating system, the monetary authorities have much more freedom in implementing monetary policies because there is no more strict linkage between gold holding and money supply. They can provide additional money whenever they need it. Under gold standard system, you can supply additional money only when it is supported by additional gold because they are supposed to maintain gold convertibility. However, in the absence of strict linkage between gold and money supply under free floating system, the monetary authority can freely supply additional money and thereby the system can easily cause inflation because there is no *external discipline* or mechanism to control money supply.

Another serious problem under the free floating exchange rate system is **instability and volatility** in foreign exchange system. There is always the possibility of wide exchange rate fluctuation. Under this system, the exchange rate is supposed to change every day reflecting the supply and demand conditions in the market. However, if there is a big change in demand or supply of one currency, the rate in the market changes dramatically. If we have a very volatile and instable foreign exchange market and the rate changes wildly everyday, the international trader will sense a high level of uncertainty and risk in doing international trade, thereby the international trade will not increase as expected.

Fixed Exchange Rate System (Bretton Woods System)

In a fixed exchange rate system, exchange rates are either held constant or allowed to fluctuate only within very narrow boundaries, such as plus or minus 1% margin around par value. If an exchange rate begins to move too much, governments can intervene to maintain it within the boundary previously stipulated. From 1944 to 1971, exchange rates for all the countries were fixed to the U.S. dollar according to the Bretton Woods agreement (made in Bretton Woods, New Hampshire, 1944). They also agreed to maintain their exchange rate within 1% margin for fluctuation. Another part of the agreement was to fix the value of the U.S. $ as 1/35 ounce of gold. Since all currencies were pegged to the U.S. $, whose value was pegged to a certain amount of gold, the values of all other currencies were indirectly pegged to gold through the U.S. $. Governments intervened in the foreign exchange markets to ensure that exchange rates drifted no more than 1 percent above or below the initially set rates.

Unfortunately, the value of the anchor currency (U.S. $) of this system became very weak as the Balance of Payment conditions of the U.S. deteriorated so dramatically in the late 1960's. Three elements can be attributed to this weakening of the dollar value. First, U.S. exports started to shrink significantly since the late 1960's. Secondly, the amount of government expenditure to support the Vietnam War increased astronomically. Finally, U.S. MNCs started to make extensive FDIs, which caused a massive outflow of money from the U.S. No country wanted to have their assets tied in terms of the dollar because of this weakened value of the anchor currency ($). They started to dump their dollar and replace their assets with other currencies. The chaos continues even if the U.S. took several measures to fix the problems.

As of December 1971, a conference among representatives of various countries concluded with the Smithsonian Agreement, which called for the devaluation of the U.S. dollar by about 8 percent against other currencies. In addition, boundaries for the currency values were expanded to within 2.25 percent above or below the rates initially set by the agreement. However, the "dollar crisis" continued, and as of February 1973, the dollar was again devalued. By March 1973, most governments of the major countries were no longer attempting to maintain their home currency values within the boundaries established by the Smithsonian Agreement.

Advantages of Fixed Exchange Rate System

One of the biggest advantages that we can have under fixed system is the **stability** in the exchange market. The rate doesn't change that much every day. Even if it changes a little bit, we know that the rate is still supposed to be maintained between the narrow boundaries already set up by the government. Thus, MNCs have a pretty good idea about what kind of rate they will have in the future. Under a fixed exchange rate environment, the managerial duties of an MNC are less difficult that the floating system.

Disadvantages of Fixed Exchange Rate System

Under this system, each country has an obligation and **burden to maintain their exchange rates at the stipulated level or within the range pre-determined**. However, when they start to build up a huge amount of balance of payment deficit, there will be a great pressure in the market to depreciate their currency. In this case, in order to defend their fixed rate and to eliminate the devaluatory pressure, they need to buy out their own currency in the market (to create an artificial demand for their own currency). In order to buy out their own currency, they have to pay for that in terms of foreign currency that they hold. In other words, under this system, in order to defend their fixed rate, **they may have to use a large amount of foreign currency** that they hold. For many countries that already have a serious balance of payment deficit, this can be a serious burden to carry. **If they fail to deal with this devaluatory pressure for lack of enough foreign currency reserve**, the whole system will break down and the country will suffer a **chaotic situation** as witnessed in recent currency crisis in many Asian and Latin countries in the late 1990s.

Jamaican Agreement (1976)

After a serious turmoil in foreign exchange system in early 1970s, finally, all the IMF (International Monetary Fund) member countries met together in 1976 at Jamaica to find out the solution to deal with the chaotic situation and entered into Jamaican Agreement. Under this agreement, they Bretton Woods system was officially abolished and IMF members countries were allowed to have their own system. As the result of this, some countries decided to maintain **the fixed exchange system** by pegging their currency to another currency such dollar and British pound and maintain the rate within very narrow margin for fluctuation. Some countries decided to go back to a floating exchange system. However, the system that decided to have this time is not exactly the same floating system we had before. Instead of having a "clean floating" system we had before where the exchange rate was solely decided by supply and demand in the market, they decided to have a **managed (or dirty) floating system** where a government frequently intervene in foreign exchange market . This exchange system lays somewhere between fixed and frees floating system. It resembles free floating system in the sense that exchange rates are allowed to fluctuate on a daily basis and yet it is similar to the fixed exchange system in the sense that governments intervene in the market to prevent their currencies from moving too much in a certain direction or to maintain their exchange rate within optimal ranges. These countries include India and Russia. Some countries decided to have an **independent floating system**. This system may be the closest to the "clean floating" system in the sense that the countries who adopted this system rarely intervene in foreign exchange market and basically let the market decide the exchange rate with no clear direction. These countries intervene in foreign exchange market only to prevent the undue fluctuation in exchange rate. These countries include Canada, US and Japan. Even if there are a few more variations, foreign exchange systems of the most of the IMF countries fall into one of these three types.

Since every country has its own right to select their foreign exchange system under Jamaican Agreement, some countries switch their foreign exchange system to another one occasionally. For example, China used to have a fixed exchange rate system for a long time. However, they changed it to a "crawling peg", where their pegged exchange rate has been periodically adjusted within 0.5 % margin by the government . Most recently, they announced that they would go back to the fixed exchange system in 2010.

Government intervention in open market

Government Intervention

Each country has a government agency that may intervene in the foreign exchange markets to control its currency's value. In the United States, for example, the government agency whose duty is to maintain the exchange rate at the optimal rate is the Federal Reserve Bank (the Fed). Using a special fund called "Exchange Rate Stabilization Fund", the Fed constantly intervenes in Foreign exchange market by buying or selling foreign currencies and U.S. dollar in the foreign exchange market. In order to maximize the effect of foreign exchange market intervention, we need to coordinate with other countries' agencies to control the exchange rate.

Direct Intervention

The Fed's direct method of intervention to force dollar depreciation is to exchange dollars that it holds as reserves for other foreign currencies in the foreign exchange market. This so-called "flooding the market with dollars" places downward pressure on the dollar.

This will require the Fed to buy foreign currencies because if you want to buy foreign currency, you will pay in U.S. dollar. This will increase the supply of dollar and thereby decrease the value of the U.S. dollar. If the Fed desires to strengthen the dollar, it can exchange foreign currencies for dollars in the foreign exchange market, thereby placing upward pressure on the dollar. This will require the Fed to sell foreign currency they hold because if you sell foreign currency, you will be paid in dollar, which will reduce the supply of dollar and thereby increase the dollar value. To make the direct intervention more effective, a coordinated effort among central banks is needed.

Indirect Intervention

The Fed can also influence the dollar's value indirectly by manipulating some other factors rather than directly involve in the foreign exchange market. For example, the Fed could lower interest rates by increasing the U.S. money supply (assuming that inflationary expectations are not affected). Lower U.S. interest rates tend to discourage foreign investors from investing in the U.S. securities, thereby reducing demand for dollar and placing downward pressure on the value of the dollar. Otherwise, the Fed could increase interest rates by reducing the U.S. money supply. The higher interest can stimulate foreign investment in U.S. securities, thereby creating more demand for dollar and placing upward pressure on the value of the U.S. dollar. It has commonly used this strategy along with direct intervention in the foreign exchange market.

Pegged Exchange Rate System

Some countries still use a pegged exchange system, which means their home currency's value is pegged to a foreign currency such as the U.S. dollar or British pound or to some unit of account. Those countries believe that stability in exchange rate to a specific currency is vital to operate their economy and they want to stabilize their economic relationship with a certain country. Many small African countries still peg their currencies to their previous mother countries because maintaining economic ties through trade with those countries are so crucial for their economic survival. Many Asian countries such as Malaysia and Thailand used to peg their currency's value to the dollar. However, during the Asian currency crisis in the late 1990's, they were unable to maintain the peg and allowed their currencies to float against the dollar.

Review Questions

(Gold Standard System)
What are the major contents of Gold standard System?

What is gold convertibility?

Discuss the advantages and disadvantages of Gold Standard system.

What is "Built-in Adjustment Mechanism" available under this system?

(Flexible: Free Floating System)
How money is supplied under this system?

How exchange rate is decided under this system?

What are the advantages and disadvantages of the system?

(Fixed Exchange System)
What are the major components of the system?

Discuss the advantages and disadvantages of the system.

What are the problems we experienced under Breton Woods System.

Discuss the three major forms of foreign exchange system adopted under Jamaican agreement.

What is managed (dirty) floating system?

Discuss open market intervention in a dirty floating system.

What kind of action a government can take to stop to depreciate or appreciate their own currency in the market?

CHAPTER 6. EXCHANGE RATE DETERMINATION THEORIES

At the most fundamental level, exchange rates are determined by the demand and supply of one currency in the market. For example, if Japan wants to buy more U.S. products, the demand for dollars will rise and this additional demand will appreciate the dollar value. However, if Americans want to buy more Japanese products, the demand for Japanese yen will increase. This additional demand for Japanese Yen will appreciate the Yen value and depreciate the dollar value vis-à-vis Japanese Yen. However, while the demand and the supply in the market explain the determination of exchange rates at more fundamental level, there are many other factors that could significantly affect the relative value of one currency vis-à-vis that of another currency. The above case does not provide us the whole picture of how exchange rates behave. Thus, in this chapter, we will review several theories which were developed to understand how exchange rates are determined. If we understand how exchange rates are determined, we may be able to forecast exchange rate movements in the future. The factors that determine exchange rates are complex, and there is no one comprehensive and powerful theory that can explain exchange rate behaviors. Nonetheless, most economic theories of exchange rate movements seem to agree that three factors have an important impact on future exchange rate movements in a country's currency: the country's price inflation, its interest rate, and market psychology.

Prices and Exchange rates

Implication of the Law of One Price

The Law of one price postulates that in a perfect market free of transportation costs and restrictions such as visible and invisible trade (such as tariffs), identical products must be sold for the same price in different countries when their price is expressed in terms of the same currency.

The Purchasing Power Parity Theory

The theory of purchasing power parity in its simplest form argues that the exchange rate must change so as to equate the prices of goods in both countries. **The purchasing power parity condition exists if one can buy exactly same amount of goods and services in a foreign country when he converts his currency to that foreign currency.** If the law of one price is true for all goods and services, **purchasing power parity** must be maintained between the two currencies. The *Purchasing Power Parity Theorist (PPP)* states that exchange-rate should change in the direction to maintain purchasing power parity when two countries have two different inflation rates. When two countries have different inflation rates during the same period, eventually, purchasing power parity will be lost and the parity condition will be lost. In order to restore the parity under this kind of condition, foreign exchange rates should move in the direction to offset inflation rate differentials and to restore purchasing power parity. The following illustration can help you understand the purchasing parity condition more clearly.

EXAMPLE 1:

Assume the cost of a Big Mac in the US and the UK is as following:

	Time Period 0	Time Period 1	
US	$2/BigM	$4/BigM	**100% Inflation**
Ex Rate	$2/£	$2/£	
UK	£1/BigM	£1/BigM	**0% Inflation**

Time Period 0 = Base period
Time Period 1 = FUTURE

In this case, at the time period 0, Purchasing Power Parity exists because a Big Mac costs the same in both U.K. and U.S. (Ex Rate = $2/£). However, at Time Period 1 Purchasing Power *Imparity* exists because now it takes $4 to purchase a Big Mac in U.S., but still only £1 to purchase that same Big Mac in U.K., with no change in the exchange rate yet.

To restore PPP at Time Period 1, the exchange rate should change from $2/L1 to of $4/£1, 100 % change, which is equivalent to the inflation rate differentials between the two countries. (US; 100% - UK 0% = 100%)

Thus, the proposition of this theory is that the % change in exchange rate, which is required to maintain the purchasing power parity, should be approximately equal to inflation rate differentials between the two countries. However, **the direction for change is opposite**, which means the higher inflationary country's currency should be devaluated and lower inflationary country's currency should be appreciated.

In summary, the theory suggests that the magnitude of the change in exchange rate needed to restore PPP is equivalent to the inflation rate differentials between the two countries but the suggested direction for change is opposite. In the example above, the U.S. dollar should be depreciated by 100 % (equivalent to inflation rate differences) change in opposite direction (higher inflationary country's currency to be devaluated). This means exchange rate should change from $2/£ to $4/£.

The mathematical presentation of PPP is as follows:

$$\% \text{ change in Ex Rate} = \frac{St - So}{So} = Ius - Iuk$$

St = the future exchange rate,
So = base (current) exchange rate,
Ius = U.S. inflation rate,
Iuk = U.K. inflation rate.

We can rewrite the above equation as below to find out the formula to predict the future rate St:

$$St = So\,(Ius - Iuk) + So$$

EXAMPLE 2;

Assume,

Ius = 20%,
Iuk = 10%,
So = \$2/£

Then, the future exchange rate (St) is;

$$St = 2\,(20\% - 10\%) + 2$$

St = \$2.20/£ (\$ depreciated by 10%)

Since the U.S. inflation rate has gone up versus the U.K. inflation rate, the U.S. dollar would depreciate. In this example it depreciates by \$.20 or 10% [(2.20 – 2.00)/2.00 X 100].

This PPP theory is intuitively appealing because when inflation goes up in a country it means that overall prices in that country are higher than other country. When overall prices in a country go up, this country loses its price competitiveness in the international market, thereby, its export will decline, which will contribute to its Balance of payment deficit. And this will drive down the value of its currency.

Even if PPP theory suffers some drawbacks and limitations, the PPP theory is quite useful to predict future exchange rate particularly under floating exchange rate system and very valid over the long term period.

The International Fisher Effect (IFE)

The relationship between interest and inflation was originally defined by Irvin Fisher. Fisher effect theory tells us that interest rate reflect expectations about likely future inflation rate. In the countries where inflation is expected to be high, interest rates also will be high since investors want compensation for the decline in the value of their currency. Thus, interest rates always reflect expected inflation rates in a country. *International Fisher Effect* proposes that since expected inflation rate is already reflected in interest rates, it is the interest rate that will directly influence exchange rate rather than inflation rate.

The International Fisher Effect in its simplest form argues that the future spot rate should move in an equal amount but a different direction to the interest differentials between the two countries. When two countries have different interest rates, it will inevitably cause interest arbitrage between the two countries. In other words, capital will fly from low interest countries to high interest countries to take advantage of interest differentials between the two countries. In order to deter this interest rate arbitrage by equating the effective rate of return (rate of return adjusted after exchange rate) between the two countries, exchange rate should move in the direction to offset and nullify the interest rate differentials between the two countries, and the % change in an exchange rate must be approximately equal to interest rate differentials (Versus inflation rate differentials in PPP Theory). Mathematical illustration of the simple version of this theory can be seen below;

$$\%\text{ change in Ex Rate} = \frac{St - So}{So} = Rus - Ruk$$

So = current exchange rate,
St = future exchange rate,
Rus = interest rate of US,
Ruk = interest rate of UK.

The above equation can be rearranged as shown below to find out the formula to predict future rate St:

$$St = So\,(Rus - Ruk) + So$$

EXAMPLE;

Assume,

Rus = 10%,
Ruk = 20%,
So = \$2/£,

Then;

$$St = \$2\,(.10 - .20) + \$2$$

$$St = \$1.80/£$$

In this example, the U.S. dollar appreciates by \$.20 or 10%.

Original version of International Fisher Effect

The original version that leads to the simple version discussed above is illustrated below;

Assuming that;

X= \$ amount of principal
ef= effective rate from foreign investment,
rf= nominal foreign interest rate
rh= nominal home interest rate
So= current spot rate
St= future spot rate,
%S= % change in exchange rate = $\frac{St-So}{So}$

Using the above terms, we can calculate the effective rate of return from foreign investment shown below;

Return from Foreign Investment: $X(1+ef)=\frac{X\,(1+rf) \times St}{So}$ ← $\left[\frac{St}{So} = \frac{So}{So} + \frac{St-So}{So}\right]$
(principal & interest in \$)

$= 1 + \%S$

We replace $\frac{St}{So}$ in above equation with $1 + \%S$

Then, we can rewrite above equation as $X(1+ef)= X(1+rf)(1+\%S)$ -- (1)

Solve (1) for $ef = (1+rf)(1+\%S) - 1$ ---(2)

To find out %S that will equate effective rate of return from foreign investment (ef) to domestic return (rh):

We set $ef = (1+rf)(1+\%S) - 1 = rh$ --------------- (3)

Then, we solve equation (3) for %S (% change in future spot that will equate the effective return from foreign investment to domestic return)

Thus, % change needed to equate the effective return from domestic return (%S) would be;

$$\%S = \frac{1+rh}{1+rf} - 1 = \frac{rh - rf}{1+ rf} = rh - rf \text{ (approximately)}$$

$$\%S = \frac{St - So}{So} = rh - rf,$$

In order to forecast future spot rate (St), we need to solve the above equation for

$$St = So\,(rh-rf) + So$$

The Fisher Effect

The original Fisher Effect defines the relationship between the nominal interest rate and the inflation rate. It holds that the nominal interest rate consists of two components; one is a real interest and the other one is an expected rate of inflation. The nominal interest rate need to incorporate an inflation premium that is sufficient enough to compensate lenders or investors for an expected loss of purchasing power. Thus, nominal rate will increase when people expect high inflation but when they don't expect high inflation, nominal interest will decrease.

Interest Rate Parity Theory

The Interest Rate Parity theory postulates that the difference between a forward rate and spot rate equals the difference between a domestic interest rate and a foreign interest rate. When there are different interest rates between two countries, it is very likely that investors may try to do interest arbitrage. When an investor in country A observes that the interest rate in country B is higher than that of his own country, s/he may want to invest in country B converting his own currency to that of country B. However, s/he should also consider the risk of possible loss due to exchange fluctuation at the time when s/he needs to convert his/her invested amount back to his/her own currency at the maturity. To cover this potential risk in the future, it is very likely that the investor will make a forward sell contract for the amount of principal and interest simultaneously with his/her initial investment in foreign country (covered interest arbitrage). IRP theorists believe that the forward rate not the future spot rate will be influenced by the interest differentials between the two countries, That's why they argue that the spread between a forward rate and a spot rate should be equal but opposite in sign to the interest differentials between the two countries. According to the IRP theory, in order to deter covered interest arbitrage, forward rate should move in the direction to equate effective rate of return from foreign investment to domestic return.

<u>Proposition</u>: % premium or discount in forward rate must be approximately equal to interest rate differentials between the two countries.

Assuming;

X= $ amount of principal
ef = effective rate of return from foreign investment
rf = nominal foreign interest
So = current spot rate
Ft = FWD rate
%F = annualized % premium/discount in Forward rate

Using the above terms, we can calculate the effective return from foreign investment in case of covered interest arbitrage as shown below:

*note that the exchange rate to be applied in case of converting back to original currency is Ft (forward rate not future spot rate).

Effective Return from foreign investment: $X(1+ef)=\frac{X(1+rf) \times Ft}{So}$
(principal and interest)

$$\left\{\frac{Ft}{So} = \frac{So}{So} + \frac{Ft-So}{So}\right\} = 1 + \%F$$

We can rewrite the above equation replacing $\frac{Ft}{So}$ with $1 + \%F$ as below;

$$X(1+ef) = X(1+rf)(1+\%F) \text{----- } (1)$$

To find out the ef (effective rate of return from foreign investment),

Solve (1) for $ef = (1+rf)(1+\%F) - 1$ -----(2)

To find out the annualized % premium or discount in FWD rate (%F) that will equate <u>ef</u> to domestic return (rh),

we set $ef=(1+rf)(1+\%F) - 1 = rh$ ------------------- (3)

and then solve (3) for %F (ann. % prem/disc in forward rate);

$$\% F = \frac{1+rh}{1+rf} - 1 = \frac{rh - rf}{1+ rf} = rh - rf \text{ (approximately)}$$

We can rewrite the above relationship as shown below to calculate equilibrium forward rate (Ft) using IRP theory;

$$\% F = \frac{Ft - So}{So} \times \frac{12}{n} = rh - rf,$$

We can solve the above equation for Ft (equilibrium forward rate);

$$Ft = So(rh - rf) \times \frac{n}{12} + So$$

Efficient Market Theory

If foreign exchange market is efficient, all information will be immediately reflected in the forward rate. Then, forward rate will be the unbiased predictor of the future spot rate. If forward rate truly reflects future spot rate, then % premium or discount in forward rate should be equal to the % change in future spot rate. This relationship can be written mathematically as shown below;

$$\frac{Ft - So}{So} = \frac{St - So}{So}$$

(% Premium/discount in forward rate) (% change in spot rate)

If the above relationship (equation) holds,

Then Ft = St

Synthesis of Exchange rate determination theories

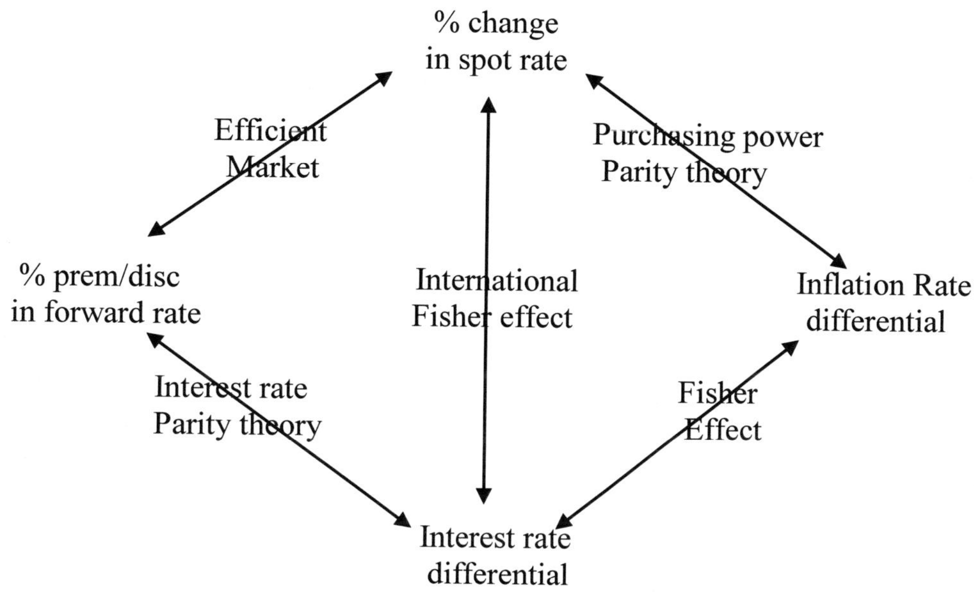

Exchange Rate Forecasting

Forecasting Techniques

The numerous methods available for forecasting exchange rates can be categorized into four general groups: (1) technical, (2) fundamental, (3) market-based, and (4) mixed.

Technical Forecasting

Technical forecasting uses historical exchange rate data to predict future values. Technical forecasting of exchange rates is similar to technical forecasting of stock prices. When they use this method, what they try to do is to find out some systematic patterns in exchange rate movement from the past historical data. If the pattern of currency values over time appear random, then technical forecasting is not appropriate.

This method appears to be widely used by speculators who frequently attempt to capitalize on day-to-day exchange rate movements. With the abundance of technical models existing today, some are bound to generate speculative profits in any given period. Speculators using technical exchange rate forecasting often incur large transaction costs due to frequent trading. In addition, it can be time-consuming to monitor currency movements in the search of any systematic pattern. From the corporate point of view, use of technical forecasting may be limited in that it typically focuses on the near future, which is not that helpful for developing corporate policies. Also, it rarely provides point estimates or a range of possible future values, as pointed out by Goodman. Because technical analysis will not typically estimate future exchange rates in precise terms, it is not, by itself, an adequate forecasting tool for financial managers of MNCs.

Fundamental Forecasting

Fundamental forecasting is based on fundamental relationships between economic variables and exchange rates. When this method is used, a statistical model is developed that contains several economic variables that can potentially influence the future exchange rate.

Example:
For simplicity, assume the firm's forecast for the Canadian dollar is dependent on only two factors that affect the pound's value:

1. Inflation in the U.S. relative to inflation in Canada.
2. Income growth in the U.S. relative to the income growth in Canada. (measured as a percentage change).

The first step is to determine how these variables have affected the percentage change in the pound value based on historical data. This is commonly achieved with regression analysis. The independent (influential) variables may be set up as follows:

1. Previous quarterly percentage change in the inflation differential (U.S. inflation rate minus Canadian inflation rate), referred to as I_{t-1}.
2. Previous quarterly percentage change in the income growth differential (U.S. income growth minus Canadian income growth), referred to as Y_{t-1}.

The regression equation to predict Canadian Dollar (CD) can be defined as

$$CD_t = b_0 + b_1 I_{t-1} + b_2 Y_{t-1} + \mu_t$$

where b_0 is a constant, b_1 measures the sensitivity of CD_t to changes in I_{t-1}, b_2 measures the sensitivity of CD_t to changes in Y_{t-1}, and μ_t represents an error term.

Market-Based Forecasting

Market-based forecasting is the method to predict the future rate based on all the information currently available in the market. For example, there will be a conference among the major economic powers in near future to discuss the exchange rate of Chinese currency (Yuan). They are expected to put pressure on the Chinese government to appreciate their currency. Then, it is most likely that the Chinese Yuan will appreciate sooner or later. The most frequently used information source available in the market is the forward rate since the forward rate reflects all the currently available information about the future exchange rate and it is the market's best estimation of future rate as of today.

Mixed Forecasting

Since no single forecasting technique has been found to be consistently superior to the others, some MNCs may prefer to use a mixed forecasting method, which is a combination of the above three methods already discussed. Various forecasts for a particular currency value could be developed using several forecasting techniques. Each of the techniques used could be assigned weights in such a way that the weights total 100 percent, with different weights for different techniques based on their reliability. The actual forecast of the currency by the MNC would be a weighted average of the various forecasts developed.

Forecasting Services

Several consulting firms, including Business International, Conti Currency, Predex, and Wharton Econometric Forecasting Associates start to provide services to meet the MNCs necessity to forecast exchange rate. In addition, some large investment banks such as Goldman Sachs and commercial banks such as Citibank offer forecasting services. Many forecasting services use at least two different types of methods to forecast and then determine the weighted average of the forecasts. Some forecasting services, such as Capital Techniques, FX Concepts, and Preview Economics, focus on technical forecasting, while other services, such as Corporate Treasury Consultants Ltd. and WEFA, focus on fundamental forecasting. Many services, such as Chemical Bank and Forexia Ltd., use both technical and fundamental forecasting. In some cases, the technical forecasting techniques are preferred by the forecasting firms for short-term forecasts because its ability to give some information about the timing of the exchange movement. Fundamental techniques are favored for long-term forecasts because of its more scientific approach and ability to tell the magnitude of exchange rate changes. However, given the recent volatility in foreign exchange markets, it is quite difficult to forecast any currency values accurately no matter what kind of methods or services is used. Thus, the responsibility of MNCs' financial manager is rather how to evaluate the accuracy of the provided services than actually developing a forecasting model.

Review Questions

(Purchasing Power parity)
What are the exact meanings of purchasing power parity and imparity?

What is the proposition presented by Purchasing Power Parity theory?

If PPP theory holds, how exchange rate is supposed to change?

How can you calculate an equilibrium exchange rate in future if PPP theory holds?

(International Fisher Effect Theory)
What is interest arbitrage?

What is the proposition presented by International Fisher Effect Theory?

If IFE theory holds, how exchange rate is supposed to change?

How can you calculate an equilibrium exchange rate in the future if IFE theory holds?

(Exchange rate forecasting methods)
Identify four different methods to forecast exchange rate and discuss the advantages and disadvantages of each method.

Practice Questions

1. We have following information.
   US exp. inflation: 50% UK exp. inflation: 30%
   The current exchange rate: $ 3/£
   Assuming Purchasing Power Parity theory holds, what will be the equilibrium future rate?

2. We have following information.
   US interest rate: 20% Mexico interest rate:30%
   The current exchange rate: $0.20/peso
   Assuming International Fisher Effect theory holds, what would be the equilibrium future rate?

Answers: 1) $3.60/£ 2) $0.18/peso

PART B: THE ENVIRONMENT FOR INTERNATIONAL BUSINESS

CHAPTER 7. POLITICAL AND ECONOMICAL ENVIRONMENT

Political System

The business environment in a foreign country is very different from domestic business environments. One of the major factors that contribute to such a different business environment in a foreign country is the political system.

A political system is supposed to integrate all parts of society into one sustainable operating political unit. A major challenge of any political system is to bring different groups of people together and develop an allegiance to the unit. A country's choice of political system significantly influences the way business is conducted domestically and internationally. Theoretically, any political unit has two choices for their political system even if there is a wide variety between these two systems. One is democracy and at the end of the political spectrum, there is the totalitarian system. MNCs normally prefer democracies because democracies usually allow more economic freedom and ensure individual rights including ownership of private properties.

Democracy

The ideology of modern democracy has been inherited from the ancient Greeks, who believed all citizens should be equal and should enjoy freedom and participate in the political decision making process. However, the complexity of the modern societies and sheer increases of the total population made it impractical for citizens to get directly involved in the decision-making process. Accordingly, many countries started to adopt different variations of democracy, in which citizens elect representatives to make decisions on behalf of them rather than they directly participate in the decision making process. Most of the contemporary democratic systems share the following elements.

1. A participation in the political decision-making process.
2. Freedom of opinion, expression, press, and religion.

3. Majority ruling.
4. Less internal and external control on information flow.
5. An independent/fair court system (to ensure fair trial).
6. A relatively open society with equality among the citizens

The Freedom House survey observed that there were 117 electoral democracies in 1998, more than double the number of countries that were called democracies in the early 1970s. Even if democracy is one of the most popular forms of political system since the French revolution, as Winston Churchill once called, democracy can be one of the worst forms of government because of its inefficiency and difficulties to have a consensus in the decision making process. Another problem that international business managers have to deal with is a new type of democracy that has emerged since the early 1970s, which are characterized by its frangibility and instability. Many South East Asian, Latin and Eastern European countries are typical examples. Their instability is typically derived from internal fragmentation and division between the different interest groups, different regions, different ethic groups and strong influence still exercised by militaries. It is interesting to watch how these newer forms of democracies would eventually develop in terms of political freedom and civil liberties.

Totalitarianism

At the other end of the political spectrum, there is a system called totalitarianism. Totalitarian governments can take many different forms. In theocratic totalitarianism, religious leaders are also the political leaders. A typical example of this type of totalitarians is some Islamic countries in Middle East such as Iran. Another type of totalitarianism is secular totalitarianism. In this type of totalitarianism, the government often controls the people through military power. Examples of this form are found in previous Iraq under Saddam Hussein. Communism is another form of secular totalitarianism in which political and economic systems (and philosophies) are virtually inseparable and tightly controlled by the government. Some communist countries such as China, Cuba and Vietnam, started to adopt some elements of the capitalistic system to improve their economies. However, they are still communist countries with strong authoritarian control over the political process.

The major characteristics of typical totalitarian regimes are presented below.

1. Political power is monopolized by a man or a small number of people.
2. Minority controls the majority and no opposition is permitted.
3. Inequality among the citizens is often observed.
4. The society is very much closed to the rest of the world and information flow is tightly controlled by the government.
5. The citizens' freedom and civil liberties is very much limited.
6. There is no guarantee for fair and independent trial.

Political Risk Analysis

Political risk represents the potentially adverse impact of a country's environment on the multinational corporations (MNC's) cash flows. Recently political risk analysis became more important than ever because so many countries try to rearrange their political-economic system and we also witnessed the emergence of so many leftist governments in Latin America. Besides, there are several other reasons why MNCs should carefully analyze the level of political risk of one country. First, it can be used to predict future business environments in the monitored countries where the MNC is currently doing business. If the political risk level of a particular country begins to increase, the MNC may consider divesting its subsidiaries located there. Country risk analysis can also be used by MNCs as a screening device to avoid an investment. Events that heighten a country's risk tend to discourage U.S. direct investment in that particular country. Political risk analysis is not only used to make major decisions such as investment or divestment but it also can be used to improve the accuracy of Net Present Value calculation for foreign projects by incorporating the level of political risk in the decision making process.

<u>Political Risk Factors</u>

An MNC must assess a country's risk not only in countries where it currently does business but also in those in which it expects to market exports or establish subsidiaries. Several risk characteristics of a country may significantly affect performance, and the MNC should be concerned about the degree of impact likely for each.

As one might expect, there are many country characteristics related to the political environment that influence an MNC. The extreme form of political risk is the possibility that the host country will take over a subsidiary. In some cases of expropriation, some compensation (the amount decided by the host country government) is awarded. In other cases, the assets are confiscated and no compensation is provided. Such events can take place peacefully or by force. Some of the more common forms of political risk include

- Confiscation
- Expropriation
- Blockage on the fund flow
- Breach of Contract (Concession Agreement)

- Freezing the Assets
- Operational restrictions (equity or market share)
- Heavy tax or frequent tax probe

Types of Political risk

Definition

Political Risk is defined as the risk of drastic changes in a country's business environment which is caused by the political instability. The political risk is different from sovereign risk, which represents the risk of non-payment by a government. The major essence of the political risk is discontinuities and uncertainties in a country's business environment. There are two different kinds of political risks to be assessed.

Macro Risk;

This is the type of risk that can cause a dramatic and abrupt change in business environment which will influence all foreign operations in the host countries such as nationalization of all foreign operation in the country.

Micro Risk:

This type of risk causes less dramatic but more prevalent changes in business environment which will influence only some specific firms or specific industries. Certain industries are more intrinsically vulnerable to this type of risk such as resource extraction (oil and gas) industry or defense related industries.

Techniques to assess political risk

Once a firm identifies all the macro and micro factors needed to be considered in the political risk assessment, it may need a system to evaluate these factors and determine a country risk rating. There are several techniques available to assess the level of political risk:

A. Checklist Approach

This approach identifies all the political and financial factors (both macro and micro) that contribute to a firm's assessment of country risk. Some factors (such as real GDP growth) can be measured from available data, while others (such as probability of having a war or government change) must be subjectively measured in terms of numerical form if it is necessary. Those factors thought to have a greater influence on country risk should be assigned greater weights. Both the measurement of some factors and the weighting scheme implemented are strictly subject to the evaluator's judgment.

B.- Delphi Technique

The Delphi technique requires the evaluator to collect independent opinions of the group of people called "specialists" on country risk without discussion among themselves. The specialist group members can be the employees of the MNCs or journalists who have been staying in the target country for a long time, political scientists or outside consultants. The MNC can average these country risk scores by assigning the weights for each assessor.

C. Quantitative Analysis

Another approach to asses the degree of political risk is to develop a statistical model and by identifying the major factors that seemingly influence the level of country risk. Discriminatory analysis is a commonly used statistical method for this purpose. This analysis is designed to identify which factors help to distinguish (or discriminate) between two groups of countries: a tolerable-risk country and an intolerable-risk country.
One of the major problems of this approach is, just like any other quantitative models, even if this statistical model tells us the magnitude of the political risk and which variable is the most crucial factor, it provides very little information about the timing of the major political shakeups.

D. Inspection Visits

This approach requires extensive traveling to a country and numerous meetings with government officials, firm executives, and/or consumers in an attempt to collect more relevant and confidential information about the target country. Such meetings help MNCs clarify any uncertainty and questions they may have by collecting the ample first hand information not biased by assessors' prejudice or preoccupation. In this sense, this method may be the best way to make a final confirmation on the assessment already made by one of the other methods.

Forecasting Services

Most of the MNCs take the political risk analysis seriously. However, they don't have experts specializing in this area within the firm simply because of inefficiency of permanently hiring these experts. Thus, when the necessity to analyze the political risk arises, MNCs normally outsource the services from other institutions. Some of the institutions that provide the political risk forecasting services are:

a. ASPRO/SPAIR Index by Shell Oil co.
b. BERI index by Business International Corp.
c. PSSI index by Haedel and West
d. IRIS index by PRS group.

Reducing exposure to the Political Risk

The most severe form of political risk is the risk of host government takeover. This type of takeover may result in major losses such as nationalization, confiscation or expropriation of your properties on foreign soil. It is particularly true when the MNC or the home country of the MNCs does not have any power or leverage to negotiate with the hostile host government. There are several strategies that can be used to reduce exposure to a host government takeover;

A. Use a Short-Term Horizon

This approach requires shortening the payback period and recovering invested capital as soon as possible delaying any additional major repair, replacement or investment in order to minimize the damage in case of confiscation or nationalization of your properties. MNCs often even gradually divest from the host country by partially selling off its assets to local investors or the government over time.

B. Differentiated Technology

If an MNC can bring in much superior or unique technology to its subsidiary that cannot be duplicated locally or internationally, it would not be that easy for the host government to take over and operate the operating unit without such techniques. If the subsidiary can effectively and secretively incorporate the technology in its production process, it would not be easy for the host government to takeover because they know that it will be a useless facility if they secure the unique technology, which is the core part of the production process.

C. Hire local labor and manager

If MNCs hire a great number of local employees for their subsidiary, they could put the pressure on their government to avoid any government take over. If you hire high level local managers who used to be high ranking government officer, they will work hard to draw a favorable decision for the company. It is a very effective strategy particularly in the country where almost every aspect of their economy is tightly controlled by the government. That's one reason why many MNCs hire ex-general in many developing countries where militaries can still exercise a considerable amount of political power.

D. Maximizing local financing

If the subsidiary borrows loan from local banks to finance the project or build the facilities in host country, when the host country tries to take over your properties there, you can minimize the damage because the significant portion of the facilities was originally financed by a loan from local banks. In this case, the production facilities that you already built using local loan are not yours. It is actually the local banker's properties. This kind of mutual hostage will definitely reduce the exposure to the risk of host government take over because they know they will gain very little from this take over while this kind of action significantly jeopardize their reputation in international community.

E. Purchase Insurance

Another approach to deal with high level of politics observed in a host country is to buy an insurance provided by one U.S. governmental agency; the Overseas Private Investment Corporation (OPIC). The amount of insurance premiums paid by a firm depends on the degree of political risk assessed in the host country and risk characteristics of the firms who want to operate in the host country. The World Bank also established an affiliated agency called the Multilateral Investment Guarantee Agency (MIGA) to cover a political risk for MNCs in conjunction with FDI in politically unstable developing countries. Normally MIGA insurance covers the risk of expropriation, confiscation, nationalization, breach of contract, currency inconvertibility, war, and civil disturbances.

Inverted U-curve Theory;

The assumption that political instability and risk is related to economic deprivation is, in general, supported by existing data. When one examines a number of countries at one point in time, or a single country over time, a somewhat unusual pattern of political instability emerges. On a continuum from very low levels of economic development to very high levels of economic development, the pattern of political instability resembles an inverted "U", with political instability peaking in the middle stages of economic development. This theory is so called the "inverted U-curve Theory". Underlying assumption for this theory is that the degree of political instability, which will eventually influence the level of political risk, will be decided by the amount of frustration that people have in the society. Another crucial assumption of this theory is the amount of frustration the people have will be a function of the difference (gap) between people's expectations about their life and economic reality such as their actual income. As the gap widens, political instability increases. This indicates that the more they feel the differences between their expectations and the economic reality, the more they feel frustrated and this will brew more instability in the society (such as street demonstration or protest against their government, etc). According to this U-curve theory, the people with the lower level of national income generally do not expect that much about their life because they have had the same kind of lifestyle for such a long time.

In the early stages of economic development, the expectations of a country's citizens are focused primarily on survival – finding shelter, food, clothing, etc. Their level of income may be low but they don't expect that much either. Thus, the gap between the economic reality and their expectations is relatively narrow. This indicates they may have a relatively stable life with less amount of frustration even if their national income is low. However, as a nation moves toward greater economic development, its citizens' economic expectations rise, and often rise rather quickly and dramatically. As the standard of living improves, people imagine even better economic conditions. Generally, economic expectations rise more rapidly than actual economic conditions. Consequently, the "gap" or relative economic deprivation increases as one move from very low levels of economic development to the middle stages of development. This will make them more frustrated and brew a high level of political instability in newly industrialized countries. Inequitable distribution of wealth typically observed in many newly industrialized countries can easily amplify the situation and make their political system very vulnerable and instable. Interestingly, however, as one move towards high end of economic development, people's expectations continue to rise but at slower pace as they become more realistic. Besides, even if people's expectations continue to rise, their income also rises and this high level of income can support their high expectations. Thus, the gap between their expectations and their economic reality will be minimized and thereby they will have relatively less frustration in their life. This will stabilize overall political situation and demonstrate relatively less amount of political instability.

The "Inverted U-curve" theory can be summarized as below.

Political risk = Political Instability = Amount of Frustration = f (expectation- reality)

Degree of Economic Development	People's expectation	Economic Reality	Amount of Frustration	The level of Political Instability
Less developed	Low	Low	Low	Low
Newly Industrialized	High	Low	High	High
Developed	High	High	Low	Low

This relationship between the level of economic development and the degree of political instability can be illustrated in following graph.

Inverted U-Curve and Political Instability

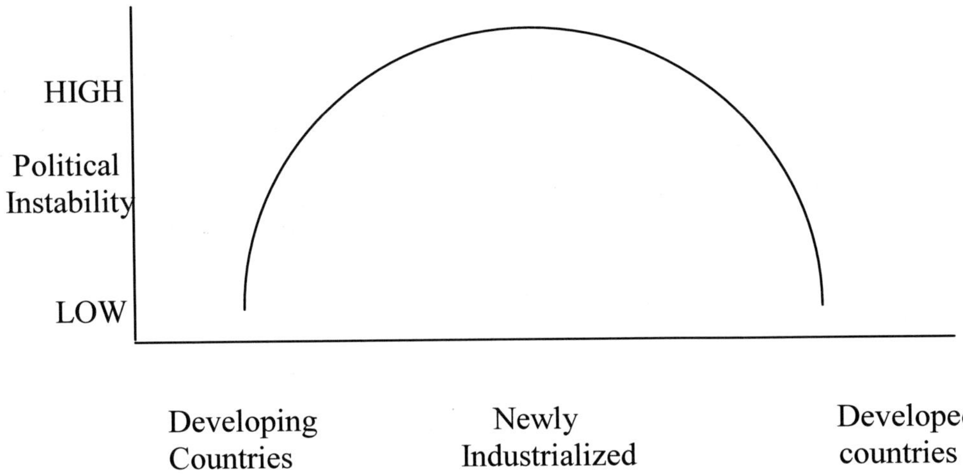

The Economic System

Any political system needs an economic system to solve two major economic problems: how to produce and how to distribute?

The classification of economic systems is based on two criteria's: The way the resources are allocated and the type of ownership that they have. Based on the first criterion, we can identify two broad types of economic systems – a market economy and a command economy even if there is a wide variety in between these two systems.

Market economy

In a pure market economy, the amount of goods and services that a country produces is solely determined by the interaction of supply and demand in the market. If demand for a product in the market exceeds supply, price will rise, signaling producers to produce more. If supply exceeds demand, prices will fall, signaling producers to produce less. In other words, market is the heart of economic system where the scarce resources are allocated most efficiently without external intervention in a pure market economy.

Command economy

In a pure command economy, the amount of goods and services that a country produces and distributes are decided by the government. In this type of economy, they don't even have market because everything is produced using the government production facilities and all the output will be distributed by the government plan. Historically, command economies were often found in communist countries where collectivist goals were given priority over individual goals. Since the demise of communism in the late 1980s, the number of command economies has fallen dramatically.

Ownership

The second criterion to classify economic systems is the type of ownership. There are two different types of economy, **Private ownership** versus **Public ownership** economy.

In a **private ownership** economy, the citizens are allowed to have their private properties and assets. Since citizens are allowed to have their private assets and properties, they have a stronger urge to work harder than in a country where the private ownership is prohibited. Private ownership also ensures that entrepreneurs have a right to the profits generated by their own efforts. This gives entrepreneurs an incentive to search for better ways of serving consumer needs. That may be through introducing new products, by developing more efficient production processes, by better marketing and after-sale service, or simple through managing their business more efficiently than their competitors. In a **public ownership** country, all the assets and properties and production means belong to the government and individual citizens are not allowed to have private assets or properties. In addition, all businesses are state owned, the rationale being that the government can then direct them to make investments that are in the best interest of the nation as a whole, rather than in the interests of private individuals. Generally speaking, this type of economy fails to provide motivation to work hard because people know that even if they work hard and produce more than they are supposed to, they cannot keep this extra output produced working hard.

Synthesis of Political/Economic System

Any political unit, whether it is democratic or totalitarian, need some kind of economic system to feed their people and to solve two fundamental economic problem; how to produce and how to distribute. Commonly, a Totalitarian system has a planned economy and public ownership; it is the case for most of the communist countries. A Democratic society usually has a market economy and private ownership, like the typical capitalist countries. However, no economy is purely Market or Command anymore. Most countries have mixed economies with different degrees of government ownership and freedom.

As we discussed earlier, two main economic problems need to be addressed by any political unit; how to produce and how to distribute. A Socialist, Karl Marx, proposed a joint production system, or communism, where all citizens work together using the publicly (government) owned production means and everybody is supposed to have equal distribution.

Karl Marx, 1818-1883

However, his theory never really worked in practice because this system failed to provide a motivation for the people to work harder. Under this system, nobody wanted to work harder because everybody knew that even if they work hard they will have an equal share. Consequently, production suffered and total output in the society dropped significantly. The problems that developed with Socialism and Communism were insufficient and inefficient production, lack of incentives to work hard and low level of output.

On the other hand, the problems that developed in most of the capitalistic societies are inequitable distribution. This means the rich got richer and poor get poorer, and most of the means of production were owned by a small number of rich people. Even if the majority of the capitalistic societies produce an enough amount of goods and their overall economy and GNP increase, the poor gets poorer. It indicates none of both systems is perfect. Thus, so many political units have been trying to correct their problems by introducing some variation from their original political and economic ideology and trying to adopt some elements that do not belong to their original system. The following chart summarizes some of the problems in each system and the variation that has developed to correct those problems.

	Problems	Correction	Variation
Communism	Insufficient production	Add capitalistic elements: Private ownership, and introduce the market concept	**"Market Socialism"** maintains socialistic structure, but has added Capitalistic elements to increase production and efficiency
Capitalism	Inequitable distribution	Add socialistic elements: public ownership and heavy taxes on the rich	**"Democratic Socialism"** maintain democratic structure but to introduce some socialistic elements to achieve distributive justice

Transition to a Market Economy

Many countries are undergoing transition from a communist system to market economies because of the failure of the communist system and central planning to generate economic growth. The breakup of the Berlin Wall, the collapse of the Soviet Union and many Eastern European communist dictatorships since the late 1980's renewed Western interest in doing business in those countries that previously had been denied. These countries were classified as command economies. Several command economies in transition have shown strong economic growth (such as China and Vietnam) since the transition process began, some have experienced growth reversals, and others have shown little or no growth at all.

Review Questions

Discuss the major characteristics of democracy and totalitarianism.

Identify two criteria to classify economic system

What are the two major forms of political-economic syntheses?

Identify the typical problems in both socialism and capitalism.

What is the major variation of each system; socialism and capitalism?

What is the definition of political risk in International Business context?

What is the difference between the political risk and sovereign risk?

What are the possible net consequences of investing in a politically risky country?

Discuss the "Inverted U-curve theory".

CHAPTER 8: CULTURAL ENVIRONMENT

Cultural environment is one of the most important and challenging topic in international business as this permeates the entire functional aspects of international business.

Why study culture?

If you want to become a competent international business man, you need to improve your **cultural intelligence (CQ)**, which is defined as an "ability to deal with the people from different culture. Culture is the most important source dictating human behavior and, understanding people's behavior is a very important issue in International business study. However, understanding the foreign culture is often very difficult because the culture has very many different layers. That is why the culture is often compared to an iceberg, where the visible part you see above the water is only a very small piece of the whole.

Surf (front) culture, the visible part above the surf, is the part you easily see such as clothing and food.

Sub (back) culture, the invisible part below the surf, is the part you can't easily see such as attitudes, perceptions, or assumptions.

Culture is also often compared to a peach because it has so many different layers such as beautiful visible skin at the most outer side, soft juicy meat inside, and hard core that you can't eat! The physical appearance of a peach is also deceiving. Even if all the peaches look good, tempting, and delicious, in many cases, actual taste can be significantly different from what you originally expected from its appearance. For this reason, some people suggest the following model for culture. At the most superficial level, you can see all the visible part of culture such as artifacts, foods, clothing, products, and physical appearance. Immediately below this level, there is a social norm and vale system that dictate their behaviors. At the deepest level, which you can't easily see, there is an implicit part of culture which contains people's assumptions and perceptions.

Definition of Culture

It is very difficult to define what a culture is because culture contains a wide variety of social phenomena. That's why we have more than 200 different definitions of culture. One of the most famous and widely accepted definitions of culture is:

> A learned, shared, compelling interrelated set of symbols whose meaning provide a set of orientation for the members of the society. Culture is learned, after birth, from other members of society. Cultural values also shared with other members in the society not monopolized by one man. Cultural values are also imposing and we cannot refuse the norms set by our own culture. Culture is also very much interrelated with other aspects of the society.

Another widely accepted definition that we can use for practical purpose is:

> culture is the various aspects of society (such as value, rituals, symbols, rules, beliefs & artifacts) that distinguish the members of one society from the members another society.

Some researchers believe that **Culture is a man-made environment** because it is us, the members of the society, who create our own culture. Nonetheless, our own behaviors are confined by the culture that we created. Thus, culture is an environment that we create under which we have to conduct our own behavior.

Values, Rituals, Heroes, and Symbols (Hofstede, Geert: Cultures and Organizations. Intercultural Cooperation and Its Importance for Survival. - London: Harper Collins Publishers, 1994 (1st. ed. 1991).)

Hofstede (1991) provides the following "Onion Diagram" to explain the multiple layers of cultural components. He argues that cultural differences can be very well characterized using the four terms "Values, Rituals, Heroes, and Symbols". Hofstede illustrates these terms "as the skin of an onion, indicating that symbols represent the most superficial and value the deepest manifestation of culture, with heroes and rituals in between."

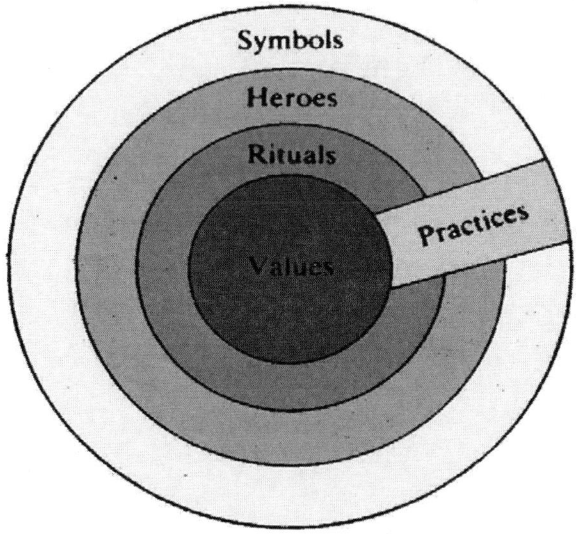

Symbols are any kind of pictures, objects, gestures, or words which carry a particular meaning only recognized by the members of one culture. To the category of symbols belong:

- words, idioms, jargon, accent
- flags, status symbols
- brand names, clothes, hair style, colors, pins...

Heroes are role models that posses characteristics that are highly prized in a culture. They can be alive, dead, real, or imaginary. Almost anybody can function as a hero:

- sport, music, or movie stars (e.g. Madonna)
- politicians and historical people (e.g. Abraham Lincoln)
- cartoon heroes, heroes from books (e.g. Harry Potter)
- people from one's own family (e.g. one's own father or mother)

Rituals are conventionalized behavior patterns that are occur in particular situations. Examples for rituals are business meetings, church services, morning routine. These are activities which are take place on a regular basis in a particular course. Rituals play also a significant role in language:

- Small-Talks
- Greetings
- Agreeing and Disagreeing

Usually the original meaning has been lost; e.g. "How are you?" is more likely to be understood as a form of greeting rather than a serious concern about someone's health.

Values are "the core of culture". They are taught in early childhood and most important for one's decision what is right or wrong. Values can also be seen as priorities, things we like most and choose before others. Personal values differ among the members of one culture but are normally respected by all of them.

Source

Hofstede, Geert: Cultures and Organizations. Intercultural Cooperation and Its Importance for Survival. - London: Harper Collins Publishers, 1994 (1st. ed. 1991).

Cultural Contrast

Cross-cultural anthropologists, Samovar, Porter, and Jain, proposed **cultural contrast** as an effective starting point to discuss culture. The following table displays various cultural attributes that can be contrasted between the U.S. and traditional culture:

	U.S.(Modern)	**Traditional Societies**
1. **Nature**	Master over nature…earth belongs to us like our personal property Natural disaster: Scientific phenomenon	Servant to nature we belong to earth Natural disaster: Act of angry God
2. **Material**	Very materialistic, the more the better Nothing wrong with material pursuit	Less materialistic; Too much Material ruins the soul material pursuit is selfish & immature
3. **Change**	Accept change accept new ideas love new products	Reluctant to change against ancestor's will change is work of evil
4. **Action vs. Thinking**	Action oriented any action better than inaction dynamic trial and error ; improvement	Thinking oriented inaction better than stupid action static no trial and error: no improvement
5. **Ourselves**	Individualistic "Me" centered privacy & uniqueness	Collective "Us" centered sharing & conformity
6. **Ideas**	Pragmatic Practical	Idealistic non-practical
7. **Future Life**	Optimistic life is full of joy	Pessimistic life is sea of agony
8. **Relationship with Others**	Horizontal Egalitarian equally born	Vertical Hierarchical unequally born

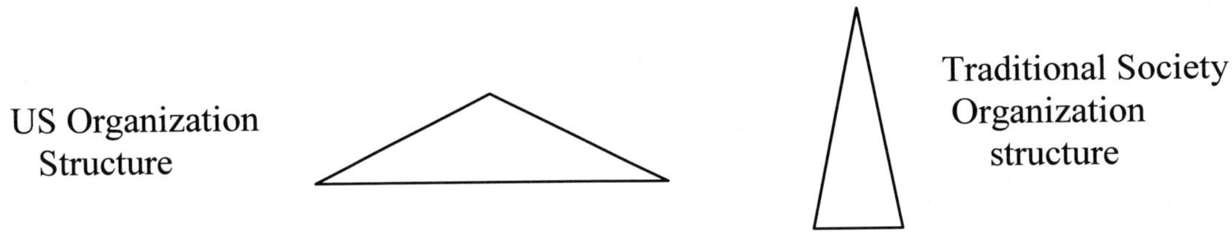

Language (Communication)

Language is one of the most important and integral part of culture. Language is the primary means by which a culture transmits its beliefs, values, and norms. It gives people means of interacting with other members of the society. The ability to make efficient communication is one of the important qualifications to become a competent international business manager.

Language can be divided into two types: verbal (or formal) language and non-verbal (or silent) language.

Verbal language is a formal or official way to communicate. It is not only a simple device to convey thoughts. It is a special device to perceive the world and to share people's experiences with other members of society. Language and culture is inseparable. You cannot learn a foreign language without learning their culture because it is deeply embedded in the language they use. When you learn a foreign language, you internalize the foreign culture to some extent at subconscious level, which is embedded in that language. Edward Sapir and Benjamin Whorf concluded that language not only serves as a mechanism for communication, but as a guide to social reality. Their studies resulted in what today is called **The Sapir-Whorf hypothesis.** It proposes that language not only serves as a mechanism to transmit the perception that people have but also the language itself influences people's perceptual process. This hypothesis suggests that depending upon what kind of languages you speak, the way you speak, think and act can be different. For example, if you become very fluent in one foreign language, you already internalize the foreign cultural value embedded in that language and you tend to act like them and think like them. This hypothesis was used during the colonial period when mother countries put a great deal of pressure on the colonial people to use the mother country's language. The mother country believed that as long as colonial people use their own local language, they will keep on thinking independently and this would make it difficult to control the people in the colonies.

Any communication, either domestic or international, can be depicted by the following process:

Communication Process

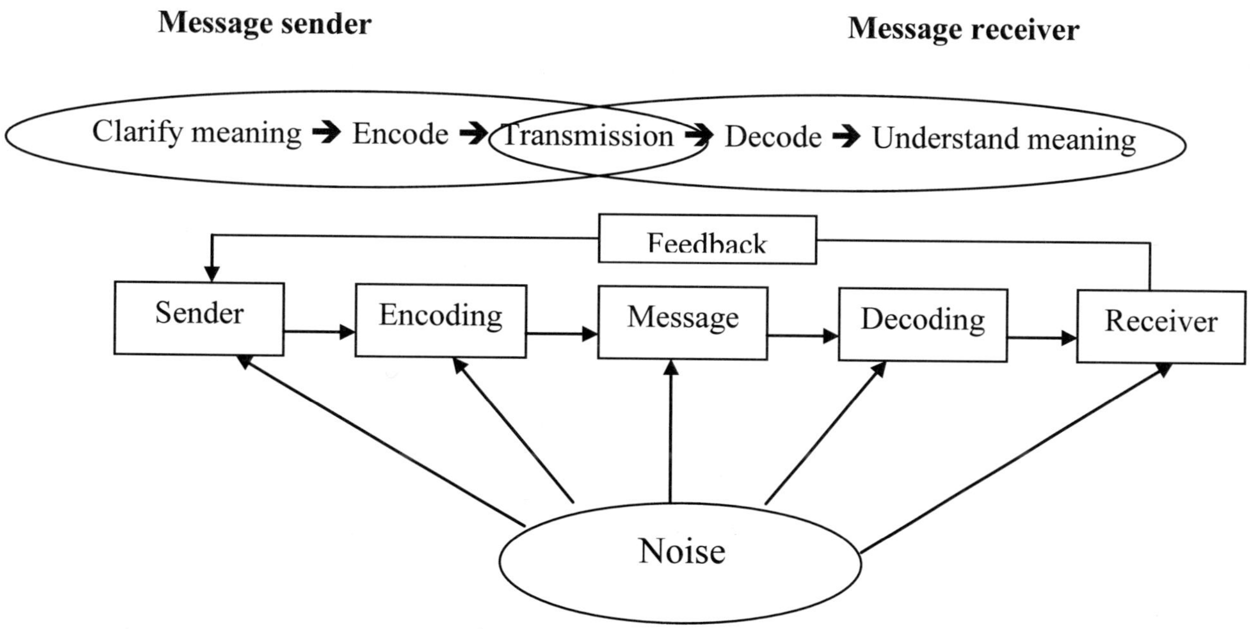

First, a person subconsciously clarifies the meaning he wants to convey in his mind. Then, he selects the right words (encode) to use to convey that meaning. The Transmission is where the individual physically speaks out the words. For effective communication to take place, the receiver must successfully decode the sender's message, and successful decoding in the way the message sender encodes should allow him to understand the meaning. However, in cross-cultural communication, there are a number of sources of noises that impede the efficient and clear communication between the message sender and message receiver.

1) *Incompatible language*: In cross-cultural communication, one of the most typical problems is the fact that the message sender's language is not compatible to that of the message receiver. Sometimes even simple words can cause problems due to limited ability to command a foreign language. For example, several years ago a Japanese exchange student studying in the United States was going to a friend's house for a Halloween party. The student went to the wrong house and the homeowner, who saw a stranger approaching, told him to "freeze". However, the student did not understand the meaning of that word in that situation. In the confusion, the homeowner tragically shot the exchange student. Perhaps the student thought he was saying "please" because in the Japanese language there is clear distinction between the "l" and "r" sound and they don't have an "f" sound.

2) Encoding and Decoding. Even if we use the same language, the same word can be interpreted in different ways. For instance, the British word "flat" means "apartment", "lift" means "elevator", "ale" means "beer". The way they encode by selecting the word like "flat" is different in the way that the average American decodes it. Again, intercultural communication breaks down.

3) Past experiences can also influence communication. As discussed earlier, language is a special device to share past experiences. If, the message sender and receiver do not share the same experiences in their lives, it is very difficult to have an effective communication. For example, most average Americans are very familiar with the expression "Where's the beef?", but to foreigners or Americans who has lived in other countries for a long time they would have some troubles grasping the true meaning of this expression.

4) The differences in *communication patterns* can also cause a lot of noises in the cross-cultural communication process. For instance, Americans tend to speak in a linear pattern, and be straightforward and direct. However, in some other cultures, people speak in a spiraled pattern, and they go tangents.

some traditional
countries

5) Tone of voice and silence
Tone of voice

Another cross-cultural problem arises from the tone of voice. The figure below shows typical patterns for Anglo-Saxon, Latin and Oriental languages. For some neutral societies, ups and downs in speech suggest that the speaker is not serious. However, in most Latin societies this "exaggerated" way of communicating shows that you have your heart in the matter. Oriental societies tend to have a much more monotonous style; self-controlled, it shows respect. Frequently, a person in a high position has a lower and flatter voice.

A British manager dispatched to Nigeria found out it was very effective in raising his voice for important issues. His Nigerian subordinates saw this unexpected explosion by a normally self-controlled manager as a sign of extra concern. After success in Nigeria he was dispatched to Malaysia. Shouting in Malaysia was a sign of loss of face; his colleagues did not take him seriously and he was transferred.

Silence

We become nervous and uneasy once we stop talking. However, we have very different styles of discussion. For the Anglo-Saxons, when A stops talking, then can B start talking. It is not polite to interrupt. The even more verbal Latin integrates slightly more than this; B will frequently interrupt A and vice versa to show how interested each is in what the other is saying.

The pattern of silent communication shown in the following figure is for oriental languages that frightens the Westerners. The moment of silence is interpreted as a failure to communicate. However, this is a misunderstanding. Let us reverse the roles; how can the Westerner communicate clearly if the other person is not given time to finish his or her sentence, or to digest what the other has been saying? It is a sign of respect for the other person if you take time to process the information without talking yourself.

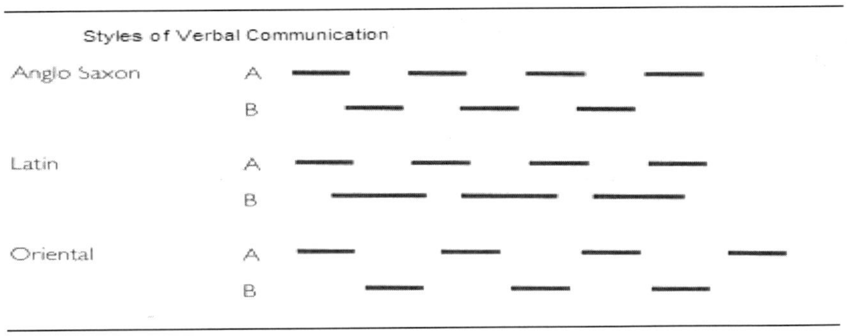

6) Different cultures may have different *sources of metaphors*. A metaphor may be thought of as an impressive or efficient way to express an opinion, but it can create problems when communicating with a foreigner. Americans tend to base many of their metaphors to sports, such as the sayings "it's a long shot", "dropped the ball", or "ball is in his court". On the other hand, a traditional culture could tie their metaphors to other sources such as nature.

7) Preferred topics can differ between cultures. In the U.S., discussions on religion or political beliefs, which are very private, are usually avoided whereas a foreigner may find these topics as a way to show his intelligence.

A practical advice to minimize the blunders when communicating with foreigners, both in business and on a personal level, would be, first, never to use slang or colloquial expressions. Foreigners learn the language from textbooks, which rarely contain those languages. Therefore, it is helpful to deliver grammatically perfect sentences and to speak the language the way it is written. Second, if the individual does not understand what you are trying to say, don't repeat yourself, but use other words to describe what you are trying to say. A third advice may be to "thicken" your question if you have some questions. Thickening a question means you can ask the same question in many different ways repeatedly to make sure you and your counterpart clearly understand each other's position. It would be a good idea to try to summarize, or re-cap, what you are saying to avoid potential confusion and misunderstanding. Finally, you need patience and honesty in cross cultural communication. Your foreign communication partner may need a lot more time to digest and interpret what you said. They may need more time to "decode" (comprehending) the message than you conveyed more time to "encode" (finding an appropriate words). Cross-cultural communication already presents a variety of problems. Once you lose your trust in communicating, your chance to mend and to restore the lost trust may be very slim because both parties' capability to command foreign languages is limited. Thus, it is advised that you better be brutally honest from the beginning.

Non-Verbal (Silent, Body) language:

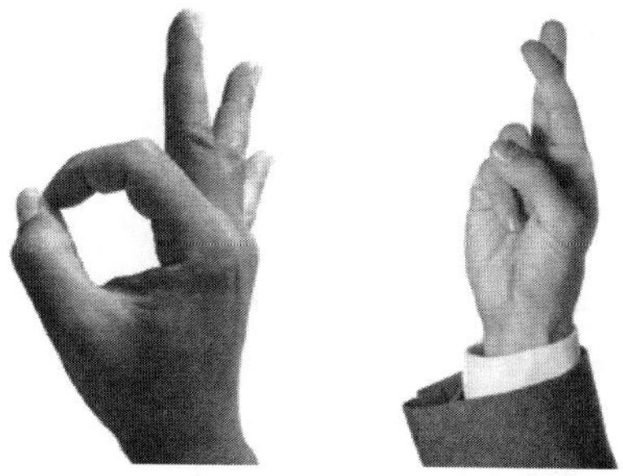

Definition (Samovar,Porter and Jain)

Silent language is defined as all stimuli, humanly or environmentally generated, except verbal ones that have potential message value for the sender and/or receiver. It is the silent way of communicating. Sometimes there is no choice but to use non-verbal language in cross-cultural communication. The forms of non-verbal language can be any gestures, facial expressions, objects and artifacts, or paralanguages that are used to convey ideas. However, one thing that you have to remember is that non-verbal language is not universal. Most of the international communication is in the form of silent language. However, sometimes it might be even more confusing or embarrassing than formal/official language. For example, when a typical average American encounters another American for the first time, they first try to make eye contact and then try to greet. This first move, eye contact can be considered very rude behavior in other cultures since they consider the eyes to be the window to their souls and feel that they are peeped when you try to make an eye contact. Also, the finger gesture with your palm up to have someone come to you is very common in the U.S., but in some countries they only call their dogs in that manner. Americans would raise one finger to call a waiter to their table, but in many Asian countries, they make a loud clapping sound. In some Latin culture, they scratch on the table. Likewise, burping is not considered socially acceptable behavior in the US, but in some countries it signifies that one has enjoyed the meal very much.

Functions of Nonverbal language

Our nonverbal behaviors perform a variety of functions during interaction. Five rather specific functions of nonverbal communication can be identified: first impressions, relational messages, affect, self-presentation, and manipulation of others. It will be helpful to look briefly at these five functions so that we can learn to identify them as they operate during an encounter.

A natural starting place for studying the communicative functions of nonverbal cues is *first impressions.* Since our first reactions to others supply the framework, within which all the other nonverbal functions operate. These first judgments color our perceptions of everything else that follows.

The second function, *relational messages*, are the nonverbal cues people send to reach other that help to explain how they like each other, themselves, and the relationship they are in. We offer people this type of information in many forms. We position and space our bodies as a mean of signaling whom we want to include and exclude from our conversations. We use body orientation and space to show friendliness and affection. We smile, touch, nod, and the like to communicate our feeling about what is happening and how we feel about it.

Affective, or emotional states as they are often called, is also communicated by nonverbal cues. Our emotions are reflected in our posture, voice, facial expressions, and eyes. Be it fear, joy, anger, or sadness, we express these emotions and feelings to others and they in turn attach meaning to them.

Fourth, we use nonverbal elements as one way of *presenting ourselves* to other people. We manipulate a host of nonverbal cues as we try to influence what others think of us. The car we drive, the clothes we wear, the smile on our face are messages that we send to others to help them decide who we are and whether they wish further contact with us.

Finally, we *manipulate nonverbal symbols*, either consciously or unconsciously, to alter the thinking and behavior of others. Our nonverbal actions often influence how others will act and how they will think. We use nonverbal elements just as we use words to affect how people feel and even what they might learn.

Attitudes

Another big element in culture is people's attitudes about certain things. Some noticeable differences associated with attitude are:

<u>Time</u>

- People's perception about the speed of time may be very different. According to a study conducted on this topic, when asked to estimate the duration of 1 minute, actual average amount of time, a Mexican group turned out to be 1 minute 40 seconds and that of North American group turned out 45 seconds.
- People's perception about the punctuality can differ significantly from culture to culture. A culture may take deadlines seriously while another one doesn't care very much about it. Deadlines or due dates are only a point of time that you start to think something seriously.
- The shape of time in a typical Western society may be described as a straight line - where people and timing is so critical and lost time can never be made up. However, many traditional societies perceive time as circular one where there is no beginning and no ending, and for them, time comes back again and again like the moon and the sun.

Wealth Accumulation

In many capitalistic countries, the most preferred form of wealth is the accumulation of money or valuable securities such as stocks and bonds. However, in many countries, they measure wealth by the number of wives a man has, or how many sons he has, or the amount of land or cattle he owns.

A society's perception of wealth accumulation itself may also differ significantly. Western societies see wealth accumulation as good and positive, whereas some other societies do not like one person to have so much more than others, and even deny the wealth accumulation by one person. For example, in a Mexican peasant society if a farmer is very successful, he is pressured to sponsor a big, expensive fiesta (party) for the whole community. After he sponsors the big fiesta for the whole village, he will gain the honor but materially he will be put back on par with other village man. Thus, the whole society refuses wealth building by one man.

Gender (Male versus Female)

The social status of the female can be significantly different from culture to culture. In some societies females are treated equally and with respect. However, in some countries females in the society are strictly second class citizens and in some extreme cases, they are treated like slaves. The role of the female in a traditional society can often limit the jobs available to them because women are considered only for household positions or child nurturing.

Group Membership

Society needs some way to evaluate a person's potential ability and interpret his status by that person's memberships in various groups. Generally speaking, we have two different types of group membership that can be used to serve this purpose depending upon what kind of culture they have.

-*Ascribed membership:* This type of membership is given to the individual at birth by their ethnicity, religion, region or hereditary social classes.

-*Acquired membership*: This kind of membership can be obtained after birth through various social affiliations such as education and political party.

In many traditional countries, ascribed membership is frequently used to assess the partiality of the individuals and in certain countries, acquired membership is a more prevalent way to assess the individual's potential ability.
The implication of the attitude regarding group membership for international business is that sometimes it can be a tremendous hurdle for the company to mobilize the human resources effectively if the society emphasize too much on the ascribed membership when assessing the potential ability of the employees.

Giving of gifts

In some cultures the *philosophy* of giving gifts is to build better human relationships while in the American culture, a gift is a way of showing appreciation.

The *frequency* of giving gifts and *value* of the gift may differ from country to country depending upon how they value the significance of the human relationship.
Some countries may simply consider gift giving as a way to invest in the relationship for future, whereas in the U.S. it is perceived as an *illegal bribe.*

Age

In the U.S. culture people don't always think highly of the elderly population, and in many cases, they are often neglected and the result has been many "gray orphans". It is the opposite case in many Eastern countries where they equate old age with wisdom and show their elders lots of respect.

Cultural Dimensions

It is almost impossible to identify all the little differences in people's attitudes about certain things. Thus, many cross-cultural anthropologists started to develop some major dimensions that we can use to distinguish one culture form another (Early, Hall, Triandis, Hofstede, 1988, Hampden-Tuner and Trompenaars, 1992 and Globe project, 2004).

High context vs. Low context: Communication style (Hall)

One very effective way to distinguish one culture from another is to examine their communication styles. In particular, as has been noted by Hall, the amount of context embedded in the communication patterns plays a key role in explaining many differences in culture. Context is the information that surrounds a communication and helps convey the message. In high-context culture, such as Japan and many Arabic countries, messages are often highly coded and implicit. As a result, the receiver's job is to interpret what the message means by correctly filtering through what is being said and the way in which the massage is being conveyed. This approach is in sharp contrast to low-context societies such as the United States and Canada where the message is explicit and the speaker says precisely what he or she means. The following figure provides an international comparison of high context/implicit and low context/explicit societies.

In high-context cultures, messages are implicit and indirect. One reason for this tendency is to avoid confrontation and embarrassment and make it easy to have a consensus. More often than not, direct and explicit expression can be an impediment to have a consensus in collective culture. That's why many collectivist cultures prefer this type of communication style.

In low-context cultures, people often meet only to accomplish goals and objectives. Thus, they prefer efficient way to communicate and they waste no time to discuss the topic directly and clearly. They try their best to minimize ambiguity in their communication to avoid any confusion in the future. Consequently, the message receiver's job is to take the message literally and they are not allowed to have any room to interpret the message in their own way.

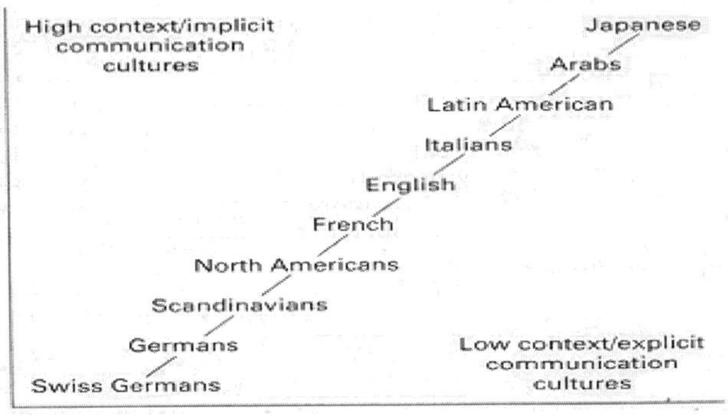

Doing (Dynamic) vs. Being (Static) : Preference to Action vs. Thinking (Triandis)

Some cultures view being (having a deep experience of life) and being-in-becoming (evolving as a person to "higher" levels of understanding) as much more valuable. Traditional Asians de-emphasize doing. One's work should not be the center of one's life and should not take all of one's time. People should have fun, should experience deeply, should reach higher levels of understanding. This type of culture is more cohesive, coherent, rigid and well-bounded and constrained. As a result, they will maintain an unchanging nature and be static. They discourage anything which could unbalance them or perturb their equilibrium and homeostasis.

Whereas doing culture is an action oriented culture. Typical western cultures value action. North Americans, for instance, have a high regard for 'the man of action." You are supposed to take an action and reaction quickly when something happens. According to a research, the reaction time in people in doing oriented culture is much shorter than those in thinking oriented culture ($r = 0.30$) and higher on scales of aggression, autonomy, dominance, and achievement. In cultures with a doing orientation, the emphasis is on quantity of production; and supervisors tend to impose structure. In cultures with a being orientation there is emphasis on interpersonal sensitivity and supervisors tend to be very considerate of others. In cultures emphasizing being and thinking, there is emphasis on training and personal change.

High Contact vs, Low contact: Amount of physical Contact (Triandis)

Cultures differ in the amount of contact that is appropriate. The distance between bodies in ordinary conversation can vary from many feet to a few inches; orientation of the bodies can vary from face to face to looking away from the other; touching the other with one's hands may be normal in some areas but taboo in others; eye contact can vary form looking into the other's eyes to looking away.

In general, people around the Mediterranean, the Arabs, and the South Americans are high-contact cultures; they touch, look closely, and shout. But in China, India, Japan, Pakistan, Thailand, and northern Europe, people prefer to not touch. North Americans are generally low-contact people (Watson, 1970).

When a high-contact person meets a low-contact person at a cocktail party, the high-contact person approaches him and the other retreats, so it can look as if one is chasing the other. The low-contact person sees the high-contact person as intrusive, pushy, and overbearing, trying to get too familiar; the high-contact person sees the low-contact person as cold, remote, haughty, and arrogant.

Apollonian vs. Dionysian : Expression of emotions (Benedict/Mead/Triandis)

Another interesting way to distinguish cultures is to investigate their way of handling their emotions. In a Dionysian culture, people believe that expressing one's emotions is appropriate and hiding them is inappropriate. Formality and protocol is not that important in this type of culture. In this type of culture, people favor intimate interpersonal relations; supervisors are most liked if they engage in such relationships. They approve recklessness, exaltation and passion to break away from the usual routine. By contrast, in Apollonian cultures, people are culturally trained to control their emotions. Any educated and mature adult is supposed to control their emotion. Releasing his emotion is considered to be childish. The people in this type of culture emphasize restraints, rules, moderation and sobriety. In Apollonian cultures, there are more emphases on protocol and formality; supervisors must express approval or disapproval in highly measured ways, or even indirectly.

> **More on Dionysian and Apollonian:** Nietzsche's designation of two different Greek art forms and artistic tendencies, reflecting two fundamental human and natural impulses. He invoked the names of the gods Apollo and Dionysus to identify and distinguish them in his discussion of the origin of the tragic art and culture of the Greeks, which he traced to their confluence, associating Apollo with order, lawfulness, perfected form, clarity, precision, self-control, and individualization, and Dionysus with change, creation and destruction, movement, rhythm, ecstasy, and oneness.

Masculinity vs. Femininity: (Hofstede)

Masculinity is defined by Hofstede as "a situation in which the dominant values in society are success, money, and things." Contrary to some stereotypes and connotations, femininity is the term used by Hofstede to describe "a situation in which dominant values in society are caring for others and the quality of life." Countries with high masculinity index, such as Japan, place great importance on goal achievement, recognition, advancement, and challenge. Individuals are driven by performance and achievement in term of recognition and wealth. Countries with a low masculinity index (Hofstede's femininity dimension), such as the Scandinavian countries, tend to place great importance on cooperation, a friendly atmosphere, and caring for others. They focus more on the quality of life than on achieving goals. Cultures with a high masculinity index tend to favor large-scale enterprises, and economic growth is seen as more important than conservation on the environment. Fewer women hold higher-level jobs, and these individuals often find it necessary to be assertive. There is high job stress in the workplace, and industrial conflict is common. Cultures with a low masculinity index (high femininity) tend to favor small-scale enterprises, and they place great importance on conservation of the environment. Many women hold higher-level jobs, and they do not find it necessary to be assertive.

Individualism vs. Collectitivsm; (Early and Traindis)

Collectivist culture has a tendency for people to belong to groups and to look after each other in exchange of loyalty. This type of culture encourage consensus-building, teamwork, togetherness and we-ness, mass experiences, social sanctions and social regulation, structured socialization, peer loyalty, belonging, homogeneity, identity formation through allegiance to a group. This culture employs numerous self-preservation mechanisms and strict hierarchy, obedience, discipline, discrimination (by sex, by race, above all, by age and familial affiliation).

Major traits for this dimension:

a. *Collective:* It is an "us" oriented culture where the group is more important than individual. Uniformity and conformity have high values. Individuals of collective cultures usually have a "keep me in the loop" attitude.
b. *Individualistic:* It is a "me" centered culture where uniqueness and one's privacy are traits of the culture. Independence and freedom is very important in this type of culture. Their basic attitude is "to leave me alone".

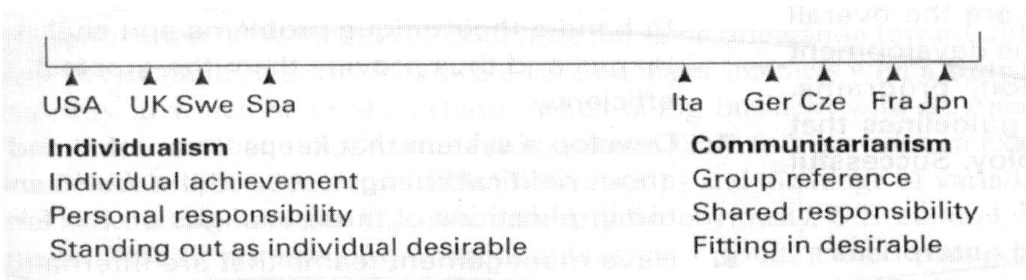

Hofstede found some correlations between this cultural dimension and national income. The industrialized wealthy countries have higher individualism scores and poorer countries higher collectivism scores. United States, Canada, Australia, Denmark, and Sweden, among others, have high individualism and high GNP. Conversely, Guam, Pakistan, and a number of South American countries have low individualism (high collectivism) and low GNP. Countries with high individualism also tend to have greater support from the Protestant work ethic, greater individual initiative, and promotions based on market value. Countries with low individualism tend to have less support for the Protestant work ethic, less individual initiative, and promotions based on seniority.

<u>High Unceraintу Avoidance vs, Low Uncertainty Avoidance:</u> <u>Level of anxiety (Hofstede)</u>

Uncertainty avoidance is "the extent to which people feel threatened by ambiguous situations, and have created beliefs and institutions that try to avoid these." The people with high uncertainty avoidance culture work so hard and tend to have stronger inner urge to reduce the level of anxiety. Countries with high uncertainty-avoidance cultures have a great deal of structuring of organizational activities, more written rules, less risk-taking by manager. Work and career are the important things in their life and general attitude about work is "live to work" and they perceive high level of anxiety and tension in their daily life and work place. Examples include Germany and Japan. People with low uncertainty avoidance tend to feel less anxiety and tension in their daily life and more willing to accept a certain amount of the risk and life goes on in spite of this. Examples here include Denmark and Great Britain. Low uncertainty-avoidance societies have organization setting less structuring activities, fewer written rules, and more risk-taking by managers. People's general attitude is "work to live" and the life is relatively easy going and less stressful.

<u>High Power Distance vs. Lower Power Distance:</u> <u>Attitude toward power (Hofstede)</u>

A power distance dimension is defined by Hofstede as "the extent to which less powerful members of institutions and organizations accept that power is distributed unequally." Countries in which people blindly obey orders of their superiors tend to have high power distance. In many societies, lower-level employees tend to follow the "crime of obedience" even if they can not justify their own action.

Organizations in low power-distance countries generally will be decentralized and have flatter and horizontal organization structures. By contrast, an organization in high power-distance countries will tend to be centralized and have tall and hierarchical organization structures. Organizations in high power-distance countries will have a large proportion of supervisory personnel, and the people at the lower levels of the structure often will have low job qualifications. Some other major traits of this dimension are shown below:

a. *High Power Distance:* Inequality is inevitable to maintain the society. The distance between power and non-power holders is high, and powerful people are thought to have the right to use their power the way they like.
b. *Low Power Distance:* There is equality between power and non-power holders and they are considered to be close in terms of status. Those with power must use it legally or they would be challenged.

<u>Universalism vs. Particularism</u>: <u>Obligations (Hampden-Turner and Trompenaars)</u>

Another interesting dimension that can provide a significant implication for international business manager is Universalism vs. Particularism. People in Universalistic cultures believe that rules and policies must be universally applied without exception. Whereas, Particularistic cultures believe the rules and regulations should be applied with more flexibility depending on the situation. In cultures with high universalism, the focus is more on formal rules than on personal relationships, whereas, people in particularistic culture focus more on personal and individual relationship than on formal rules. In a particularistic culture, rules are often violated to give a personal favor and policies are often modified to give a favor to a specific individual or group.

Trompenaars and Hampden-Turner asked a series of interesting and hypothetical questions including the following one to identify this dimension.

You are riding a car driven by a close friend. He hits a pedestrian. You know he was going at least 35 miles per hour in an area of the city where the maximum allowed speed is 20 miles per hour. There are no witnesses. His lawyer says that if you testify under oath that he was driving 20 miles per hour it may save him from serious consequences. What right has your friend to expect you to protect him? How would you testify?

- My friend has a definite right as a friend to expect me to testify to the lower figure.
- He has some right as a friend to expect me to testify to the lower figure.
- He has no right as a friend to expect me to testify to the lower figure.

Some of the major traits for dimension are as below:

a. *Universalistic:* In these cultures, individual is first obliged to society. Social justice is more important than the justice for individual. Law and regulations are followed without exception.
b. *Particularistic:* Unlike in universalistic cultures, in particularistic cultures individual's first obligation is to the individual. A friend would perjure himself to save a friend rather than looking for social justice. Corruption levels are high since personal relationships are important. Nepotism and favoritism are quite prevalent. Individuals would consider an exception before following the law. The rules and policy are frequently modified or bent to give special favor for specific individuals.

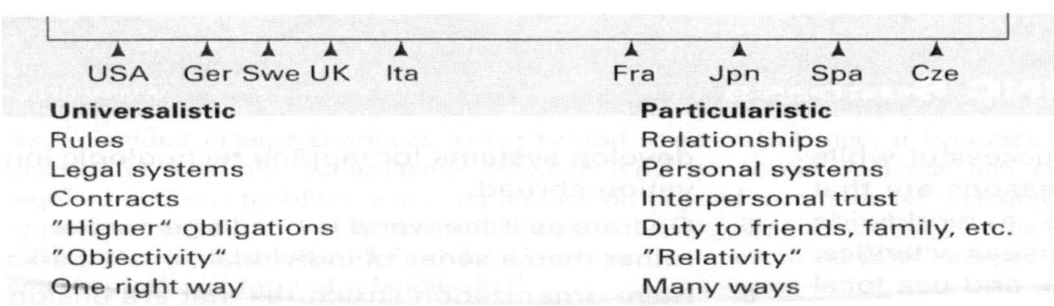

<u>Progressive (future oriented) vs. Regressive (past oriented)</u> <u>: Time orientation (Vaknin)</u>

One interesting dimension that we can also use to distinguish one culture from another is people's orientation toward time. The degree to which cultures are past-oriented or present oriented as opposed to future oriented is very different depending on their culture. In regressive culture like Russia and Venezuela, The past is more important than future in their life and they look to the past – real or imaginary – for inspiration, motivation, sustenance, hope, guidance and direction. These cultures tend to direct their efforts and resources and invest them in what IS. They are, therefore, bound to be materialistic, figurative, substantive, and earthly. They are likely to prefer old age to youth, old habits to new, old buildings to modern architecture, etc. This preference of the Elders (a term of veneration) over the Youngsters (a denigrating term) typifies them strongly. These cultures are likely to be risk averse. In progressive culture like the U.S., Italy and Germany, the future is more important than the past or the present. They look to the future to get inspiration, motivation, sustenance, hope, guidance and direction. These cultures invest their efforts and resources in an ephemeral future (upon the nature or image of which there is no agreement or certainty). These cultures are, inevitably, more abstract (living in an eternal Gedanken [thought] experiment), more imaginative, more creative (having to design multiple scenarios just to survive). They are also more likely to have a youth cult: to prefer the young, the new, the revolutionary, the fresh – to the old, the habitual, the predictable. They are risk-centered and risk-assuming cultures. Trompenaars recommends that when doing business with future-oriented progressive cultures, effective international managers should emphasize the opportunities and limitless scope that any agreement can have, agree to specific deadlines for getting things done, and be aware of the core competence or continuity that the other party intends to carry with it into the future. When doing business with past–oriented regressive cultures, he recommends that managers emphasize the history and tradition of the culture. They should find out whether internal relationships will sanction the types of changes that needs to be made, and agree to future meetings in principle but fix no deadline for completions.

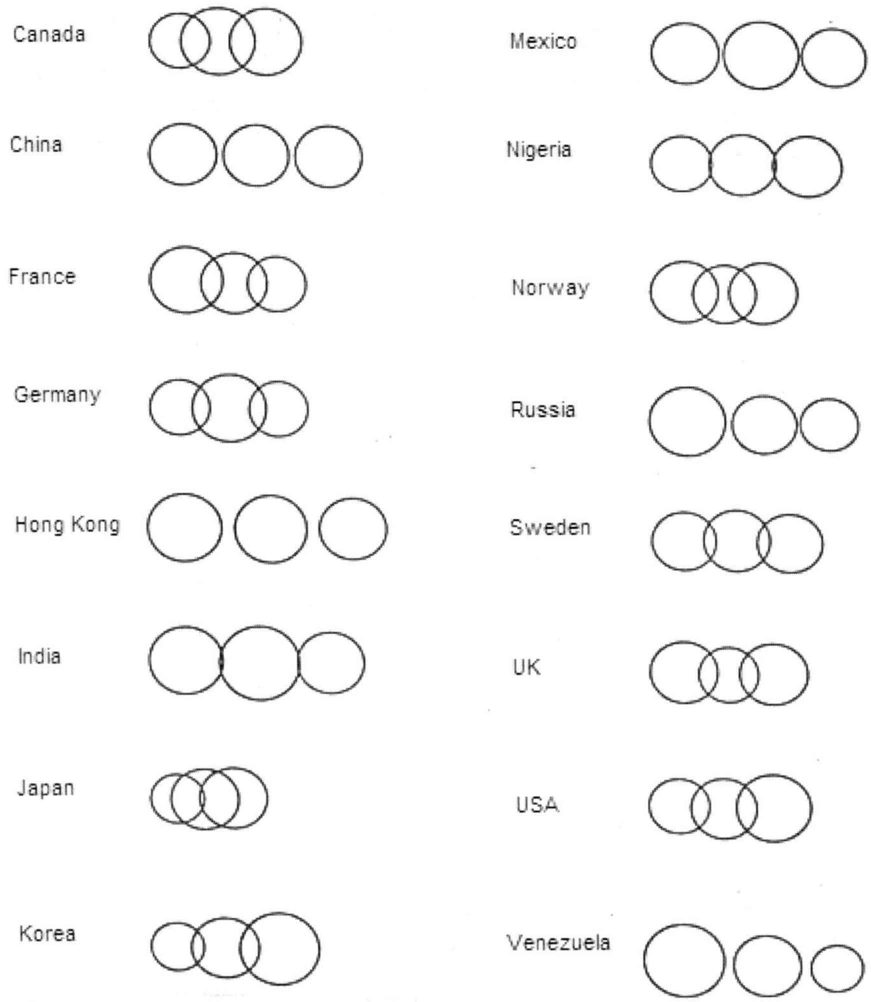

Cultural Clustering (Ronen and Shenkar)

Many researchers have been interested in classifying the cultures and develop cultural clusters based on the similarities among the countries. However, the motivation for these cultural clustering can be significantly different depending upon their academic disciplines.

Why do we need cultural clustering?

The prime motivation of many political scientists who have been clustering the culture based on the region is to understand the sources of international conflicts In a specific region and to develop a regional strategy to deal with them. A typical example of this type of clustering is the work of Huntington's (1993) "The Clash of Civilization"and Inglehart's

(1998) "The World Values Survey." Historians have also tried to understand the past history of human contention and to predict a pattern of future conflicts. (Toynbee, 1947). The major motivation of the economists who are interested in cultural clustering may be to understand the sources of variances in degree and level for economic development (Cattell, 1950; Myrdal,1968; Harrison, 1992.) The cross-cultural anthropologists' motivation is undoubtedly to understand the sources of variations in human behavior, value and attitudes. In business field, the researchers in management area are more interested in how to make an efficient HR staffing & training and how to reduce expatriate failures and to find an efficient managerial and leadership style through cultural clustering. (Ronen and Shenkar, 1985; GLOBE, 2004). In marketing area, they try to find a more efficient regional marketing tools and strategies to maximize the efficiency of limited resources . In this book, three most recent and influential cultural clustering will be discussed.

Ronen and Shenker's clustering

Probably the most referenced research regarding cultural clustering is that proposed by Ronen and Shenkar. The results of their cluster analysis classify the world cultures into eight identifiable clusters; Anglo, Nordic, Germanic, Latin America, Latin European, Arabic, Near eastern and Far Eastern based on their similarities on work-related variables using "a statistical procedures known as "smallest space analysis". Several cultures such as Brazil, Japan, India and Israel are classified as unclassifiable or independent. The results provide a useful structure for understanding the relationship between the workers attitudes and value and cultural commonalities within a group and the dissimilarities among the groups.

Huntington's clustering

He argued that since the Cold War was over and the Soviet Union collapsed, natioanlism as the source of international conflict has been replaced by the culture and civilization. He identified eight different cultures with a possible ninth: Western, Latin American, Islamic, Sinic, Hindu, Orthodox, Buddhist and Japanese, and the possible ninth, African. Huntington argues that this cultural organization (civilization) better describes the current world political structure than the classical notion of variegated sovereign states. He proposed that to understand the sources of current and future international conflict, culture (instead of the nation state) must be accepted as the locus of war. Thus, he insisted that Western nations may lose their prowess if they fail to capture the irreconcilable source of international conflict correctly and fail to develop an adequate strategy to deal with ever escalating international tension.

GLOBE (2004) researchers used the following nine (9) dimensions to classify the cultures based on their scores for cultural "practice" (actual) and cultural "value" (desired) and present the country cluster as below.

Cultural Dimensions;

1) Performance Orientation
2) Assertiveness
3) Future Orientation
4) Humane Orientation
5) Institutional Collectivism
6) In-group Collectivism
7) Gender Egalitarianism
8) Power Distance
9) Uncertainty Avoidance

Based on the scores of the above nine (9) cultural dimensions, they classify the cultures into ten (10) distinctive clusters and present the country cluster as below.

1) Germanic Europe
2) Nordic Europe
3) Anglo Europe
4) Latin Europe
5) Latin America
6) Eastern Europe
7) Middle East
8) Sub-Saharan Africa
9) Southern Asia
10) Confucian Asia

They re-configured the above country cluster using a "Multi-dimensional scaling" procedure to assess the degree of overall distance among the ten cultural clusters, across the nine dimensions that they investigated and draw a cultural map as below. The vertical North-South axis of the meta-configuration separates the five Western clusters from the five eastern cultures. For quadrants are identified. The first quadrant consists of Middle East, Sub-Saharan Africa, and the Eastern Europe clusters. The second quadrant consists of Latin America and Latin Europe clusters. The third quadrant consists of Anglo, Germanic Europe, and Nordic Europe clusters. The fourth quadrant consists of Confucian Asian and South Asian clusters.

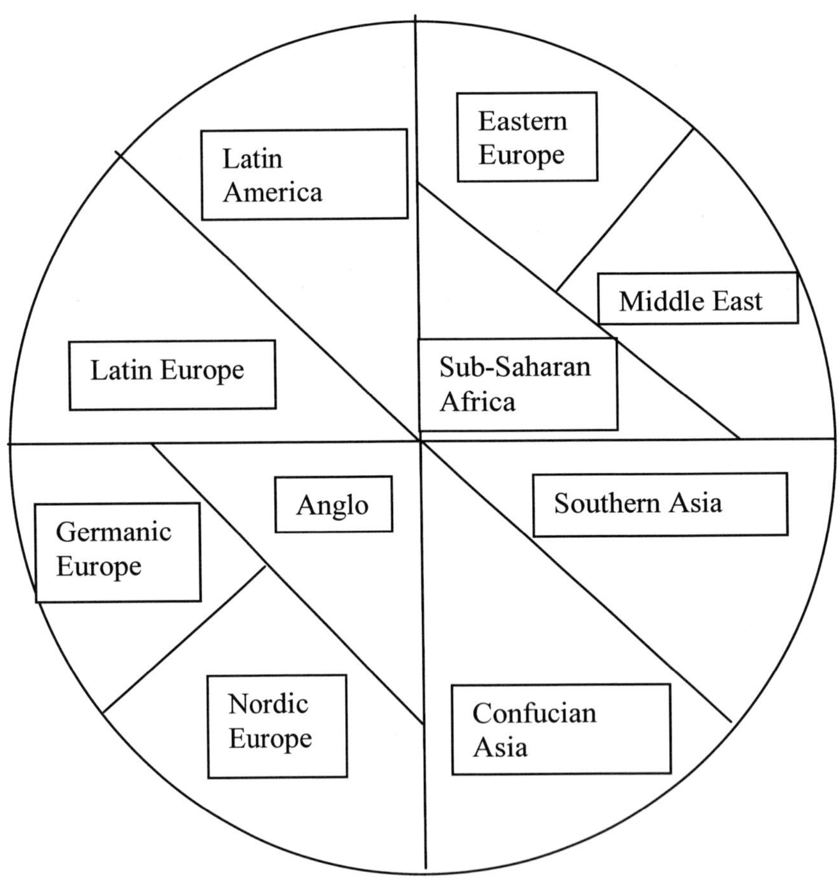

Attitudes toward Cultural Differences

There are basically three different attitudes that people adopt when they face different cultures.

Ethnocentrism (Sumner)

Ethnocentrism is defined as the view of things in which one's own group is the center of everything; all others are sacred and rated with reference to their own culture. The basic attitude of the individual who hold Ethnocentrism is "I am the center of the universe and my culture is standard and superior to any other culture."

Symptom: Individual's judgment is immediate and based on "self reference criteria". For example, an ethnocentric person would criticize other culture's diet patterns, such as Southeast Asians eating monkey brains or Americans eating bloody rare steaks, as being gross or disgusting.

Danger: Ethnocentric behaviors can be insulting to many foreigners and can provoke retaliation.

Attributions: All people are actually born to be ethnocentric. Most of the countries' national anthems, flags and their name often reveal this attitude.

As you can see below, people tend to perceive the world within their own cultural frame of reference or through their own cultural window.
Hypothetically, when the people in the culture A see a round shape object like K they will perceive the object like a triangular shape without sharp angle since they look the round shape object within their cultural window, which has a triangular shape. Whereas, the people in culture B will perceive the same round shape object X as a kind of square shape without sharp angle since they interpret and perceive the object within their own cultural frame, which happens to have a square shape.

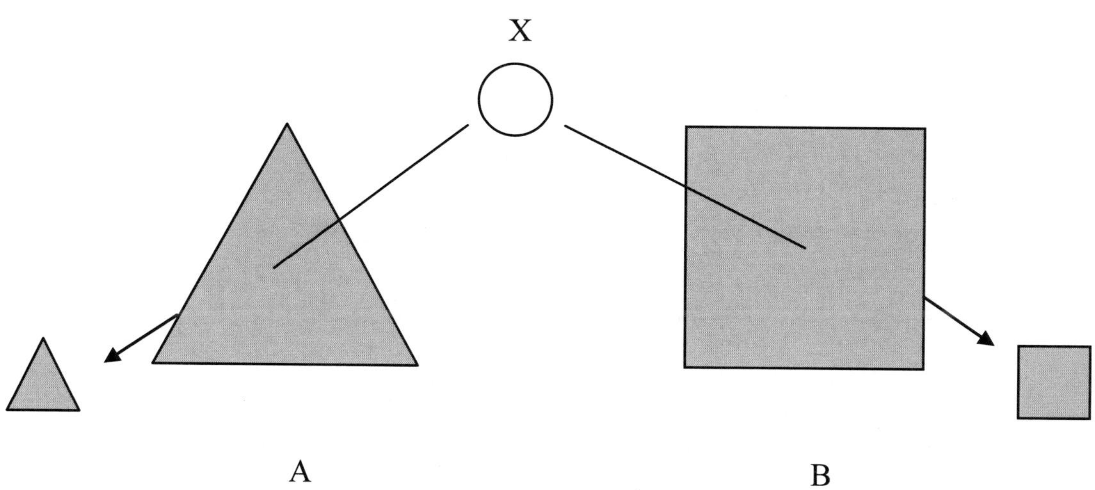

Thus, culture is a kind of window through which people look at the world. For example, when a researcher asked a group of American boys what a diamond shape (see below) represents to them, the majority of American boys responded by saying a baseball field. However, when the same picture was shown to the Mexican boys, the majority of them thought of a bullfighting ring.

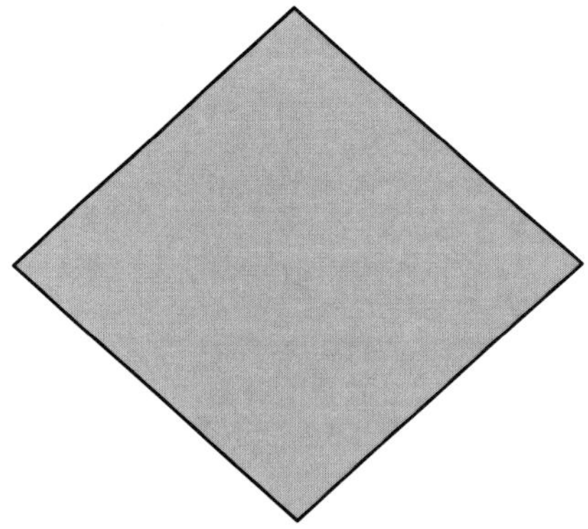

Another example may be the fact that, in the United States, we call China, Japan and Korea, Far Eastern countries. That is because we are culturally trained to look at the world from the West to East because most of our ancestors came from Europe, which is east to us. However, when we look at the world from East to West, those countries are there right across the Pacific Ocean not that Far East after all.

The *main reasons* why people are ethnocentric are cultural ignorance, lack of understanding and insensitivity.

The main *consequence* of ethnocentric behavior is that people may stereotype other cultures based on extremes, in-group versus out-group distinction, and think in terms of "us versus them." Sometimes even with hatred to the out-group along with distrust and a sense of them being inferior. Even though ethnocentrism is very common, it is not desirable particularly for International managers. If an international businessman holds this kind of attitude, he can easily aggravate their foreign business partners and lose your opportunities to do business with them. **One most important thing we have to remember about the culture is that there is no superior or inferior culture yet there are only differences among cultures**. We must remember not to confuse culture with material civilization and the level of economic development.

<u>Polycentrism</u>

Polycentrism can be defined as the view of things in which one believes that every aspects of a foreign culture is superior to his own culture, and therefore, every aspects of the foreign culture must be respected and observed. This attitude can come from shallow experiences and very limited exposure to other cultures where one only sees the good parts of it. The possible *consequences* that MNC's can suffer when their managers have this kind of attitude are:

- There can be high agency costs. The managers who like locals and local culture so much may lose their effectiveness as American manager working for American firms. There is no guarantee that this type of person would work for the best interest of his parent company.
- A multi-national company may lose uniformity and consistency in the implementation of policies, which may lead it to become more of a "multi-domestic company" that a multi-national company.

<u>Geocentrism</u>

It is the view of things in which one looks at positive aspects of both his home and host cultures, and accepts the differences between them without bias. Under this view, the individual could maintain the same distance from each culture. The *attributions* of this attitude come from extensive cross-cultural first-hand experiences and in-depth knowledge. The outcome of this attitude is having a high level of cultural sensitivity with multiple cultural frames of references when looking at cultural differences.

Cultural Diversity

Potential Advantage of Cultural Diversity

There are several benefits of having cultural diversity in an organization. There is emerging evidence that culturally diverse groups can enhance creativity and innovation, lead to better decisions, and result in more effective and productive performance.
Obviously one of the main benefits of cultural diversity is the generation of more and better ideas. Because team members come from many different cultural back grounds, they often are able to create a greater number of unique (and thus creative) solutions and

recommendations. Culture is a unique and special way to perceive the world. Thus, people's way to look at the problem and their way to solve the problem can be significantly different depending upon what kind of cultural back ground each member has. A second major benefit is that culturally diverse groups can prevent the pressure for linear groupthink, which often requires conformity and put the pressures on individual members to reach consensus under the name of efficiency. The members of culturally diverse groups can avoid this problem because they are expected to be same and thereby less pressure to conform. As a result, it may take a longer time to reach consensus but they can make more careful decision after they deliberate all different perspectives with open-mindedness.

Potential Problems Associated with Diversity

In general, cultural diversity in an organization can cause a problem to create a sense of unity among the group members and result in a **lack of cohesion in the unit.** This kind of situation obviously present a problem in the unit's inability to make a coordinated effort to solve the problem and attribute very dysfunction behaviors amplified based on their ethnocentric attitudes. Unfortunately, when culturally diverse groups come together, they often bring **preconceived stereotypes** with them. At this point it would be very beneficial to understand the difference between stereotyping and sociotyping.

Stereotyping vs. Sociotyping

Typical stereotyping involves a belief about a group of people, about a category. Examples are such as "blacks are lazy," "Jews are shrewd," and "American Indians are alcoholics." Each of these beliefs is an oversimplified, over generalization, or exaggerated statement. Some of these stereotypes might be totally false; some might be based on half-truths or might have a kernel of truth. Thus, *stereotypes are overgeneralizations, oversimplified, or exaggerated beliefs associated with a category or a group of people.* The holders of such beliefs are construed to be relatively rigid in their adherence, and the beliefs are often emotionally colored. The principal difference between stereotyping and social classification, or sociotyping, done in the social sciences is that stereotyping is an emotionally rigid process whereas sociotyping is a scientific process. The sociotype of a group or a social category is flexible, and probabilistic, and it is revised as new data becomes available. For instance, when communication scholars compare self-disclosure patterns of males and females, it is done on a statistical basis, the object being to ascertain the distinguishing characteristics of males and females, if any. Statistical generalizations for males and females are developed. Such statistical generalizations about a social category are called sociotypes. If our research showed that females are more self-disclosing than males we would consider this generalization to be a sociotype rather than a stereotype. In summary, Stereotyping is an oversimplified, overgeneralization, or exaggerated statement based on prejudice or extreme cases. Sociotyping is a scientifically generated, probabilistically reliable, and internally acceptable generalization.

Another potential problem observed in a culturally diverse group is **inaccurate communication or inability to communicate accurately.** One source of the problem is misunderstanding caused by words used by a message sender. Another source of potential problem is misinterpretation of the behavioral cues. Many Japanese say "hi" and nod their heads, but this does not necessarily mean that they agree with what you said. They simply want to be polite and to avoid the embarrassment and confrontation.

One research reveals that multicultural diverse teams have a great deal of potential to be either very effective or very ineffective. As illustrated below, Kovach indicates that if cross-cultural groups are led properly, they can indeed be very effective. However, if they are not managed properly, they can be highly dysfunctional and ineffective. In other words, diverse groups can be more powerful than single-culture groups if it is adequately managed and a proper leadership is provided.

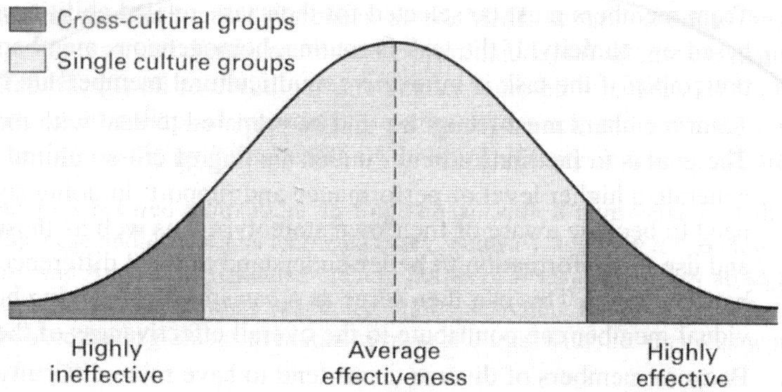

Source: Based on Dr. Carol Kovach's research, conducted at the Graduate School of Management, University of California at Los Angeles (UCLA), and reported in Nancy J. Adler, *International Dimensions of Organizational Behavior,* 2nd ed. (Boston: PWS-Kent Publishing, 1991), p. 135.

Conditions for Effective multicultural team

One crucial question raised in conjunction with cultural diversity is under what kind of condition this multicultural team functions most efficiently. Previous research indicates that multicultural teams are most effective when they are assigned of the tasks that require creative thinking and innovativeness. They are far less effective when they are assigned to routine tasks. Adler argues that Cultural diversity provides biggest asset for teams with difficult, discretionary tasks requiring innovation. Diversity becomes less helpful when employees are working on simple tasks involving repetitive or routine procedures. Consequently, diversity will provide more benefits at the initial planning and development stage of projects rather than action and implementation stage. This also implies that the senior level managerial team who are often required to develop more creative solution and strategies can get more benefits from diversity than lower level staff whose job is typically routine work.

Another important conditioning for effectiveness of the multicultural team is goal-path clarity. Given the same level of job assignment, if a clear path and instruction to reach or achieve the goal is presented, multicultural teams can function more effectively by pooling their resources and talents acquired from their different cultural backgrounds. Last factor that can also influence the effectiveness of the multicultural team is the leadership style. If the team has an authoritative leader, the group may be able to make a quick decision not eventually have difficulties to implement the decision made by this type of leader and cause a great deal of repercussion and resistance in implementing stage. The democratic and participatory leader will take time to solicit members' ideas from the beginning stage and can make a consensual decision which will ensure the efficient operation and implementation.

Cross-cultural Transactional Analysis

Original transactional analysis was developed to understand and explain how people behave when they encounter other people and what kind f psychological position that take when they meet other people. This can be applied in cross cultural setting as below.

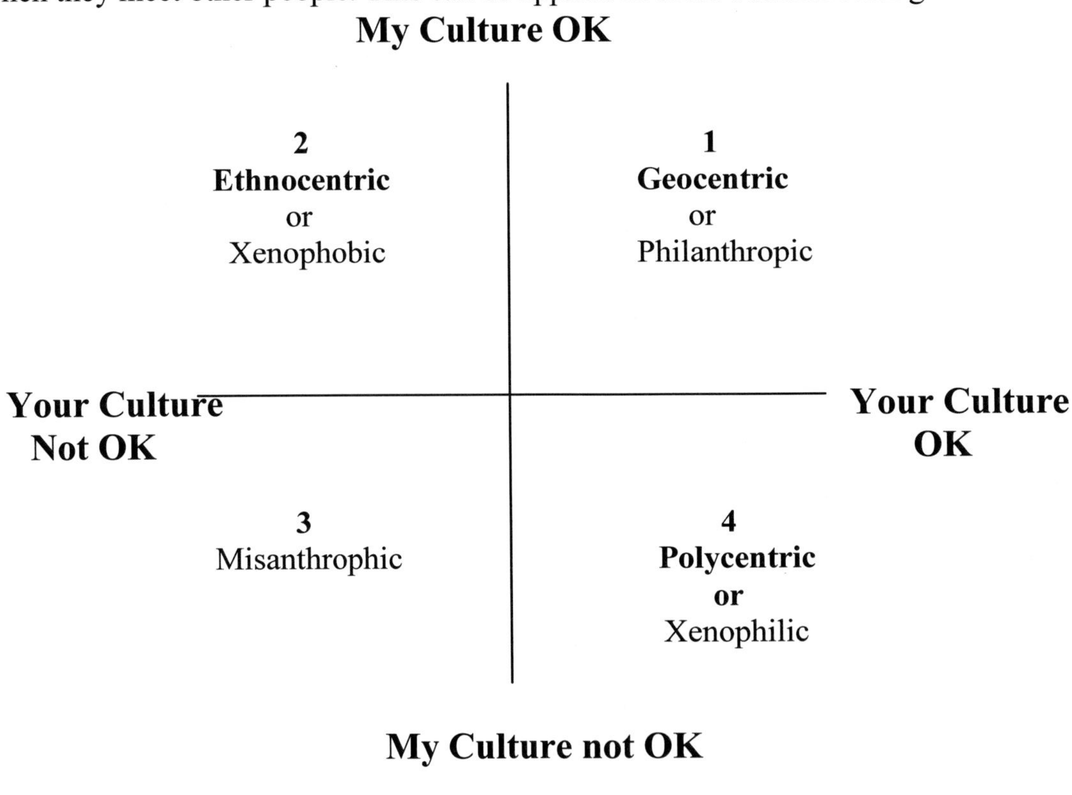

Source: "Enhancing Managerial Cross-Cultural Awareness and Sensitivity- Transactional Analysis Revisited", Hoon Park and Kline Harris, The Journal of Management Development, Vol. 10, No.3, 1993, pp. 22-29.

Although regrettably most individuals fall into the Ethnocentric (the 2nd) quadrant, it is not desirable for a multi-national company manager to be in this category. However, it is also not desirable for a multi-national company manager to fall into the Polycentric quadrant (4th) either. As mentioned, the majority of people fall into the Ethnocentric quadrant with a smaller number in both the Geocentric quadrant and the Polycentric quadrant. Thus, any cross-cultural training program should focus on how to move people's undesirable position (ethnocentric or polycentric) to more desirable position such as Geocentric position.

Ego States

Another very important part of Transactional analysis is to understand the people's ego state when they encounter foreigners. There are several ego states that people might have when encounter foreigners.

1. Child Ego State:

The person who has this type of ego state is characterized as uninhibited release of emotions such as hate, anger, or excitement toward the foreigners or foreign culture. The person with this type of ego state release his emotion based on distorted perception of foreign culture.

Verbal expressions; "All Jews"..., "Yankees...", "Disgusting", "Stupid", "Ridiculous".

Non-verbal actions: scowling, frowning, giggling, grumbling, shouting, or teasing.

2. Parent Ego State:

The person who holds this ego state is very judgmental, critical, persuasive, and preaching. This type of person tries to preach foreigners assuming that they are uneducated and ignorant. This type of ego state is often more dangerous than the Child Ego State in cross-cultural contact because the individual who has this type of ego state can easily insult foreigners by trying to preach them.

Verbal expressions: "Why don't you"..., "You should do," "You better not this", "It is illogical or irrational to do...", "Poor...".

Non-verbal actions: clicking tongue, shaking head, pointing finger.

3. Adult Ego State:

The individual who hold this type of ego state doesn't criticize or blame foreign culture but he is simply curious or experimental, and tries to understand rather why they behave than condemn them or release his emotion unchecked.

Verbal expressions: "How come"..., "Aha, I see...", "How would you feel... "What makes you ..."

Non-verbal actions: attentive, responsive, and inquisitive.

Culture Shock

Culture shock is defined as accumulated stress and strain caused by removal of familiar environment and being forced to meet daily needs where behavioral cues do not work. It is a special and more often than not a traumatic experience that people have when two different cultures collide.

Symptoms of culture shock are:
- Self-doubt and loss of confidence.
- Inability to think logically
- Blaming, and criticizing the host country
- Loneliness.
- Anxiety.
- Psychosomatic problems such as headache, diarrhea, and insomnia.

Cultural Adjustment

Gullahorn and Gullahorn, former Peace Corp workers, developed **W-Curve** as displayed below to explain the cultural adjustment process.

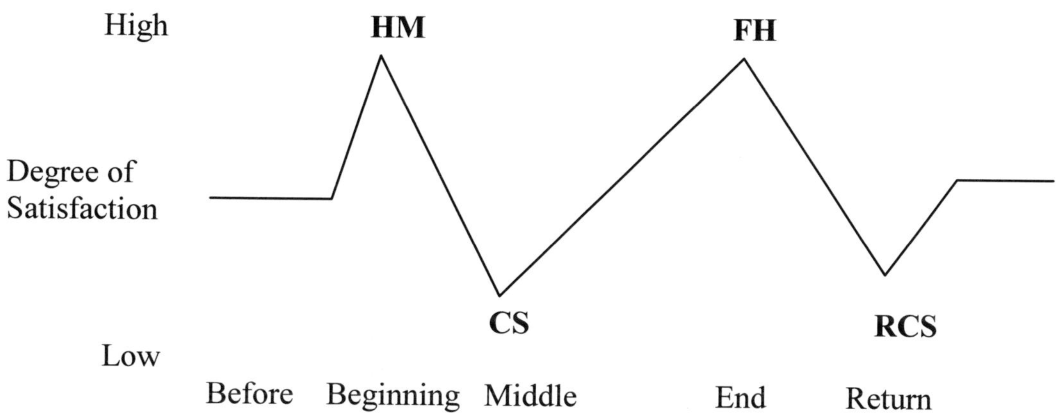

Beginning: Honeymoon (**HM**) stage; pleasantly shocking experiences

Middle: Culture Shock (**CS**) stage where you develop a lot of hostility and animosity toward the host culture.

Ending: Feel at Home (**FH**) stage where you begin to feel comfortable again in foreign country

Return: Reverse Culture Shock (**RCS**) stage when you return home country, you feel alienated in your own country.

It may seem odd that an individual would experience reverse culture shock, however when he returns, and finds that everything has changed he may feel lost and forgotten. It is often called the "Rip Van Winkle Syndrome". Many companies now try to help their managers through the reverse culture shock stage.

Review Questions

Why do we have to study culture?

What is CQ ?

Discuss the various definition of culture.

What is Sapir-Worf hypothesis and its implication?

Identify some major differences between American culture and tradition culture/

Discuss five steps in cross-cultural communication and identify the potential sources of noises in the process.

Discuss the definition of silent language and identify potential sources of problem when using it.

Identify ten (10) cultural dimensions and discuss the components of each dimension.

Identify three different attitudes that people can have when they look at the foreign culture and discuss attributes and consequences of each attitude.

Discuss the Cross-Cultural Transactional Analysis and identify the major components of each quadrant.

What are the three different ego states and their major characteristics?

What is the definition of culture shock and its typical symptoms?

Identify each stage of W-curve developed by Gullahorn and Gullahorn and discuss the typical symptoms of each stage.

Chapter 9. Government Influence on Trade

Even if the world economy is becoming more and more intertwined and globalized, not a single country actually allows the goods and services to be transferred across their national boundaries unchecked. For various reasons, still most of the countries want to exercise a certain amount of control over the goods and services moving across the national boundaries. In most of the cases, the government control is imposed on the importation from foreign countries.

Reasons for import restrictions

Unemployment Argument

If a country imports too much, the domestic firms cannot sell much of their product thereby they may have to shut down their plant. If this happens, many people in the country will lose their jobs. In order to avoid this kind of situation and to reduce possible unemployment, the government can consider a restriction on the importation of foreign goods. However, there are a few negative aspects to this argument. If the citizens can't buy cheap foreign goods, they will be forced to purchase more expensive domestic goods. As product prices increase, the individual's real income (actual amount of goods that people can buy with their fixed income) decreases. Also, in this case there is always a possibility of retaliation from the foreign country whose products can no longer be sold because of the restriction. For example, if the U.S. put restrictions on steel made by European Union, then E.U. might retaliate with restrictions on importing U.S. beef. In this sense, this could only cause a transfer of unemployment from one industry (steel) to another (beef) in the U.S.

Cheap Labor Argument

Many human right activist groups insist that we should not buy the goods produced in the countries where workers and children are exploited by cheap wage. These groups are very much concerned about the well being of foreign workers and children and try to protest against the violation of human rights in many foreign factories. These foreign factories are called "sweatshop", where the overall working condition is horrible and often inhuman. However, this argument also creates a great deal of controversy in international trade negotiation. Many people believe that stop buying the goods from those countries is not the right way to help them even if their labor is exploited. Stop buying the goods from those countries will eventually make them lose their job and it will only deteriorate their living condition worse than before. Many recent reports including U.N. reports confirm this allegation. Most of the countries, which are criticized for labor exploitation, argue that this is a kind of intervention on their domestic affairs and another form of protectionism disguised under the name of humanitarianism. Thus, unless proved otherwise there are some other parallel efforts arranged to help foreign workers and children, it is very difficult to convince them and to avoid such criticism. Rather than simply taking away their job by not buying their products, it may be more effective to put pressure on the local government to enforce more strict work environmental law and child labor law. Another way to improve the conditions is to provide an auxiliary education program like what Nike started recently. Nike recently tried to initiate after work school programs in certain countries to help those children who work at their factory to get education. This will not only help their foreign employees get better education but also help Nike enhance their public image as global citizen.

Infant Industry Argument

This argument is mostly adopted by developing countries who wants to impose restrictions to protect small and young domestic firms who has no global competitiveness yet. Such industries cannot benefit from economies of scale because their domestic market is too small and they cannot enjoy the benefit of a learning curve because their experiences are very limited. Those reasons would prompt their government to use this argument to protect them in their developing stages. However, the problem of this argument is that the citizens in the country may have to pay more to buy very expensive domestically produced goods even if cheap foreign goods are available. Another typical problem is once they impose restrictions on foreign goods based on this argument; they want to keep this restriction indefinitely to shut out all foreign products from the market even if their domestic firms gain some level of competitiveness.

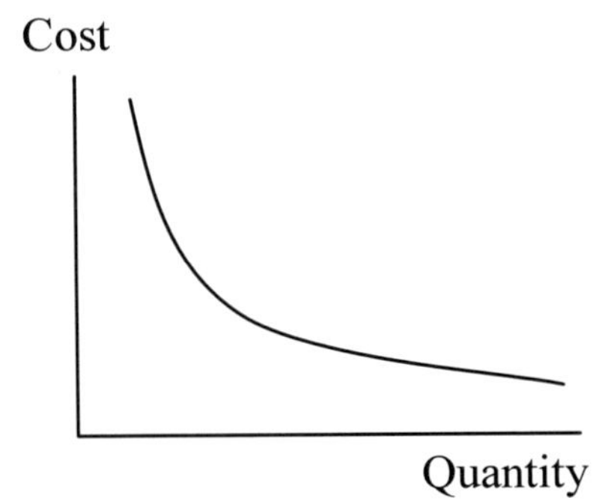

Economies of Scale
(Unit cost of manufacturing decreases as total output increases)

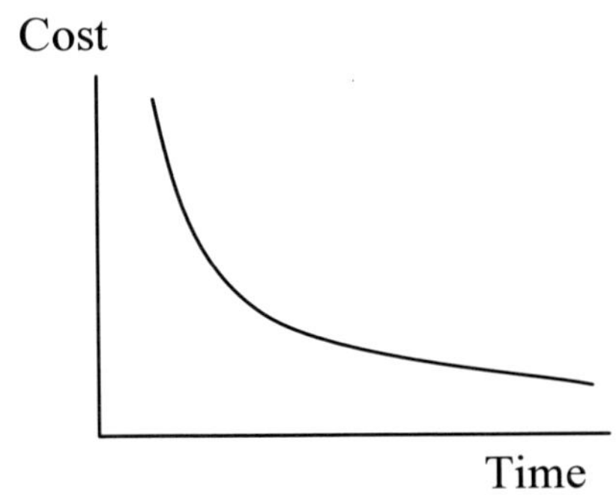

Learning Curve
(you learn to produce more efficiently as time passes)

Industrialization Argument

When some developing countries try to restructure their economy from agriculture orientee economy to manufacturing oriented economy, they may want to impose import restrictions. The rationale behind this restructuring of their economyt is that historically the prices of agricultural products remained the same level for last several decades, but the prices of manufactured products have experienced rapid increase over time. In other words, as seen below, Term of Trade (defined as below) for many countries whose economy is agriculture oriented one has been deteriorated for last several decades.

$$\text{Term of Trade} = \frac{\text{Price of Export (Agricultural products)} \;\rightarrow}{\text{Price of Import (Manufactured Products)} \;\uparrow} \Longrightarrow \text{Restructuring}$$

Thus, for those countries, which produce and export agricultural products and import the manufactured products, they will continuously lose more money that they can earn. This is the reason why, so many developing countries with agriculture-oriented economy now try to convert their economy to manufacturing oritneted economy.

However, one of the most serious problems here is the question of who should bear the cost of transition from agricultural oriented economy to a manufacturing oriented economy. During this transitory period, the citizens have to make sacrifices by buying expensive domestic product while the companies who can enjoy this government protection can make a profit. The domestic firms will get the most benefit at the sacrifice of the general public's well being and they never pay it back to the citizens who sacrificed their well being under the name of industrialization. This is one of the typical problems of inequitable distribution that many newly industrialized countries experienced in the process of industrializing their economy.

National Income Argument

A country whose national income decreases may try to minimize imports in an attempt to increase their national income or at least to stop decrease in their national income. The rationale behind this approach is *Keynesian Theory* where national income (Y) is decided as following:

$$Y = C + I + G + (X - I)$$

Y = National Income	G = Govt. Spending
C = Consumption	X = Exports
I = Investment	I = Imports

Thus, if a country wants to increase their national income (Y), then they may try to control imports to a minimum. However, this action will provoke retaliation from their trading partner. For example, the U.S. would lower its imports from its trading partners, Japan. in an attempt to increase their national income, and then the U.S. income may go up temporarily. However, when Japan's national income goes down as we impose restriction on their product, they may want to retaliate. If they retaliate successfully by imposing restrictions on our products, then the U.S. national income could go down too, making both countries worse off. The problem with this argument is the possibility **"beggar-thy-neighbor"** situation where both countries are left worse off when they have trade war by imposing restriction on each other's products. If countries want to improve their national income, they should try to change one of the other factors (such as C, I and or G) in the national income equation to avoid this problem rather than imposing import restriction.

Political Argument (Sanction)

Sometimes a government may want to impose sanctions on a certain country to protest undesirable or reprehensible political behaviors or to punish a country that violates the international laws and regulations. Since the U.S. has the enormous amount of leverage due to its largest market in the world, if the U.S. stops buying from a certain country or stop selling certain products to a certain country, it can devastate the target country's economy. Using this unique economic position, sometimes, the U.S. government tries to exercise economic muscle to achieve political objectives. However, if the sanction is not imposed properly or if the target country effectively deals with the sanction imposed, the sanctions sometimes can hurt its own country more than the sanctioned country.

Balance of Payment Argument

When a country has a large amount of Balance of Payment deficit or Trade deficit, the government may want to impose restriction on foreign products in an attempt to reduce Balance of Payment deficit or trade/merchandise deficit . For example, the U.S. now has a record high Trade Deficit so it has a legitimate reason to impose restrictions on the goods imported from the countries such as Japan and China which have huge amount of trade surplus with us. However, even in this case, some political and strategic considerations should be incorporated. Since the U.S. believes free trade is one element of the pure form of democracy, as an undisputed champion to promote world peace, it is very difficult to take any serious protective action that can escalate an international conflict with our traditional ally such as Japan. Even if the U.S. has a huge amount of trade deficit with China, we are still very reluctant to take any drastic action to curtail importation from this country because we need their help to ease the global financial crisis and to stabilize geo-political environment in the region.

Various forms of Trade barriers

Tariff

Once a country decides to control international trade, particularly importation from a foreign country, the most common form of import restriction is **Tariff**. It can be categorized based on the objectives or assessment methods as below.

Based on Objectives

a. *Revenue Tariffs;* to increase government revenue from imports.
b. *Protective Tariffs;* to protect domestic industries.
c. *Progressive Tariffs;* to discourage luxurious imports.
d. *Retaliatory Tariffs;* to retaliate against foreign tariffs.
e. *Countervailing Tariffs;* to offset the effect of foreign tariffs (Surcharge: a special short term countervailing tariff)
f. *Punitive Tariffs;* to punish unacceptable behavior.

Based on Assessment Methods

a. *Specific Duty System;* imposing a fixed amount of tariff for each unit imported. (e.g. $10/unit)
b. *Ad Valorem System;* imposing % of the value of imported goods. (e.g. 10% of the value to the goods)
c. *Compound Duty;* combination of specific and ad valorem duties. (e.g. $5/unit + 5% of the value)

Traditionally, tariffs have always been the main trade barriers. However, WTO (World Trade Organization) has been working very hard and put a great deal of of pressure on its members to reduce tariffs in order to facilitate free world trade through its multilateral negotiation. Consequnetly, overall tariffs barriers have been reduced significantly for the last couple of decades. However, so many countries still don't want to import from other countries with Mercantilistic attitudes. Accordingly, a significant part of traditional tariff barriers have been replaced by invisible non-tariff barriers. Thus, Non-tariff barriers become more serious barriers than before recently and became the major focal points of international trade negotiations.

Non-Tariff Barriers (NTB)

Government Subsidies

Many foreign companies could successfully reduce their manufacturing price significantly only because their government provides a considerable amount oif subsidies. These can be in the form of lower taxes, low interest rate loans, duty drawbacks or research and development support. The government subsidies help foreign firms reduce their price and build an **artificial competitiveness**. As discussed earlier, this is one of the reasons why many U.S. companies cannot effectively compete with foreign firms who receive a great deal of their governmental help.

Exchange Rate Manipulation

Exchange Rate Manipulation is another serious form of NTB. In some cases, a foreign government deliberately devalues its currency to make its products cheaper and this devaluation will then make the U.S. products more expensive because the U.S. currency vis-à-vis their currency will be appreciated. For example, if the Chinese government devalues their currency, Yuan(RMB) from $1:Y5 to $1:Y10, U.S. products would then be twice as expensive in Chinese market. China has been accused of manipulating their currency value and deliberately keep it low in an attempt to increase their export and discourage importation from other countries.

Problems at the Customs House

Sometimes governments try to frustrate anybody who wants to import from a foreign country by making custom clearing process much more cumbersome. This can take the form of deliberate administrative delays or purposefully making documentation complicated. Occasionally, they also apply double standards when they inspect the quality of the imported product. They apply very high quality standards only for imported product in an attempt to block the importation from other countries.

Quota (Quantity Limitations)

Many countries set a quantity limitation on the goods imported from foreign countries. Generally, quota can be classified into two types; Absolute quota and tariff quota. Absolute quota means importation beyond a certain quantity limit set by local government will be absolutely prohibited. Under tariff quota, it is still allowed to import the goods from foreign countries beyond the quantity limit established by local government. However, very high tariff rate will be applied beyond this limit.

Buy Local Policy

In many countries, government has regulations to force the purchase of local products. More often that not, government agencies which normally procure large amount of goods are required to buy local goods by law even if cheap and quality foreign products are available. Also, governments can impose a regulation where locally produced goods must contain a minimum percentage of local parts produced domestically (Local Content Bill).

Exchange Control

In many countries particularly where they have chronic balance of payment deficit problems, citizens are not allowed to hold any foreign currency. They must sell all foreign currency to their Central Bank as soon as they obtain them. When they need foreign product, they have to go to the central bank and have to buy the foreign currency to settle the importation. If a citizen fails to justify why they have to buy foreign product or if an equivalent product is available in the domestic market, they cannot buy the foreign currency that is absolutely needed to settle the international trade. They not only control the foreign exchange this way but also apply multiple exchange rate system, where central bank buys currency at low rate but sells at high rate to put maximum burden on the importer.

Complicated/burdensome import procedures

In order to get an import license, very tough qualifications are needed in many countries. In other words, governments may require certain amount of capital or certain number of employees before issuing a license to import. Also, an importer may have to get approval for each single case and have the burden of proof that the product in question is not available anywhere in the domestic market, so the company may have to do an extensive search just to find this proof. Governments can also impose a strict linkage between export and import. In this case, only those who have previously exported will be given a chance to import. Moreover, an import deposit, usually with no interest being paid on it, may be required to place the maximum financial burden on the importer.

US trade related laws

Super 301

This is an article of the U.S. Trade Act that requires the U.S. government to prepare a list of countries ("hit list") that systematically restrict access of U.S. products to their markets. If a trade dispute with one of these countries cannot be resolved through negotiation, the law requires imposing trade sanction on that country immediately.

Section 201, Trade Act (Safeguard provision)

This provision allows U.S. industries, which are seriously injured or threatened by dramatic increase in imports, to petition for import relief such as a quota. Then, the President makes the decision whether to provide relief and the amount of relief (limitation on the quantity imported).

Both provisions permit the U.S. government to "escape" temporarily from its obligations to settle the trade disputes within WTO's framework.

Review Questions

Identify the various arguments frequently used to support import restrictions and discuss some potential problems associated with each argument.

Discuss the various forms of Tariff based on their objectives.

Discuss three different methods to assess the amount of tariff.

Identify and discuss various forms of NTB (non-tariff-barriers).

What is "Super 301" of US trade act?

What is "Section 201" of US trade act?

CHAPTER 10. ECONOMIC INTEGRATION

After World War II many countries started to work closely to improve mutual understanding in an attempt to avoid another round of catastrophic war. More recently, many countries also started to have a strong necessity to work together to improve their competitiveness and strengthen economic ties to survive under an ever globalized world economy. Thus, many nations and states started to make strategic alliances by establishing some forms of economic integration. If countries want to have an economic integration, they have several choices depending upon what level of integration and cooperation that they want to have.

Various forms of Economic Integration

Free Trade Area

This is the most basic form of economic integration that a country can choose. If they create FTA, there will be no **internal tariff (**tariff among the member countries**)** charged among member countries, and each affiliated country has its own independent external tariff (tariff against non-member countries) system between themselves and towards non-member countries. For example, since the U.S., Canada and Mexico are the members of North American Free Trade Area, there is no internal tariff (no tariff among the member countries) but each country will have its own tariff system against non-member country like Japan. Some other examples of a Free Trade Area that previously existed are EFTA in Europe, and CARFTA in the Caribbean.

Customs Union

This is a little more advanced form of economic union than FTA. When they create customs union, like FTA, there is no internal tariff charged among member countries. However, the members of Customs Union will have the same common external tariffs, which are charged to non-member countries. An example is the old European Customs Union called Benelux, which included three countries (Belgium, Luxembourg, and the Netherlands).

A recent example of this type of integration is MERCOSUR in Latin America, whose members are Argentina, Brazil, Paraguay, Uruguay, Bolivia and Chile.

Common Market

The next level of economic integration is the Common Market. When they decide to have a common market, like the Customs Union, there is no internal tariff among the member countries but they will have a common external tariff against non-member countries. However, in addition, the member countries of common market usually agree to abolish restrictions on factor (labor and capital) mobility. The idea is to try to facilitate free flow of production factors as well as free flow of finished products.
Examples are the Early European Union, which was previously known as the European Common Market. Another example is the Central American Common Market (CACM).

Economic Union

This contains all aspects of the Common Market plus more harmonized efforts to coordinate and implement the same economic policies among the member countries. What they try to do through Economic Union is not only guarantee the free flow of goods and production factors but also try to cooperate with each other to achieve common economic goals. This is the theoretical direction of European Union.

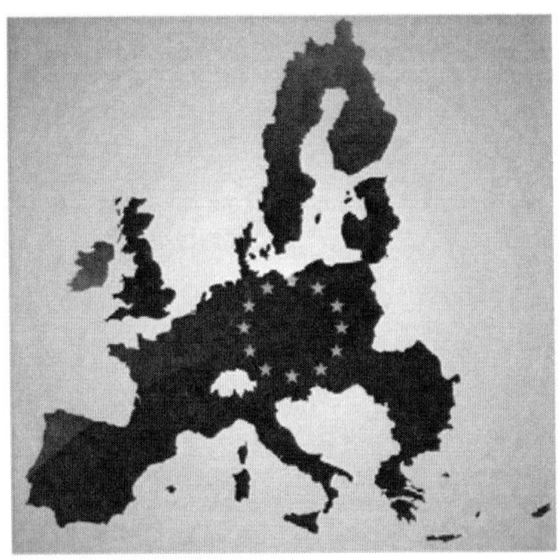

Complete Integration

It is the form that strives to achieve unification of economic, social and political systems by creating a supranational authority such as the U.S. or previous Soviet Union. This represents the last stage of integration that will eventually require a creation of federal government by surrendering their political sovereignty.

Summary of Economic Integration

Level of Integration	FTA	Customs Union	Common Market	Economic Union	Complete Union
1.No Internal Tariff	yes	yes	yes	yes	yes
2.Common Ext. tariff		yes	yes	yes	yes
3.No restriction On factor			yes	yes	yes
4.Harmonize Econ. Policy				yes	yes
5.Political & Social union					yes

The basic idea behind any kind of economic integration is to eliminate or reduce trade barriers. One of the major benefits of being the member of any kind of economic integration would be economy of scale. If they can have a bigger market by eliminating the trade barriers among the member countries, firms can sell more and produce more and thereby they can reduce their manufacturing costs and prices. This will eventually help them have competitiveness in global market. Also, efficiency would be improved because with more competition in the region, only the most efficient producer would survive. Lastly, bargaining power against other economic units would be improved since they can make collaborative efforts in international trade negotiations.

However, one of the typical problems in any kind of economic integration is the fact that international trade can divert away from efficient non-member countries to inefficient member countries. This can be illustrated as follows:

A = member
B = member (inefficient)
C = non-member (efficient)

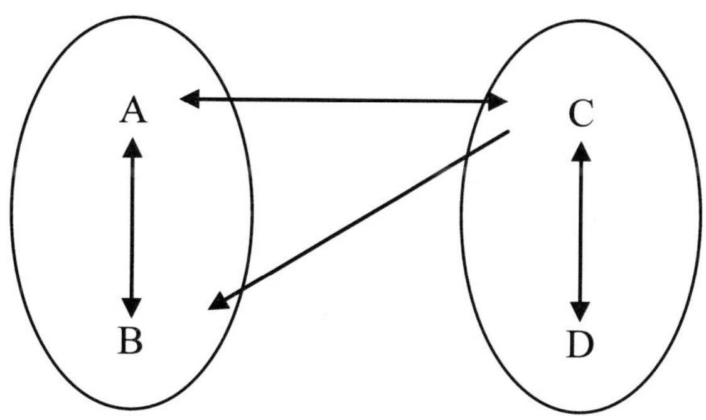

In the diagram, country A used to trade with the country C who is efficient producer before any economic integration was in effect. Economic integration was then formed between country A and B, and between country C and D. Now country A may have to trade with B, not because country B is efficient producer but only because country B is the member of same economic integration.

Another potential problem with economic integration is that international conflict and tension can easily escalate because even the small countries now think they have more leverage and power since they are the part of larger economic integration and don't want to make any concession in international trade negotiation.

Some important forms of Economic Integration

1.- European Union (Single European Act)

The major motivation to create this Union was the fear of being left alone or left behind while other economies like the U.S. and Japan continuously grew for the last couple of decades. The European economy has been stagnated for a long time and they try to get out of this economic doldrums by tightening up their economic ties with their neighboring countries. The objective was the restoration of economic competitiveness for European countries in a globalized world economy. Their basic approach to set up this union was by removing various barriers still existing among the member countries such as physical (check points on borders etc.), fiscal (red tape and customhouse problems), financial (transaction costs emerged from using different currencies) and technical (different measurement units etc.) barriers and obstacles.

However, one of the most serious challenges in establishing the E.U. was how to keep the optimal balance between nations' interests and common goals. It is not that easy to find an optimal balance between the common goals and that of each member country. Deeply rooted ethnocentric attitudes and different languages made it also very difficult to instill a sense of unity since European countries found their national identity to be too strong. Also different economic conditions in the various countries posed a challenge. Some countries wanted to lower the interest rate to boost their economy while some others wanted to raise it to cool down their economy.

One of the major tasks that they achieved was the creation of the EURO, a common currency for the whole E.U. member countries.

About the Euro: There are seven denominations of euro bills: 5, 10, 20,50, 100, 200 and 500. The bills' designs are common throughout the Euro zone, both front and back, and incorporate illustrations of bridges, gateways and windows. Coins are issued in eight denominations: 2 and 1 euro, and then, in euro cents, 50, 20, 10, 5, 2 and 1. Each denomination has a common face throughout the Euro zone. The other face, however, is decorated uniquely by issuing countries. The full range of notes and coins are shown on the European Central Bank website. All are valid throughout participating countries regardless of the issuing state or the particular design.

One of the major consequences of the creation of the E.U. were massive mergers and acquisitions because it was felt that only the "big guys" would survive in the absence of a national barrier protection. Also, there was a massive influx of FDI to become an insider to avoid increased tariff barriers against non-members.

The negative implication to the U.S. was that it is more difficult to access the European market for non-members. A positive implication to U.S. firms was that there was no longer the need to deal with so many different rules and regulations. All we have to do is to deal with one E.U. set of rules and policies.

The European Union recently made one important step to become a more politically cohesive unit by signing the Treaty of Lisbon in 2007. It is designed to **establish a new European Union in the constitutional form of a supranational European State.** According to this new treaty, it creates a Union Parliament and a Cabinet Government for the Union.

2- NAFTA (North American Free Trade Association)

This was North American response to the E.U.'s one single European approach. A basic component of NAFTA is to eliminate tariffs and non-tariff barriers among the three North American countries, the U.S., Canada and Mexico. Even if we call it Free Trade Area, in fact, the NAFTA is a little stronger form of FTA than conventional FTA.NAFTA policies have been designed to harmonize trade rules and to reduce restrictions on FDI and services among members rather than simply eliminating the trade barriers among the member countries. NAFTA is made of two agreements with our two neighboring countries.

Free Trade Agreement (FTA) with Canada was intended to expand market opportunities and increase trade between the two countries. The U.S. would be able to widen consumer choices by importing more from Canada and would improve efficiency by pooling the resources between the two countries. This integration can be termed Horizontal Integration due to the fact that it is our economic integration with other industrialized country whose economic structure and national income level are quite similar to U.S.

Free Trade Agreement (FTA) with Mexico has a little different agenda. It was a chance for the U.S. to utilize the abundant and cheap labor of Mexico. The savings from cheap labor costs could be used for more research and development to improve technology. With improved technology the U.S. could create more high tech jobs to offset the jobs lost to Mexico. Other advantages for the U.S. were that, since production facilities would be established in Mexico, it was hoped to curb illegal immigrants by creating more jobs in Mexico. The U.S. could also expand their market into Mexico and sell more in Mexico. Another ulterior motivation for this agreement is to secure a reliable and alternative source of energy since Mexico has abundant oil and gas and luckily Mexico is not a member of the OPEC. This association can be termed a Vertical Integration because Mexico, a newly industrialized country, has a very different economic structure than the U.S. Problems anticipated from this agreement were a short-term loss of mostly labor intensive, low-tech jobs to Mexico, a downward pressure on wages in the U.S. since the U.S. employers have alternative source of labor, and the lack of environmental concern in Mexico where U.S. companies could try to take advantage of lenient environmental rules.

3- APEC (Asian Pacific Economic Cooperation)

This is an economic forum for 22 pacific basin countries that account for more than half of the total world output. It is not a full fledged economic integration yet but this association carries big potential for the next decade. Interestingly, some of the non traditional Asian countries decided to join this Asian economic association to take advantage of fast growing economy in the region. Those are the U.S., Canada, Russia and Mexico.

4- Latin/Central American

Initially, most of the Latin countries preferred the weakest form of economic integration, which is the Free Trade Area, since they wanted to increase their intra-zonal trade without losing their economic sovereignty. However, they soon realized that with this weakest form of integration they could not meet their expected level of cooperation among the member countries. Thus, they decided to have a bit stronger form of integration as time passes by. Thus, the current associations have evolved from organizations of the 1960's as follows:

1960's	**1970's**
CARIFTA (Caribbean Free Trade Assoc.) →	CARICOM (Caribbean Common Market)
CARIFTA (Caribbean Free Trade Assoc.) →	CACM (Central American Common Market)
LAFTA (Latin American Free Trade Area) →	ANCOM (Andean Common Market)
LAFTA (Latin American Free Trade Area) →	LAIA (Latin American Integrated Assoc.): MERCOSUR (Argentina, Brazil, Paraguay & Uruguay)

FTAA and CARIFTA

The US government has been recently pushing the idea of Free Trade Areas of Americas (FTAA) attempting to create huge free trade areas connecting the two Americas; North and South from Alaska to Patagonia. However, the road to FTAA may not be as smooth as expected because some Latin countries (such as Brazil) believe the idea would not serve their best interest and the recent resurgence of many socialist governments in

Latin America makes it even more difficult to sell the idea. Many of them still believe in the spirit of "Calvo Doctrine" and maintain some Marxist view for foreign direct investment. Another most recent interesting development observed among Latin countries is their attempt to merge the MERCOSUR and ANCOM and create a stronger and more unified form of economic integration in Latin America.

Review Questions

Identify and discuss Five (5) major forms of economic integration and their major characteristics.

What are the major benefits of economic integration?

What are the potential problems associated with economic integration?

What are the objectives of EU and their challenges lying ahead?

What are the objectives of NAFTA and potential problems associated with it?

Who are the constituency of APEC and what is their status now?

Discuss the various attempts made by Latin countries to integrate their economies.

CHAPTER 11. INTERNATIONAL ORGANIZATIONS

GATT: The Predecessor of WTO

By the end of the World War II, 23 countries formed an association called the General Agreement on Tariffs and Trade (GATT) to negotiate reductions in international trade restrictions and work toward establishing common procedures for handling international trade. By 1995, the total number of GATT reached 117 countries. GATT's most important activity was sponsoring "rounds", or sessions, named for the place in which each began, such as the Tokyo Round and the Uruguay Round. These led to a number of multilateral agreements in tariffs and non-tariff barriers. Through these agreements, countries agreed to lower tariffs on all products from all countries by a given percentage over some specified time period. Not all countries reduced their tariff by the same percentage though. The amount of reduction depended on countries' different levels before negotiations and their bargaining strengths.

In spite of its many accomplishments, GATT had inherent weaknesses. By having so many members negotiate simultaneously on so many products and issues, closure became more cumbersome. Unfortunately, GATT provided no effective means of assuring compliance with negotiated agreements. Countries could take trade disputes to the membership, but GATT rules necessitated unanimity for trade penalties, and no country was apt to vote against itself when there were complaints against it. Instead, a GATT subgroup would investigate a complaint to determine whether the allegations were valid. If so, GATT had to depend on mutual commitment to cooperate in order to make countries alter their practices.

WTO

The World Trade Organization (WTO) became the most important international organization dealing with the rules of international trade among nations when it replaced its predecessor in 1996. Unlike its predecessor, GATT, *WTO has the authority to supervise implementation of rulings and to take retaliatory measures in case of non -compliance.

The major objectives of creating this new organization was how to promote free world trade, how to develop consistent rules for international trade and how to provide a mechanism to settle the international trade disputes. To achieve these objectives, WTO always tries to apply the following two major principles dealing with international trade issues.

1) "Multilateral agreements" among the member countries are the heart of the system. These WTO agreements are negotiated through very lengthy processes called "Round" and signed by a large majority of the world's trading nations, and ratified in their parliaments. These agreements are the legal ground-rules for international commerce. Essentially, they are contracts, guaranteeing member countries important trade rights. They also bind governments to keep their trade policies within agreed limits to everybody's benefit.

2) It also follows the principle of "Most Favored Nation Provision" where member countries should grant each other the most favorable treatment given to their best trading partner. However, the U.S. has refused to grant this to communist countries. Normally under this principle, any member providing special and favorable treatment to their best trading partner must automatically extend this to all member countries. Even if the WTO has replaced the most-favored-nation clause of GATT with the concept of "normal trade relations", people still call this provision **most-favored nation**, or "MFN".

Doha round

The Doha round of WTO negotiations began in Doha, Qatar in November 2001 with subsequent ministerials in Cancún, Mexico (2003), and Hong Kong, China (2005). Related negotiations have taken place in: Geneva, Switzerland; Paris, France; and again Geneva. This round was to have begun at the 3rd ministerial conference in Seattle in 1999, and was to have been called "The Seattle Round" but severe demonstrations disrupted those meetings, and this round's beginning was put off until the meetings at the more secure and controllable Doha, Qatar. The purpose was to agree on the Doha Development Agenda, and from there negotiate opening agricultural and manufacturing markets. The intent of the round, according to its proponents, was to make trade rules fairer for developing countries. Opponents charged that the round would expand a system of trade rules that were bad for development and interfered excessively with countries' domestic policy. The **Doha Development Round** of WTO negotiations aims to lower trade barriers around the world, permitting free trade between countries of varying prosperity. Talks have been hung up over a divide between the European Union and the United States and the major developing countries (represented by the G20 developing nations), led and represented mainly, however, by the G4 bloc.

Several other major rulings of WTO are as below;

National Treatment: All products imported from foreign countries must receive the same treatment as domestic goods in domestic market.

Protection by tariff: Quantitative restrictions (e.g.quotas) are, for the most part, illegal and not allowed in international trade.

Dispute settlement: Members may challenge trade actions of other members if they are inconsistent with the WTO agreements and rulings.

Dispute settlement: Members may challenge trade actions of other members following the next process if they are inconsistent with the WTO agreements.

Dispute Settlement Process of WTO

1. Consultation and mediation	60 days
2. Panel & panelists established	45 days
3. Final panel report to the parties	6 months
4. Final panel reports to the members	3 weeks
5. Dispute settlement and report	60days

International Monetary Fund (IMF)

This international organization was established in 1945 in order to bring economic stability and growth to the postwar world and began financial operations on March 1, 1947. Even if this organization made a humble start with only twenty-nine countries initially, it became one of the most power international financial organizations by the year 2000 with almost 200 member countries. The major objectives of the IMF are pointed below;

- To promote international monetary cooperation
- To facilitate the expansion and balanced growth of international trade
- To promote exchange-rate stability
- To establish a multilateral system of payments
- To make its resources available to its members experiencing balance-of-payments difficulties

When a country becomes a member of the IMF, it is supposed to contribute a certain sum of money, called a "quota" based on its national incomes, monetary reserves, trade balance, and other economic indicators. The quota is a sum of money that the IMF can draw on to lend its money to other countries. How much amount of money a country can borrow from the IMF will be decided by the amount of quota that each country originally contributed to the fund. This quota will also be the basis on how much amount of Special Drawing Rights (SDRs) the country can receive from the IMF when they need IMF's financial assistance. The details of SDR will be discussed later. The number of votes a country has depends on the size of its quota, which is largely decided by each country's contribution to the fund. The Board of Governors is the final authority on key matters, but it leaves day-to-day authority to a 24-person Board of Executive Directors.

IMF Assistance and controversy

In order to help the countries who suffer seriously balance of payment problems, the IMF provides a great deal of assistance to member countries. When many Asian and Latin countries had a series of economic turmoil in the late 1980's, IMF offered a tremendous amount of rescue fund to those countries to ease their financial pains. When Russia was facing severe economic challenges in the wake of the Asian financial crisis, the IMF stepped in to provide some financial help. The IMF negotiates with a country to provide financial assistance if the country will agree to adopt certain policies to stabilize its economy. Often, these policies imposed by the IMF on the troubled countries are very controversial and not very popular because there are too strict and unrealistic conditions attached to their help. There is also a heated debate about the expansion of the fund because as the world economy is globalized, many countries tend to have a problem simultaneously. Therefore, the IMF cannot effectively handle all those additional demand with the amount of fund that is currently available. Another issue associated with the role of the IMF is that some member countries believe that the IMF became more like a political organization rather than a financial organization. This is the case because some of the key members who have more voice (with larger quota) in voting try to pursue their political agenda by exercising economic muscle. For example, during the Asian currency crisis in the late 1980's, the U.S. tried to put pressure on the Indonesian president to step down in return of IMF's financial assistant to that troubled country, which drew a great deal of international criticism.

Special Drawing Rights (SDRs)

To help increase international reserves and to provide more international liquidity, the IMF created the Special Drawing Right (SDR) in 1969. The SDR is an artificially created international reserve asset. This artificial form of international money, which is often called, "paper gold" serve as the IMF's unit of account and are used for IMF transactions, operations and reserve asset for each member country. The value of the SDR is based on the weighted average of major currencies; U.S dollar, Euro, Japanese yen, and British pound. Although the SDR was intended to serve as a substitute for gold, it has not taken over the role of gold or the dollar as a primary reserve asset. Only a few countries pegged the value of their currency to the value of the SDR.

OECD

The Organization for Economic Cooperation and Development (OECD) is primarily representing the voice of the world's developed countries, and its headquarters is located in Paris, France. As of 2000, there were 30 member-countries. The OECD is often called the "rich man's club" or the "voice of the North" because it is composed of 30 of the wealthiest and most industrialized nations in the world. The OECD provides information on economic and other activities within member-countries and also provides a forum for member-governments to discuss and coordinate economic and international policies. The OECD has been instrumental in many areas, including encouraging member-countries to reduce the level of corruption and establish a code of conduct for the MNCs.

UNCTAD

UNCTAD, which is one of the U.N.'s agencies, has been catalytic to improve the relationships between developing and industrial countries regarding international commerce including trade and FDI. This organization primarily represents the group of developing and less developed countries and tries to facilitate economic coordination with the industrialized countries. One of the most important agenda's of this organization is how to improve the bargaining position of developing countries vis-à-vis wealthy industrialized countries. Also how to redistribute the wealth from those industrialized countries to developing countries through economic cooperation and cross border transactions such as trade and FDI between these two groups of countries.

Review Questions

What is the main objective and role of WTO?

What are the two major principles that WTO tries to apply when dealing with international trade issues?

What is a "Round" sponsored by WTO?

What is the meaning of "most favored nation provision", which is also known as "normalized trade relation"?

What are the major objectives and achievement of IMF?

What is SDR?

How is SDR used and how is the value of SDR decided?

What are the objectives of OECD and UNCTAD?

CHAPTER 12. FOREIGN EXCHANGE MARKET

Exchange Rate Quotation

We often find that the discussion of exchange rate is very confusing. One of the major sources of confusion is that we do have two different ways to provide the exact same rate. A *Direct Quote (value in US dollars)* is the exchange rate that is quoted as the number of my currency (hereinafter "MC") for 1 unit of a foreign currency (hereinafter "FC") (e.g. \$.005/¥1). An *Indirect Quote (units per US dollar)* is the exchange rate that is quoted as the number of FC for 1 unit of MC. (e.g. ¥200/\$1). Both of them express the same exact rate but in a different way. To convert an exchange rate from one quotation to another quotation, you simply take the reciprocal and change the signs (e.g. \$.005/¥1 → 1/(¥.005/\$1).

EXCHANGE RATES FOR SELECTED CURRENCIES

Currency	Country	Symbol	Code	Value in U.S. Dollars	Units per U.S. Dollar
pound	Britain	£	GBP	\$1.84	0.54 pound
dollar	Canada	\$	CAD	0.76	1.31 Canadian dollars
euro	European Union	€	EUR	1.23	0.81 euro
rupee	India	Rs	INR	0.0216	46.34 rupees
yen	Japan	¥	JPY	0.00902	110.79 yen
peso	Mexico	Mex\$	MXN	0.088	11.40 pesos
riyal	Saudi Arabia	SRls	SAR	0.267	3.75 riyals
rand	South Africa	R	ZAR	0.162	6.16 rand
real	Brazil	R\$	BRL	0.33	3.022 real
bolívar	Venezuela	Bs	VEB	0.00052	1,919.0 bolívars
yuan	China	Y	CNY	0.12	8.28 yuan

To avoid confusion by using better terminology, the *American Quote*, a direct quote from the U.S. point of view, was developed as a dollar expressed value of 1 unit of FC (\$.005/¥1). Similarly, the *European Quote*, which is a direct quote from a foreigner's point of view, is expressed as the number of FC expressed as the value of \$1 (¥200/\$1).

The most frequently asked question in foreign exchange market is what percentage change is made in a foreign currency value. For example, consider the beginning rate of the Peso versus the dollar was P4/$1 and the ending rate is P5/$1. We know that the Peso has devaluated here because we have to pay more pesos to buy $1, but by what percentage? The formula you can use to calculate the percentage change in a currency value is as below.

$$\begin{array}{c}\text{\% change in} \\ \text{FC value}\end{array} = \frac{(\text{End-Beg}) \times 100}{\text{Beg}}$$

However, the important thing that you have to remember when you use this formula is that you must use the *Direct Quote*. Since the original information was given in terms of indirect quote, you have to change this indirect quote to direct quote by taking the reciprocal of the original numbers and switching the currency signs. Thus, the direct quote for the beginning period would be converted to $.25/P1 and direct quote for the ending period will be $.20/P1.

If we fill in the equation with the direct quotes in the example we get the following:

$$\begin{array}{c}\text{\% change in} \\ \text{FC value}\end{array} = \frac{(\$.20 - \$.25) \times 100}{\$.25} = -20\%$$

However, sometimes, using indirect quote is more convenient to achieve a certain task. For example, we occasionally want to calculate a cross rate. A *Cross Rate* is an exchange rate between two foreign currencies:

Exchange rate between €(Euro) and $: € 2.00/$
Exchange rate between £ (pound) and $: £ 1.25/$

$$\begin{array}{c}\text{Exchange rate} \\ \text{Between € \&£}\end{array} \quad \frac{€2/\$}{€\ 1.25/\$} = €\ 1.6/£$$

The €1.6/£ represents the cross rate between Euro (€) and Sterling Pound (£). In thi s case, the cross rate can be easily calculated because the quote that we used here is the indirect quote which always has $ as a common denominator.

Instruments in the Foreign Exchange Market

Spot Market

It is the most popular type of contract in foreign exchange market. This is an agreement to deliver or to take delivery of a certain amount of foreign currency *immediately*, which means within 2 business days. When you make a spot contract, you are required to settle the contract in two business days. Buyer is required to pay and take the delivery and the seller is required to deliver the contracted amount of foreign currency in two business days. A *Spot Rate* is the exchange rate that will be applied for Spot Market.

Forward contract

It is another type of contract that you can make in foreign exchange market. This is an agreement to deliver or take delivery of a certain amount of foreign currency in *the future.* A *Forward Rate* (herein after called "FWD" rate) is the exchange rate that will be for a forward contract, usually quoted in multiples of 30 days. A key aspect of a forward contract is that the exchange rate for future delivery is to be locked in at the time of the contract, thereby reducing the risk of exchange rate fluctuation and uncertainty in the future. For example, if you make a 90 day buy FWD contract today for £1,000 at $1.50/£, you are obliged to pay $1,500 ($1.5/x £1,000) in 90 days and to take the delivery of £1,000 in 90 days. If you sell FWD contract today for £1,000 at $1.50/£, you are obliged to deliver £1,000 in 90 days and take the amount of $1,500 in 90 days.

Forward rate vs. Future spot rate

One thing that you must be clear on FWD rate is that forward rate is not the same as a future spot rate. As you can see on the table below, all FWD rates (30 days, 60 day s, 90 days) are known today and available in the market today. All the future spot rates are NOT known today. You will never know the future spot rate until the time passes. Then, what is the relationship between the forward rate known today and the future sport rate which is unknown today? Since all the information about unknown future rate is immediately embodied and reflected in currently available forward rate, **a forward rate is, in fact, the market's best estimate of the future spot rate as of today.**

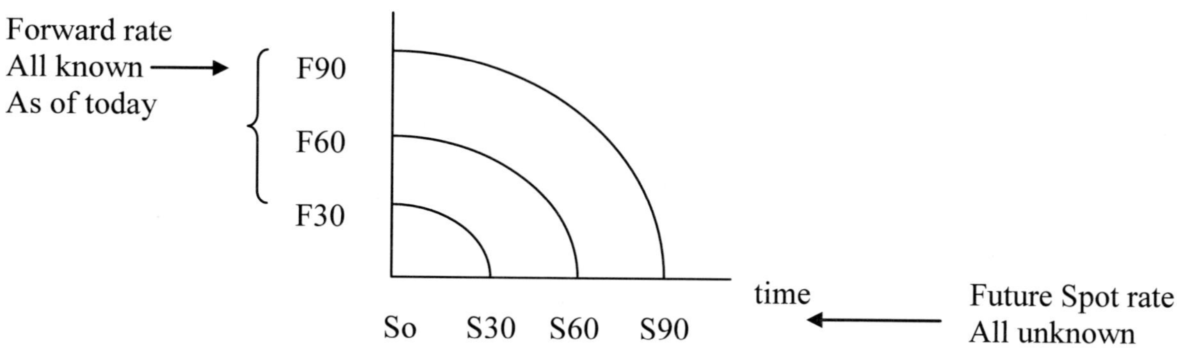

If forward rate is larger than the spot rate, the currency is now at premium
If forward rate is smaller than the spot rate, the currently is at discount.

Sometimes, we want to calculate an annualized percentage premium or discount in forward rate for a specific currency because it can be crucial information for international arbitrage and investment decision in other countries.

The following equation shows how to calculate an annualized percentage premium or discount in forward rate:

$$\text{Annualized \% Premium/discount} = \frac{Ft - So}{So} \times \frac{12}{n} \times 100$$

Where:

t = days associated with forward rate
n = # of months
12/n = annualizing factor
So = Spot rate now
F = Forward rate

EXAMPLE: Assume: So = \$.5000/CAN\$ and F90 = \$.51000/CAN\$. Then,

$$\text{Annualized \% Prem/disc} = \frac{\$.51 - .50}{.50} \times \frac{12}{3} \times 100 = +8\% \text{ (premium)}$$

In this example, Canadian \$ is now at 8% premium.

Other instruments in foreign exchange market

Currency Swap

This is a contract for the exchange of a certain amount of foreign currency with the understanding to reverse the original transaction in the future. It can be used when you need foreign currency only for *a certain period of time* since borrowing a large amount of foreign currency will definitely raise debt ratio. Besides, buying in the spot market and selling in the future spot market will make you very much exposed to the risk of exchange fluctuation since we don't know the future spot rate. Usually, the swap in foreign exchange market is a combination of spot (buy) contract and forward (sell) contract because the forward rate is the only rate that both parties can agree about future rate as of today.

Currency Future

The Chicago Mercantile Exchange handles this type of derivatives. The currency future is just like any other commodity (i.e., soybeans) future. The currency future is similar to forward contract only in the sense that you can lock in specific rate for future delivery. However, a Currency Future differs from a Forward Contract in several ways. A Currency Future only deals with standardized size (i.e., $100,000 units' contract size), and offers a delivery date as the last Wednesday of the every three month. Unlike forward contract where the contract is settled between the two individuals, currency future is described as "impersonal" contract because the contract is made between an individual and the Exchange. Another unique aspect of the currency future is the practice known as "Marking to the Market". It refers to the practice that requires a daily settlement for the differences in market rates and the stipulated rate on your future contract. The currency future market is very speculative market and the individuals can get out of the market or liquidate themselves easily anytime by taking opposite position. This is the reason why currency future's market is frequently used by investors and speculators.

Currency Options

Currency Option is another form of currency derivatives available in foreign exchange market even if it is not a highly standardized product. It is mainly handled by the Philadelphia Stock Exchange. However, many banks also sell currency option-like products. Just like any options in the stock market, when you buy currency option, you simply buy the right to buy (call option) or sell (put option) a certain amount of foreign currency for a certain period of time at the specific price (exchange rate), which we call strike price. If you buy **Call option**, that means you actually buy the right to buy a certain amount of foreign currency at the specific price regardless of future sport rate. The reason why you buy call option at the strike price is most likely that you expect the future spot rate rises above the strike price. Then, you will have a chance to exercise the option and actually buy it at the strike price and sell it at the higher rate in the market. If you buy a **Put option**, you actually buy the right to sell at the specific price regardless of future spot rate. The reason why you want to buy this type of option is most likely that you expect that future rate fall below your strike price, then you want to exercise the option and buy at the lower market rate and sell at the higher strike price that you already made a contract for. When you buy any one of these options, you have to pay a little **premium** for each unit because if you buy the right, to buy or to sell, that means the option seller will assume an obligation to sell or buy a certain amount of foreign currency no matter what. Thus, they need compensation in return of assuming this obligation. The following example will help to illustrate the points:

In this example, you buy a call option (right to buy) for £1,000 at a strike price of $1.50/£1 with an expiration date of June 30th. This option means you have the right to buy £1,000 at $1.50/L until the end of June. If you exercise the option, your option seller has to sell the amount to you no matter what. Why you want to buy this option? Because you expect the future market rate will rise above your strike price. In that case, you will exercise your call option and sell at market rate of $2£ . The difference between the market rate $2/£ and the strike price of $1.50/£ will be your profit. However, actual net profit will be a bit less than the difference because you already paid the premium to buy this kind of option.

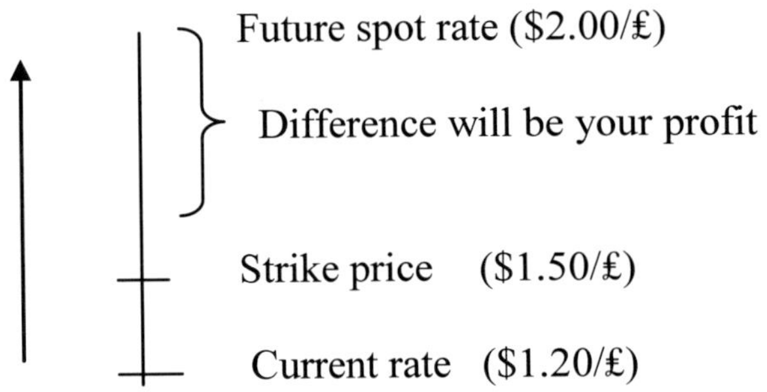

How to use the foreign exchange market?

Settlement of Trade and Foreign Debt

One very important way to use foreign exchange market is the settlement of international trade and foreign debt by transferring purchasing power from one currency to another currency. For example, a Japanese exporter sells the product to Brazilian importer. Then the Brazilian importer has to covert his currency, lair to $, which is the most widely accepted currency, and they pay to Japanese importer. Then Japanese importer will covert the $ to their own currency, Japanese Yen. Thereby, purchasing power is transferred from lair to $ to Japanese Yen and that is how the international trade can be settled.

Speculation

Another way to use foreign exchange market is speculation by using one of the instruments available in the foreign exchange market (i.e., spot, forward, & future). You buy in the spot market with the expectation that future spot rate would go up or you lock in at the specific rate in forward market or future's market expecting that the actual rate in the future's spot market will go up.

Currency Carry trade

An investment strategy in which an investor sells a certain currency with a relatively low interest rate and uses the funds to purchase a different currency yielding a higher interest rate. A trader using this strategy attempts to capture the difference between the rates -

which can often be substantial, depending on the amount of leverage the investor chooses to use.

Here's an example of a "yen carry trade": let's say a trader borrows 1,000 yen from a Japanese bank, converts the funds into U.S. dollars and buys a bond for the equivalent amount. Let's assume that the bond pays 4.5% and the Japanese interest rate is set at 0%. The trader stands to make a profit of 4.5% (4.5% - 0%), as long as the exchange rate between the countries does not change. Many professional traders use this trade because the gains can become very large when leverage is taken into consideration. If the trader in our example uses a common leverage factor of 10:1, then she can stand to make a profit of 45%.

The big risk in a carry trade is the uncertainty of exchange rates. Using the example above, if the U.S. dollar were to fall in value relative to the Japanese yen, then the trader would run the risk of losing money. Also, these transactions are generally done with a lot of leverage, so a small movement in exchange rates can result in huge losses unless hedged appropriately.

Arbitrage

Another interesting way to use foreign exchange market is *arbitrage*, buying and selling a certain amount of foreign currency almost simultaneously trying to take advantage of temporary disequilibrium or misalignment in the market. ***Two Point Arbitrage***, also called locational arbitrage, is possible when a temporary disequilibrium among regional banks exists. For example;

	Bank A	Bank B
Bid (bank wants to buy)	\$1.9999/£	\$2.0001/£
Ask (bank wants to sell)	\$2.0000/£	\$2.0002/£

In this example, the price difference is a fact. You simply can take advantage of the exchange rate difference by doing a two point arbitrage. You would buy from Bank A at the Ask price of \$2.0000/£. Then, you would sell to Bank B at their Bid price of \$2.0001/£. The key is to take fast action before the market realigns and restores equilibrium.

Three Point Arbitrage, also called triangle arbitrage, is possible when there is a temporary disequilibrium among the different foreign exchange markets. Keep in mind that these markets are kept open 24 hours a day due to time lapse among the different regions. The following example can illustrate how the triangular arbitrage can be executed. Suppose you have \$1 million for investment. First, you covert that \$ amount to € (EURO) in New York market at the rate of \$1/€1.5 and get \$1,000,000. Next, you send that amount of € to London market and convert it to P (Peso) at the rate of €1/P5. Then you will have P7.5

million. Again this money is quickly sent to Tokyo market and converted there to $ at the rate of P6/$1. This conversion will give $1.25 million.

			$1,000,000 for initial investment
New York	$1/€1.5	=	€1.5 million
London	€1/P5	=	P7.5 million
Tokyo	P6/$1	=	$1.25 million

Hedging

To avoid foreign exchange risk and minimize uncertainty, a company can also practice ***Hedging***. This is a transaction in a FWD market designed to minimize potential loss from exchange rate fluctuation. Suppose a U.S. company exports £,1000 of goods to a UK importer with 90 days credit and the expected future spot rate in 90 days is $1.60/£ . Today's 90 days forward rate is F90 = $1.50/£. In this case, one option for the U.S. exporter is to do nothing now with an expectation that they would sell spot £1,000 at $1.60 and collect $1,600 when they are paid by the U.K. importer in 90 days. However, this is very risky option because if they don't do anything, their future $ earning will totally depend on the future spot rate, which is unknown to them. The future spot rate cited above is only an expectation and it can be either $2.00/£ or $1.00/£. Depending upon the future spot rate, which is absolutely unknown to them, their future income will fluctuate widely. Most of the international traders don't like to assume this kind of risk. That's why they rather do hedging which requires the U.S. firm to make a sell forward contract for the amount of £1,000 as soon as they make an export contract. Then, the forward rate of $1.50/£ will be locked in and this rate will be applied when they deliver £1,000 in 90 days. Thus, they will collect $1,500 no matter what happens to the future spot rate. This amount may be a little less than $1,600 (they will get this amount only when the expectation is correct) but it is guaranteed regardless of future spot rate. The whole idea of hedging is to avoid the uncertainty and risk in foreign exchange fluctuation not necessarily to maximize your income.

Review Questions

Discuss the two different ways (direct vs. indirect) to express exchange rate.

Discuss the difference between the American quote and European quote.

How to calculate percentage change in the value of foreign currency?

How to calculate the cross rate between the two foreign currencies?

How is spot rate different from forward rate?

What is the most important aspect of forward contract?

Is future spot rate the same as forward rate?

What is the relationship between future spot rate and forward rate?

How to calculate annualized percentage premium or discount of a forward rate?

Discuss the various ways to use foreign exchange market.

What is the underlying assumption when you do currency carry trade?

What is currency future and how is it traded?

What is currency option and how is it traded?

What is two point arbitrage and how to execute it?

What is three point arbitrage and how to execute it?

What is hedging and how to execute it?

Practice Questions

1. Assume that prior to a major change in the exchange rate, the Japanese Yen (¥) was selling at ¥ 200 per $, and that the rate after the change is ¥ 250 per $. What would be the percentage change in the value of Japanese yen (¥)?
   a. 20% devaluation.
   b. 20% appreciation.
   c. 25% devaluation.
   d. 25% appreciation.

2. If the exchange rate between Euro (€) and U.S. dollar($) is €2.0000/$ and the exchange rate between Sterling pound (£) and U.S. dollar is £1.5000/$, the cross rate between these two foreign currencies is :
   a. £1.3333/€.
   b. £7.5000/€.
   c. €7.5000/£.
   d. €1.3333/£.

3. Assume the spot rate of the Canadian dollar is $.37 and the 90-day forward rate is $.36. The forward rate exhibits a ___________ of ____________ on an annualized basis.
   a. Discount; 11.11%
   b. Premium;11.11%
   c. Premium; 10.81%
   d. Discount; 10.81%

4. If a U.S. firm desires to avoid the risk from exchange rate fluctuations, and it is receiving 100,000 euros in 90 days, it could:
   a. obtain a 90-day forward purchase contract on euros.
   b. obtain a 90-day forward sale contract on euros.
   c. purchase euros 90 days from now at the spot rate.
   d. sell euros 90 days from now at the spot rate.

Answers; 1(a), 2(d), 3(d), 4 (b)

PART C: FUNCTIONAL OPERATION AND STRATEGY

CHAPTER 13. INTERNATIONAL FINANCIAL MANAGEMENT

We have a variety of important issues in International Financial Management. However, since this is only an introductory level course for International Business, only three issues will be addressed here. Those are: working capital management, currency risk management and international capital budgeting.

Working Capital Management

MNCs have so many foreign subsidiaries scattered all over the world and occasionally any one of these foreign subsidiaries may need additional working capital urgently. In this case, MNCs can utilize two different sources of fund to provide the addition working capital for their foreign subsidiaries; intra-corporate source vs. external source.

Intra-Corporate Fund

One way to provide additional working capital for their foreign subsidiaries using intra-corporate source of fund is to increase the equity stock of the subsidiaries. Another way is for the parent company to provide a loan to their subsidiary. Most of the MNCs prefer parental loan to equity increase since first of all, interest is tax deductible while dividends are not. Another reason is the fact that there will be less control by the host government over interest than dividend payment. If a subsidiary is paying a dividend to a parent company, it is a clear indication that the subsidiary is generating profit. If the host country notes that dividends are being paid back to a parent company, they usually want to step in with regulations or require that the money be reinvested in the country where it was earned. For these reasons, loan is more preferred than equity increase in general. The only problem associated with a loan may be the increasing of their debt rate if too much loan is provided. However, even that is not a serious problem because the loan is from the parent company. Since it is a parental loan, the subsidiary's credit rating will not be seriously jeopardized because they know that the parent would not let their subsidiary go bankrupt because the subsidiary has too much loan from them. Because of the various reasons above stated, MNCs always prefer parental loan to equity increase when their foreign subsidiaries need additional working capital.

However, when a parent wants to provide a loan to its subsidiary, they may wish to find a better way to deal with future political risk that may interrupt any future interest payments. In this case, a parent company may arrange a bit more complicated parental loan to the subsidiaries rather than a direct loan, such as a Fronting Loan. This is a loan that involves a third party bank as illustrated below:

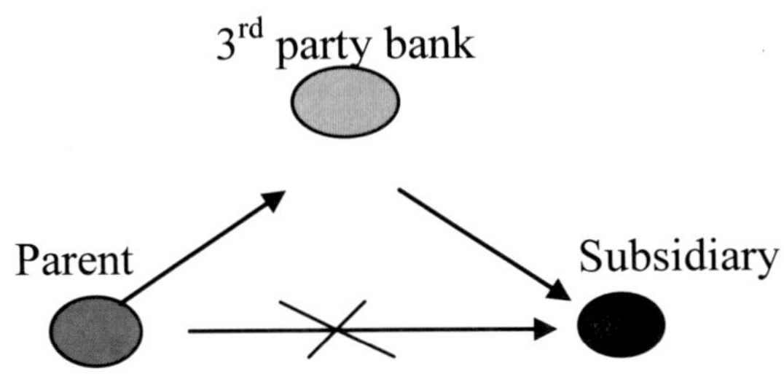

The fronting loan is not made directly with the subsidiary, but instead Parent deposits money with the 3rd party bank, which in turn loans the money to the subsidiary. The whole purpose of this indirect parent loan is to avoid possible political risk that the host country may block the interest payment in the future.

Another way to use internal source of funds is the leads in accounts payable or lags in accounts receivable, when there are numerous internal transactions between the Parent and its Subsidiaries. If a Parent has an account payable with the Sub and the Sub needs additional capital urgently, the Parent can simply settle the payable early. On the other hand, if the Parent has an account receivable to be collected from the Subsidiary, the Parent can delay collection to give the Subsidiary more working capital.

Transfer Pricing

Another way to use internal source fund to provide working capital is manipulation of the transfer price. A transfer price is the intra-corporate price charged on the goods and services transacted among the affiliated units such as between sister companies and the parent company. When a subsidiary needs additional working capital, the parent company can reduce the transfer price of the goods provided by the parent to the subsidiary. However, transfer price can also be used in MNCs to achieve so many other objects.

- If a local government is trying to block a subsidiary's dividend or interest payment to a parent company, the parent can increase the transfer price of supplies in order to siphon out some of those blocked funds.
- If a subsidiary pays too much tax, the parent can increase the transfer price, which will lower the sub's net income and allow them to pay less tax to the local government.
- If an ad valorem (% of value) tariff is imposed on imported supplies raw materials, the parent can lower the transfer price in an attempt to lower the amount of the tax that they pay to the local government.
- When a subsidiary wants to borrow the money from the bank, the parent can decrease the transfer price in order to bolster the subsidiary's credit rating. They do this since decreased transfer prices will have the effect of increasing the sub's net income and making them look good financially.
- A joint venture partner can deliberately increase the price of raw materials or supplies to increase their profit sharing. In this case the loss from increased price will be shared with other partners but the extra profit from the increased price can be solely enjoyed by the partner who manipulated the price.
- MNCs sometimes manipulate the transfer price to avoid government price control. For example, a product price can be set with various costs, which are identified by the local government, and a 5% profit margin may be allowed on top of all these cost factors. If the parent marks up the transfer price by 10%, it will still appear to be a 5% profit margin, but in reality it is 15% profit margin.

These manipulations of transfer price are often unethical, and often illegal, but they are commonly practiced by many MNCs to survive in hostile environment in the host country.

However, when MNCs try to manipulate the transfer price, they may suffer several problems. When MNCs manipulate the transfer price, it will eventually undermine the host country's efforts to control their own economy; thereby increase the conflict between the MNCs and the host government. The host government may not have hard evidence; they can sense something illegal is going on and try to investigate through frequent tax probe and so forth. This will escalate the tension between the MNCS and the host government. Also, the subsidiary's financial performance picture can be badly distorted as the result of transfer manipulation. It will become difficult to evaluate the performance of the unit on which the transfer price was manipulated. Consequently, the parent company would have to maintain dual sets of accounting books to see the actual subsidiary's performance and this would be very cumbersome. Lastly, the various objectives that are trying to be achieved can end up conflicting with one another. A company may want to increase the transfer price because they want the subsidiary to pay less income tax to the local government, but then they may end up paying more tariffs because of the increased price.

External source of funds

Working capital can also be obtained through External Funds. *A subsidiary can borrow from an International Market* such as the Euro $ Market and in this case the parent company's payment guarantee may be required because their name (subsidiary) is not well recognized in the international capital market. *A subsidiary can also borrow from a local bank* where the subsidiary is better known, which is the most preferred method for multinational companies. Advantages are that the subsidiary can borrow without the parent's payment guarantee giving limited liability to the parent in the case subsidiary goes bankrupt. This may also serve as a way to hedge against political risk. When the relationship between the parent company or home country and the host government deteriorates badly, the host government may try to confiscate a subsidiary's assets/ properties. However, if the subsidiary's properties/plants were built or purchased based on the loan from the local bank, MNCs got nothing to lose and the impact of this confiscation will be minimal. Also, the local loan from the local bank can be an excellent way to hedge against high inflation often found in many developing countries. When we have a hyper inflationary situation, if you borrow fixed amounts of loan, your burden to pay back fixed amounts of loan will be automatically alleviated as the value of local currency goes down as time passes by.

Currency Risk (Exposure) Management

Wide exchange rate fluctuations can cause serious troubles to MNCs in their cash flow and asset management. To find out the better strategy to deal with this currency risk, the financial managers of MNCS must be able to identify three different types of currency risk. The currency risk is often called currency exposure because this type of risk is derived from the fact that your assets and liabilities are exposed to the risk of exchange fluctuations.

The first type of Currency Risk (exposure) is called ***Translation Exposure***, also known as Accounting exposure. Translation Exposure is the degree to which a firm's financial statements are influenced by exchange rate fluctuation. All companies must issue financial statements at year-end (fiscal) and must translate those into the home country currency at the end of the fiscal year to file tax reporting. However, in some cases, translated book values on the financial statements can be significantly influenced simply by exchange rate fluctuations. The rate that was applied last year can be significantly different from this year. Even if the unit has the same operational result, the reported earnings can be significantly different only because of exchange rate differences. Translation exposure does not cause any changes in real cash flow. There will be only paper gain or loss from this exposure. However, that does not necessarily mean this exposure does not pose any serious problem to the MNCs. Even if this exposure does not cause any real loss or real gain, wide fluctuations in reported earnings from this exposure could create a false perception that the MNCs are risky firms. However, even if MNCs admit this exposure can present a serious problem for them, MNCs' strategy here is actually to do nothing because of the risk of backfire. Since this exposure only causes a paper loss, if they take some action to hedge against this kind of risk, it could then turn into real losses!

The next Currency Risk is ***Transaction Exposure***, which causes real cash flow changes. Transaction exposure is the degree to which a firm's actual cash flow is influenced by exchange rate fluctuations. For example, an MNC has an account payable in sterling pound. If the value of £ increases significantly before payment is due, then to pay this fixed amount of foreign currency payable, you have to spend more $. The strategies used for this type of exposure would be to use several instruments that we already discussed such as forward contracts, future contracts or options to lock in at specific rate regardless of the future spot rate.

The third type of Currency Risk is ***Economic Exposure***. This is defined as the degree to which a firm's value (stock price) is influenced by long-term and fundamental exchange rate fluctuations. If an MNC exports most of its products to one country, and if that country's currency depreciates (my currency appreciated) dramatically, this might cause a serious sales decrease. This happens since the deprecation of their currency and appreciation of my currency will make our product more expensive. Then the net result would be a reduction of profit and the stock price would fall dramatically. A strategy here to deal with this kind of situation is to diversify the market to disperse the risk from one currency fluctuation. Entry mode diversification can be another option. It is about time to think about foreign direct investment (establishment of your own production facility) because when your currency is appreciated, of course, your export may lose competitiveness as your product become more expensive. However, you can have competitive advantage in FDI because you can build the plant with less amount of capital (your currency value is stronger than before) and thereby alleviate this type of exposure in the future.

International Capital Budgeting

Another area of International Financial Management to examine is International Capital Budgeting. Capital budgeting is the process of making an investment decision when there is a limited amount of capital. One of the most widely used methods to do capital budgeting is to calculate *net present value* to evaluate a project. The rule is that a project should not be undertaken if the expected cash inflows are less than the cash outflows. Only when cash inflows are larger than cash outflows the project will be undertaken as below:

NPV =	**cash inflow**	**-**	**cash outflow**
Positive NPV =	**cash inflow** **(future value)**	**>**	**cash outflow** **(present value)**

When comparing cash inflows and cash outflows, there is one problem. The cash outflows are needed now to build a plant but the cash inflows will be made from sales of the products in the future. For this reason, the time value of money must be considered when we calculate net present value (NPV). Suppose, an individual has one million $ now and the other person will have a million $ in a year. Even if we are looking at same one million $, the first person's one million is more worth than the second person because his money generate interest for the next year. In other words, the second person's one million $ is worth less than the first person's one million $ by the amount of interest earned. Thus, if we want to compare the value of these two people's one million $, you have to discount the second person's money, which is a future money, by the interest rate.

Therefore, when you want to compare future cash inflows with cash outflows to be disbursed now, the future cash inflows must be discounted to the present value by the interest rate (r). The above equation can be restated as follows if we add tax factors (1-t) and sales revenue and cost:

$$NPV = \sum \frac{Revenue - Cost\ (1-t)}{(1 + r)^{n}} - \text{initial outlay}$$

$$(PV) > (PV)$$

However, even if the same framework for capital budgeting is applied for international projects, several factors should be additionally incorporated for international capital budgeting. The **exchange rate** will constantly influence the revenue and the cost. **Local inflation** will be a big factor to decide the manufacturing costs since it will influence the wages of the local employees and the prices of the materials locally supplied. Thus, in order to make a net present value calculation more accurately, we have to forecast the exchange rate and local inflation rate first. Another important factor, which must be considered for international capital budgeting is **tax** on foreign sourced income. A company must consider both local and U.S. tax on income earned abroad and know what kind of tax system they are dealing with since the ultimate concern is net cash inflow after tax. Another issue is what kind of rate should be used as a base **rate to discount** future cash inflows. The cost of capital, usually a base for discount when NPV is calculated, can be significantly influenced by the way foreign projects are financed. As we discussed earlier, since the local financing from local bank is the most preferred form of financing foreign project in MNCs, the projects are most likely financed by local loans from local banks. In this case the most relevant rate that will decide the discount rate may be local rate rather than that of international market of host country market. Finally, **political risk** must be considered when you make a decision for discount rate. If you are going to invest in a country where political risk is very high, this additional risk must be incorporated in discount rate and the discount rate must be adjusted upward to reflect additional risk premium.

Managing the risk of non-payment

Various payment methods for International Trade

A company must also find out an adequate payment method to minimize the risk of non-payment when they do international trade. The risk of non-payment can increase dramatically when you do international trade because your customers are located in other countries and it is very difficult to check foreign firm's credit rating from a long distance. There are several ways that international trade can be settled as explained below.

Cash Advance:
The customer pays in advance, and then the seller ships the goods. With this kind of payment agreement, the seller is not exposed to any non-payment risks. However the customers will assume the risk of non-delivery after payment or non-compliance of the product.

Open Account:
A company can simply have an *Open Account* where the goods are shipped first and then the customer pays later. A buyer loves this type of arrangement, but it poses a serious risk of non-payment to the seller.

Draft (Bill of Exchange):
A company can also request payment in the form of a ***Draft***, also known as a *bill of exchange or a trade draft.* Here, a company would hire some type of collection agent, normally a bank, to function between the foreign buyer and domestic seller. A draft is an unconditional order of payment made by the exporter to the importer or an official payment request. The implementation of the draft is as following:

The first step is to ship the goods by the exporter. The exporter will obtain a set of shipping documents including the Bill of Lading (B/L), which is the valuable security and the proof of shipment. Then the exporter will turn the shipping documents together with the Draft (payment request) to the third party collection agent (bank). The bank will present the draft (payment request) first and the importer will pay to take the shipping documents and B/L, which are indispensable to claim the cargo already arrived at the port.

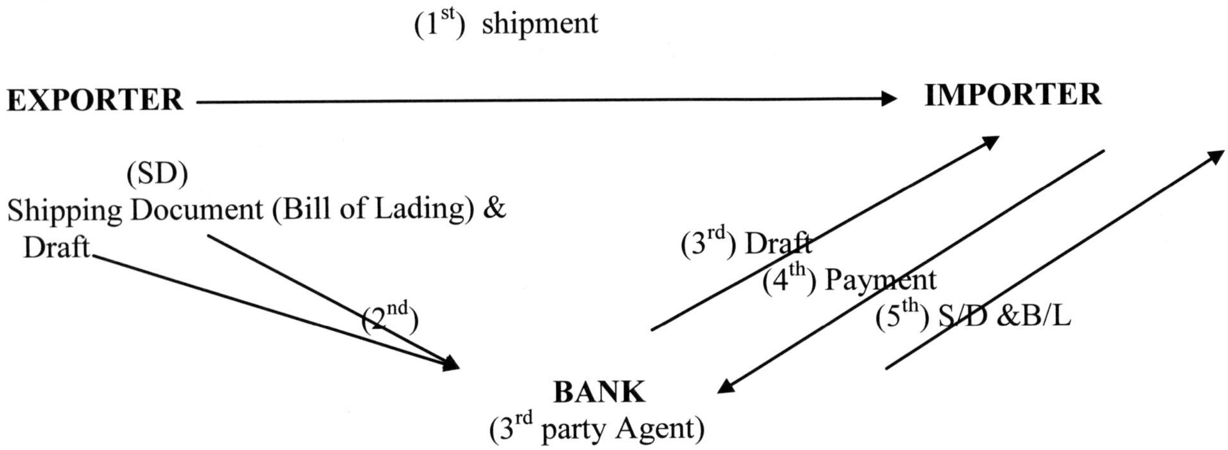

There are two different kinds of drafts. A *Sight Draft,* also called a document against payment (D/P), requires that payments be made immediately to take the shipping documents when it is presented. A *Time Draft,* also called a document against acceptance (D/A), requires only acceptance (an endorsement) of the draft in order to take the shipping documents. By endorsing (putting a signature on the back side of the draft), the buyer legally promise to pay at a later time. This kind of draft is frequently used by the international traders who have been doing business together for along time and thereby can trust each other. *Baker's accepance* is a time draft that has been accepted by the bank on which the draft was drawn, thus becoming the accepting bank's obligation. This banker's acceptance can be bought and sold at discount in the financial markets like other commercial paper.

When international traders use the Draft, it can reduce the amount of non-payment risk significantly because they hire a kind of collection agency in the middle. However, a certain amount of risk still remains when settling with a draft because under draft, the payments are still contingent upon the buyer's willingness and ability to pay. More often than not, an importer can change his mind after the shipment is made and he may not need the goods anymore. If the importer does not need the cargo anymore, they don't need the shipping documents. Accordingly, even if the draft is presented, they can refuse to pay since they don't need the cargo and shipping document anymore (even if they still need the cargo, but sometimes they are unable to pay anymore because of their financial troubles). In these cases, the draft will be a useless paper and there is nothing that the exporter can do about it. Thus, under this draft, the exporter is still exposed to a serious risk of non-payment.

Letter of Credit:

The most important instrument that you can use to reduce the risk of non-payment for international trade is a *Letter of Credit (LOC).* A Letter of Credit is a payment guarantee made by **importer's bank** (not by importer) under one condition, which is the presentation of the proper documents. In this case, "proper documents" means shipping documents (including Bill of Lading) and bank draft drawn on the importer's bank which originally issued the letter of credit. The following diagram indicates how the letter of credit is actually executed.

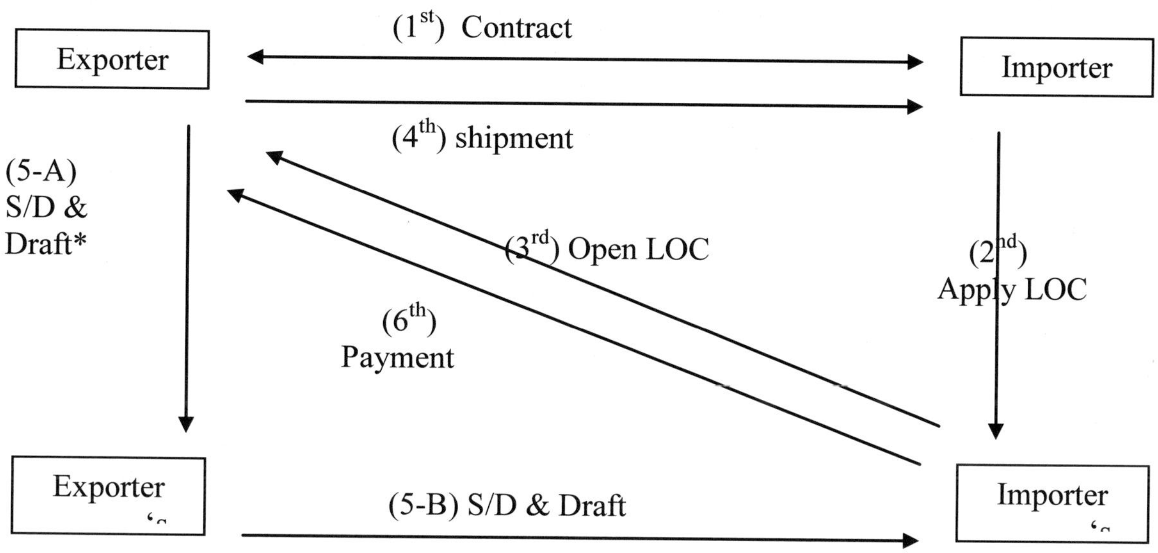

(1st) The contract is drawn up and must clarify that when the LOC is to be opened. The exporter will want to have the LOC at least before the shipping date.

(2nd) When the shipping date nears, the importer applies for the LOC to his bank.

(3rd) The Importer's Bank will open the LOC to the Exporter based on collateral collected from the importer. The exporter wants this payment guaranteed (LOC) before the shipment is made.

(4th) Since the exporter received a payment guarantee (letter of guarantee), he can ship the goods. When shipment is made, the Exporter will obtain a set of shipping documents (including Bill of Lading) from the shipping company.

(5-A) A set of shipping document and Draft (payment request which is drawn on the importer's bank) are presented to Exporter's Bank.

(5-B) The Exporter's Bank, usually in Exporter's own country, relays the S/D and Draft to Importer's Bank located in other country.

(6th) Upon receipt of proper S/D and Draft, Importer's Bank should pay exporter regardless of importer's willingness or ability to pay back to importer's bank .

The benefit of a LOC is that a major source of non-payment risk is eliminated once the exporter receives the LOC from the importer's bank. All the exporter has to do to get paid is to ship the goods and present the shipping documents together with a draft drawn on the importer's bank.Even if the LOC can reduce the risk of non-payment significantly, there are still two types of risk that remains. One is the case when the importer's bank which originally issued the LOC changes its mind and abolishes the payment guarantee made under the LOC. To avoid this kind of situation, most of the LOC's are **Irrevocable LOC's**, which means once the LOC is issued, the issuing bank cannot revoke it. The majority of International Trade is settled in terms of Irrevocable LOC's.

The other type of risk that still remains under the regular LOC is the risk of bankruptcy of the importer's bank, which originally issued the LOC. This will make the payment guarantee useless. If you are concerned about this kind of situation, you can ask for a confirmed LOC rather than a regular LOC. A ***Confirmed LOC*** is the LOC, which is guaranteed twice by two different banks, first by importer's bank and secondly by the exporter's bank. Since payment guarantee is made twice by two different banks, it is the safest way to handle the international trade. The only problem with the confirmed LOC is the fact that the importer has to pay LOC commission twice to two different banks.

We can conveniently draw the following graph to depict the amount of risk to exporter and the cost to the buyer associated with each financial instrument to settle the international trade as below.

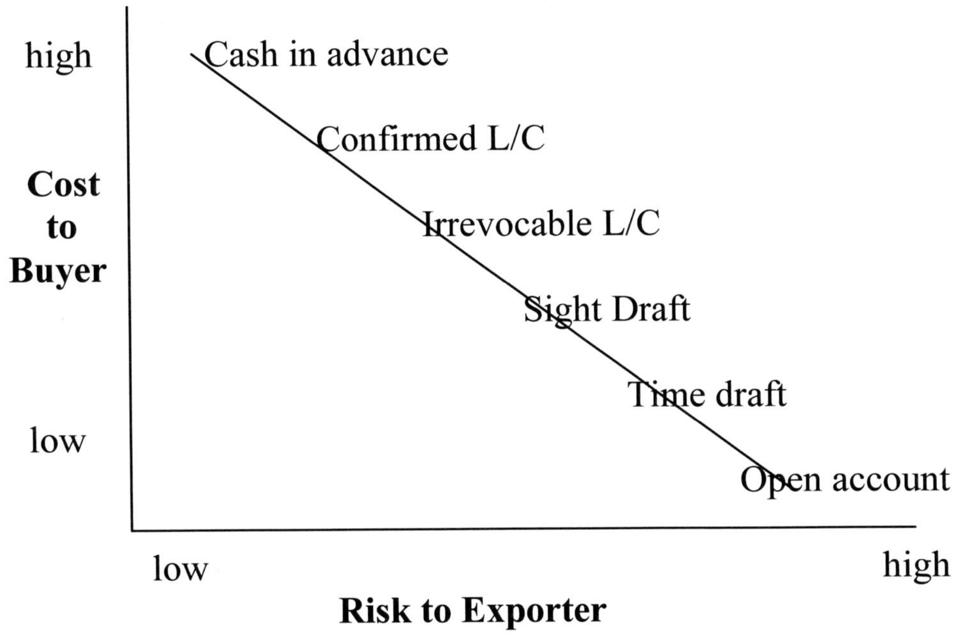

Review Questions

(Working capital management)
Identify and discuss the various ways to provide working capital for foreign subsidiaries.

What can be potential advantages and disadvantages of providing working capital in terms of equity and parental loan?

What is "transfer price" and how is it used in international setting?

What can be the potential problems of manipulating transfer price?

What is the most preferred way for MNCs to provide financing for their foreign subsidiaries and why?

(Investment decision)
What is time value of money?

Discuss the major concept of Net Present Value.

What interest rate will be most likely the base rate to discount the future cash inflow for foreign project?

Identify and discuss the major variables that influence the NPV calculation for foreign project.

Where and how can we incorporate the political risk in international capital budgeting process?

(Currency risk; Exposure)
Identify and discuss three different types of currency risk the financial managers have to deal with.

Discuss the various strategies to deal with those three different types of currency risk.

Discuss the impact of dollar appreciation and depreciation on US export and FDI.

(Settlement of Trade)
What is 'draft' (bill of exchange) and how is it executed?

Discuss the difference between Time draft (D/A) and sight draft (D/P).

What is letter of credit?

Discuss the difference between draft and letter of credit.

Discuss the proper sequence to execute letter of credit.

Discuss the various forms of letter of credit (i.e. irrevocable and confirmed LOC).

CHAPTER 14. INTERNATIONAL ACCOUNTING/TAXATION

International Accounting

At the end of the fiscal year, any business firm should meet the requirements of tax report to the authorities. This requires preparation of financial statements such as income statements and balance sheets. However, the preparation of financial statements in MNCs is not as easy as a typical domestic firm. The reason for that is MNCs have so many subsidiaries scattered all over the world and unfortunately, there is no consistent and standard international accounting rules implemented among the different countries.

Normally, there are two steps involved in international financial reporting. The first step is ***translation***. A subsidiary would first report to their local tax authority under the local rules. Then the company must re-write the subsidiary's financial statements in compliance with the U.S. accounting standard, which is GAAP (Generally Accepted Accounting Principles). After this process (rewriting) is done, the company should convert the local currency to their home currency ($ for U.S. MNCs). In this case the most crucial issue is what kind of exchange rate should be applied. We will discuss this issue later.

The second step is a ***consolidation*** of the financial reports of many subsidiaries into one financial statement for the whole MNCs organization. This process may be time consuming, but it does not have to be very complicated because this is simply a summation process of the already rewritten and translated financial statements.

The most troubled area that accountants who prepare the financial statements for MNCs at the end of the fiscal year have is how to rewrite the subsidiary's financial statements in accordance with home country principles. Also, what kind of exchange rate is applied to convert the local currency to the home currency? The first part requires a very in-depth knowledge about accounting and tax laws on foreign sourced income. Accordingly, the discussion of this issue in an introductory level international business course may not be adequate. Thus, here we will focus on the issue what kind of exchange rate will be applied when the company wants to convert the foreign currency to home currency.

Translation methods

Generally speaking, when a company wants to translate the local currency to home currency, two methods can be used: current method and temporal method. The following table sets out the differences between the two methods:

	Current Method	Temporal Method
Balance Sheet	All items to be translated at current rate except Equity. Equity is to be translated at historical rate	Monetary (cash, A/R, A/P): current rate Non-monetary (fixed assets, equipment, inventories): historic rate
Income Statement	Weighted Average for all items (no exceptions)	Weighted Average for all items except cost of goods sold & depreciation (Historical rate for those two items)
Translation Gain/Loss (where to report,	Balance Sheet – Equity section	Income Statement – part of reported earnings

As seen on the chart, there are some differences between these two methods on how they apply the exchange rates for the items on the balance sheet and income statement. However, there is another big difference between those two methods in the way they handle the translation gain or loss mentioned. The translation gain or loss is a paper loss or gain that inevitably happens when we translate the foreign subsidiary's financial statement to home currency statement. This is the case because the rate that was applied last year and the rate applied this year can be significantly different. This is the typical example of translation risk (exposure), also known as Accounting exposure that was already discussed before. No matter what kind of method is used, firms cannot avoid this type of risk and distortion derived from this type of exposure. Whether they like it or not, they have to translate the financial statements and should report them to home country tax authority. However, in most of the cases, MNCs prefer to have such distortions from this exposure (paper gain or loss) on the Balance Sheet as a part of equity section. The reason for this is that if such a paper gain or loss is reported on the income statement, as part of the reported earnings, the reported earnings for MNCS will fluctuate widely and it can generate a false sense that MNCs are really risky and dangerous firms. This is the reason why most multi-national companies prefer to use the current method where paper gain or loss would appear on balance sheet rather than on the income statement. Another reason why MNCs prefer the current method is convenience. Under the current method, most of the items are supposed to be translated at the current rate, which is the year-end rate. Thus, you don't need a lot of book keeping for the exchange rate to be applied each transaction.

FASB rulings

The Financial Accounting Standards Board publishes a set of rules for translation. The old rule, FASB #8, used to dictate that the temporal method was to be used for all companies. However, many MNCs have argued that using the temporal method could create a false sense. Finally, the FASB accepted the argument and issued a new rule, FASB #52, which states that what kind of method they have to use totally depends on what the *functional currency* of the subsidiary is. Functional currency is the currency by which the major business activity of the foreign subsidiary is conducted. FASB #52 states that if the functional currency is the local currency, in other words, if majority of the foreign subsidiary's business is conducted in terms of local currency, then the Current method will be used. Otherwise the Temporal method is to be used. Since most of the MNCs' foreign subsidiaries are doing their business in terms of local currency, their functional currency is the local currency; thereby they can use current rate methods.

International Taxation

International tax management is one very important issue for a MNC since even if MNCs produce a lot of profit from its operation in foreign countries, if they fail to manage the tax properly, all those profits that they generate can be easily wiped out. However, tax management for MNCs is not that easy because the philosophy of taxation and the way foreign countries impose tax can be very different from country to country. A company must be aware that there is always a risk of being exposed to double taxation by the foreign country and taxation by home country.

Two principles of taxation

The U.S. tax authority maintains two principles of tax on foreign sourced income. First, a ***tax credit*** is designed to avoid double taxation and to ensure tax neutrality regardless of their income sources. The purpose is to have the company pay the same rate wherever they produce their income. Under the tax credit concept for foreign sourced income, the domestic tax liability of U.S. firms on foreign sourced income will be reduced by the amount of tax that they have paid to a foreign government.

Another principle that the U.S. tax authority applies for foreign sourced income is Tax Deferral. A ***tax deferral*** was originally designed to encourage foreign business activity of the U.S. firms by delaying the collection of U.S. income tax on foreign sourced income until it is remitted back to the U.S.

The application of tax deferral depends on types of foreign operation and the nature of income generated by this foreign operation. According to the U.S. tax system, there are two types of foreign operations – a branch office or a subsidiary. A branch office is simply an extension of the international division of the parent company. It is an unincorporated business unit with no legal distinction between the branch and parent. However, a subsidiary is a legally separate and totally independent business unit incorporated under foreign laws. It can be functionally controlled by the parent company but is legally separate and an independent company.

Modes of foreign operation and its implication for tax management

This distinction between the two types of operation provides a significant implication for tax management. Since the branch office and parent company are basically legally the same company, this indicates branch office's assets and liabilities are the same as the parent company's assets and liabilities. The branch office's loss is the parent's loss. Since there is no distinction between branch's profits and parent's profits, when the branch office generates a profit, this will be immediately subject to U.S. tax even if it is not remitted back to the parent company. In other words, tax deferral will not be applied for branch office income. When branch office has some losses, the parent company's tax liability will be reduced by the amount of branch office's losses because that loss will be treated as the parent's loss. However, when the subsidiary has a profit and if they don't send it back to the U.S., then they don't have to pay tax because the subsidiary is a legally different company. In other words, in this case, tax deferral will be applied. However, if the subsidiary suffers a loss, there will be no change in parent company's tax liability because foreign subsidiary is legally separate business entity established under the foreign law. This analysis provides a significant impact on how to arrange foreign operation to minimize overall tax burden when you want to do business in other countries.

Generally speaking, **in the beginning stage of doing international business in other countries, a branch office is often preferred because most likely losses will incur and the parent company can take advantage of deducting those losses from their domestic tax liability. In the later stages of operation a subsidiary may have more experience in the country and start to generate a profit. Once the foreign operation starts to generate a profit, a subsidiary can be a better option because as long as they don't send the profit back to the U.S., they don't have to pay income tax (tax deferral will be applied for subsidiary's income).** This is the reason why most of the MNCs start foreign operations with branch and then change it to a subsidiary later when they start to produce a profit.

U.S. tax system on the foreign subsidiary's income

Unfortunately, however, MNC's use the subsidiary as a tool to avoid U.S. tax by creating a paper company, with no real substantial business going on, in tax haven countries like the Cayman Islands and the Bahamas.

As you can see in the following illustration, many U.S. MNCs don't want to send the dividend payments back to their parent company (1) located in the U.S. because they don't want to pay taxes. So, instead of sending dividend payments to the parent company, MNCs rather send that money to the paper company (2) established in one of those Tax haven countries where they don't have to pay taxes. When the subsidiary in B needs additional financing for working capital or capital investment, it will be the paper company not the parent company who will provide all the necessary funding (3). Thus, by establishing and operating this ghost/paper company in tax haven countries, many U.S. MNCs attempt to avoid U.S. tax permanently.

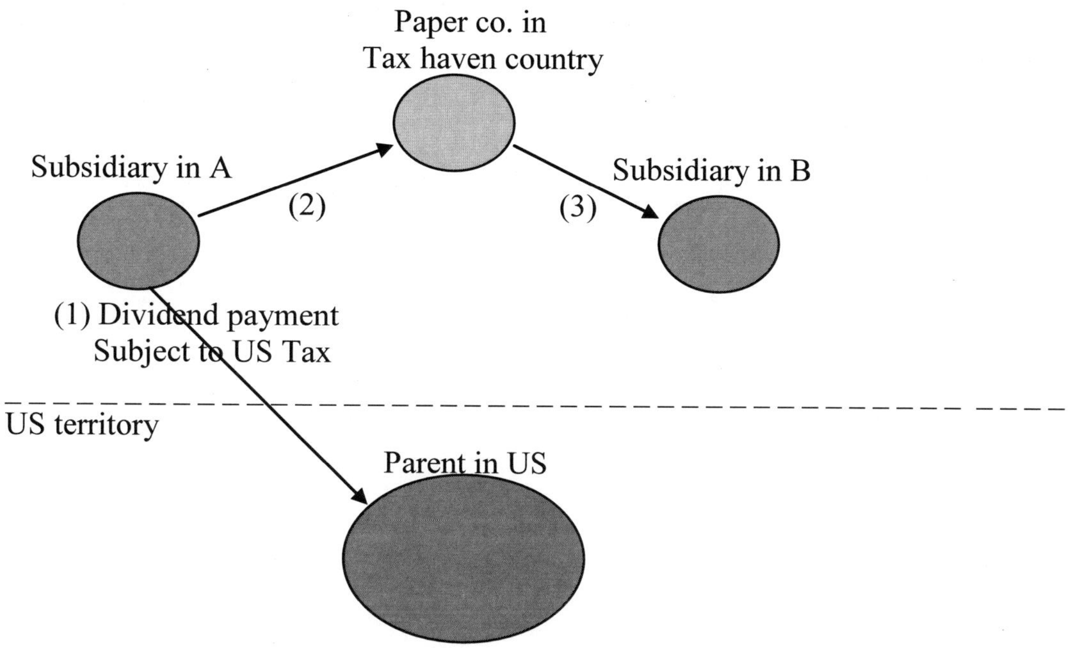

The U.S. tax authorities decided to scrutinize this practice. The U.S. tax authorities classify U.S. foreign subsidiaries into two types – a non-controlled and a controlled. In a *non-controlled foreign subsidiary* the U.S. partner is a minority stockholder, thereby the U.S. tax authorities believe that there is very little room for the U.S. partner to maneuver tax evasive planning such as manipulating transfer price. The kind of subsidiary would generate a normal, innocent income. Thereby, tax deferral would be applied for the income generated by this type of foreign subsidiaries. In a *controlled foreign subsidiary* the U.S. partner would be a majority stockholder who could dictate business decisions and can do whatever they want to do including tax evasion. Since there would be more room to maneuver tax evasive tactics, the income from a controlled subsidiary would be subject to more scrutiny.

According to U.S. tax authorities, income generated by a controlled foreign subsidiary will be classified into two types. *Active income* is considered normal, innocent business income generated through normal business activities such as buying form the third party and selling to the third party. For this type of normal business income, tax deferral will be applied. In other words, if they don't send the profit back to the U.S., they don't have to pay taxes. However, if their income is classified as passive income, it will be treated very differently. *Passive income* (a.k.a. Subpart F) is abnormal income usually generated by internal transactions among affiliated business units such as manipulation of the transfer price. This type of income is looked upon as being suspicious income. If the income of the controlled foreign subsidiary is classified as passive income, Tax deferral is NOT allowed and this income will be immediately subject to U.S. taxes even if it is still kept outside of the U.S. The following chart illustrates and summarizes how the tax deferral will be applied:

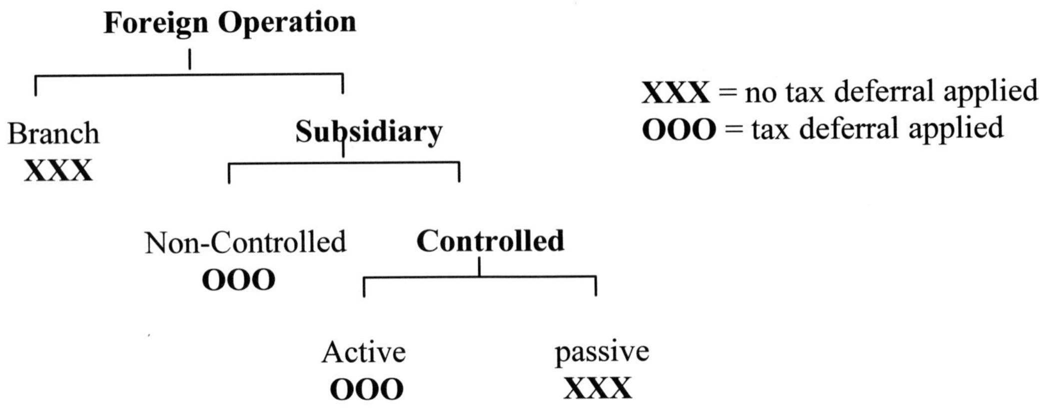
Foreign Operation
Branch
XXX
Subsidiary
Non-Controlled
OOO
Controlled
Active
OOO
passive
XXX
XXX = no tax deferral applied
OOO = tax deferral applied

Review Questions

(International accounting)
What are the two steps needed to convert foreign currency expressed financial statement to dollar express financial statement at the end of the fiscal year?

What are the major differences between current method and temporal method?

What is the major content of FASB ruling #52?

(International taxation)
Discuss the concept of tax credit and deferral on foreign sourced income.

What is the purpose of MNCs' operating offshore financing center in a tax haven country?

Discuss the tax implication of loss and profit of subsidiary and branch.

Discuss the differences in tax implication between controlled and non-controlled foreign subsidiary.

What is the most desirable sequence of foreign operation (subsidiary vs. branch) to minimize the overall tax burden in MNCs?

CHAPTER 15. INTERNATIONAL MARKETING

Global companies must carry out the basic business functions under very different business environments in a foreign country. Compared to domestic firms, MNCs usually can enjoy relatively abundant resources but still have to do their utmost to maximize the efficiency of their resources. In marketing function, the first task that MNCs have to conduct, in order to minimize their loss and potential waste, is to do a fairly accurate market potential analysis before launching any type of marketing and promotional activities.

Assessment of Potential Demand

MNCs can use many different kinds of methods to assess the potential demand in their target countries. The most preferred and most frequently used method that they can use to assess the potential demand in the target country is ***Cross-national analysis***. This method assumes that the demand for your product is a function of certain variables, such as national income [Demand = f (Variable like GNP/capita)]. The researcher will collect the two different sets of data from many different countries: one for actual sales in a country and the other one for the economic variable, which seemingly influence the demand for the product. The resulting two sets of data would be plotted on a chart to find out the best-fit regression line. The regression line is then used to assess the market potential. For example, your target country's national income is $15,000/cap. Then, you can impose that data on the regression line to find out potential demand in the target country.

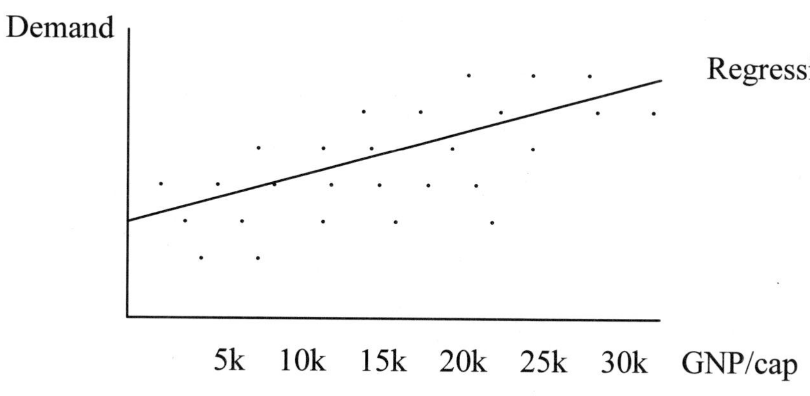

Another method that International marketers can use to assess the potential demand in the target country is ***Time Series Analysis***. This method is appropriate when you have a previous record of sales in the country and want to forecast the future demand. It follows the same principle of cross–national analysis in the sense that you also try to find a regression line with the plotted data. However, unlike the cross-national analysis, the data to be used to develop the regression line for this method would be historical data not cross national data. The researchers collect the actual historical sales data of the target country over a long period of time and plot the data in the two-dimensional spaces where the X-axis represent time and Y-axis reflect the actual sales. By plotting the data on this space, you can find the best fit regression line, which will be used to assess the potential demand by extrapolating the line into the future.

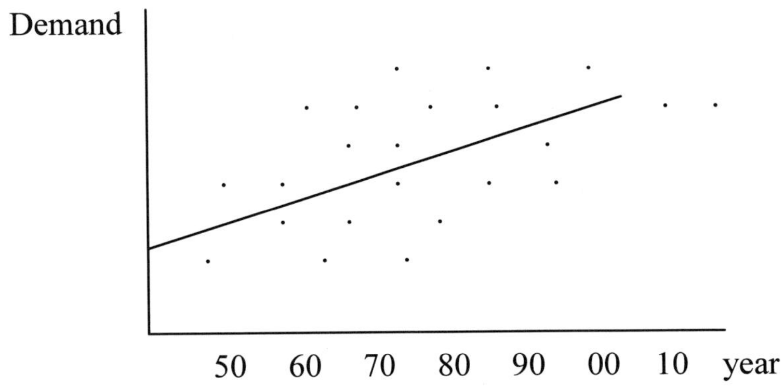

Another way to assess the potential demand in a target country is by looking at ***Income Elasticity*** %. The underlying assumption when using this method is that income is the single most important variable that will influence the demand for your product. Generally, elasticity is defined as sensitivity of one variable to another variable. The income elasticity is defined as below.

$$\varepsilon_i = \frac{\textbf{\% change in demand}}{\textbf{\% change in income}}$$

Income elasticity is represented as a percentage change in demand over the percentage change in income. The product with high income elasticity means the demand for the product will fluctuate widely depending on people's income. If people's income increases, the demand for this type of product will increase dramatically. However, when people's income goes down the demand for this type of product will also decrease significantly. Examples of these kinds of products are luxurious products such as cars and expensive furniture. For most products income elasticity is well known due to previous researches. Luxury goods usually have high elasticity while goods such as milk and bread have low elasticity. Suppose that national income in your target country is expected to increase by 100% next year. If the elasticity of your product is 1.5, then you can predict that demand for your product in your target country next year will increase by 150%.

Another way of assessing demand is by using the ***Regional Leads & Lags Method***. International market researchers found that the demand of a certain type of product displays almost identical patterns across the nations. The assumption here is that most countries will follow the same demand pattern of other countries with some time lag depending upon their level of economic development or national income.

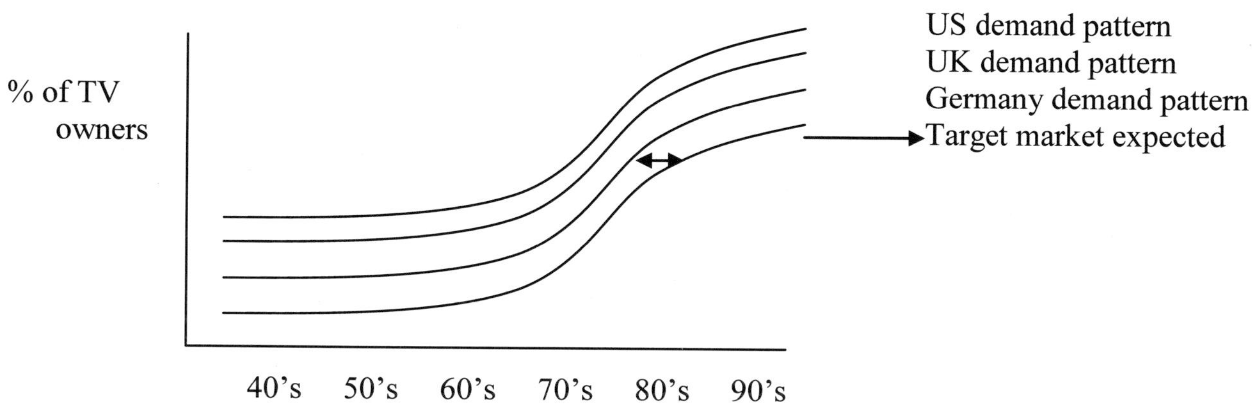

The graph shows that many countries follow almost the same general demand pattern. Thus, we can reasonably assume that your target market country will eventually follow the same demand patterns with some time lapse. If a period of time lapse (↔) can reasonably be calculated with the help of the international economists, the potential demand for your target country can be fairly predicted.

Even if we can use the above methods to assess the potential demand, usually there can be a significant difference between potential demand and actual sales. This would require an international marketer to perform a *Gap analysis* to understand why they have such a big gap between actual sales and potential demand. In a Gap analysis, a marketer would investigate various variables for marketing mix often referred to as the four 'Ps' in marketing: Product, Price, Place, and Promotion.

Product policy

When there is such a big gap between actual sales and potential demand, the first P that the international marketer has to check is its product policy.
There are several different ***product*** policies that MNCs can choose.

1. First, MNCs can take a standardized approach in product design. This is a very ethnocentric approach based on the idea that if you can sell the product in your own market, you can sell it anywhere. The underlying assumptions here are that the world is one big integrated market and that cultural differences are insignificant and can easily be defeated. When they take this kind of approach in product policy, they always try to standardize the product and sell the standardized product everywhere. This kind of approach can be easily applicable for industrial products such as machinery, equipment, etc., which are basically cultural free products. This approach can also be used if the firms

can enjoy strong brand name recognition for the product worldwide. The biggest advantage of product standardization is cost savings because they can have long production runs for each product. When quality is standardized, it also creates a spillover effect. Customers anywhere in the world can expect the same quality from this product. However, the limited product line and lack of diversity and flexibility in product design make it very difficult to serve local markets effectively and thereby they may not be able to increase their sales in the target market significantly.

2. The second approach that MNCs can take is localized approach in product policy. This is considered to be a polycentric approach in product design. The underlying assumption of this approach is that the world market is still very much segmented and cultural difference is insurmountable. If an MNC takes this type of product approach, it may need to change the product design because cultural differences are very difficult to overcome and consumers' preferences are very much influenced by their culture. This approach is applicable to consumer products, which are more culture bound. A good example of this type of product would be Campbell Soup. This company changes the taste and the contents of its soup to match the varying tastes of its foreign markets. Consumer products tie closely to how we eat and dress where cultural differences may be more pronounced. This approach can also be used when MNCs don't have strong brand name recognition for their products. In this case MNCs may try to penetrate or to increase sales by developing new product more suitable for local culture. An advantage here is that sales can be increased with more flexibility in design, which would be more effective in local markets. However, a potential problem is that the cost of manufacturing would increase as production runs are shortened because they have to make so many different products. Also another potential problem may be difficulties to exercise control quality over so many different types of products.

3. *Adaptation* is a hybrid of the previous two approaches. The company who take this approach would relentlessly push the standardized product first, and then reluctantly modify the product only when they experience serious resistance from local markets. There are several factors that make it unavoidable for MNCs to modify their product design. Cultural factor is one of the important reasons. For example, U.S. cars are too large for typical Asian country's housing. The sweetness and color of Coke have been constantly modified to serve local markets more effectively. Pizza Hut reduces the amount of cheese on their pizzas in countries where they have troubles to digest dairy products due to lactose deficiency symptom. Regulatory factors such as health and safety codes may force a company to adapt their products. Since the U.S. is one of the countries that have very stringent health and safety regulations, MNCs can reduce production costs in other countries where the rules and regulations are more lenient. Lastly, the level of economic development and national income can influence a company's decision to introduce a more luxurious or cheaper model to serve the local market more efficiently.

Pricing

When MNCs observe the big differences between potential demand and actual sales figures in the target country, the company has to check another P, which is pricing. Pricing is a very important decision whether it is domestic or international. It can directly affect the sales volume and revenue and indirectly affect profitability, market share and long term viability of the firms. MNCs normally have two alternatives when they make a pricing decision; **Uniform Pricing vs. Differentiated Pricing**

Uniform Pricing

What kind of pricing methods should MNCs adopt in a worldwide market is a very crucial question that they have to address constantly. MNCs always have a pressure from the host government to apply uniform price to avoid legal troubles. If they sell at too low price, they will be accused of dumping and if they sell too high, they will be accused of exploiting the local customers. For these reasons, MNCs try to adopt uniform price whenever possible. There are some conditions that are propitious for uniform pricing. First, when MNCs can enjoy strong brand name, they can easily apply uniform price because consumers will buy their products with relatively less resistance no matter what price set. Typical example for this case is McDonald's. They always try to apply uniform pricing (purchasing power equivalent) even if occasionally there are some deviations because of temporary exchange rate misalignments. Another case that favors uniform price is when the markets are very similar to each other in terms of consumer demographics, perception, physical distance and their income. Thus, you don't see any reason to set different prices among the similar markets. Another condition to set the uniform price is relatively less chance for "grey marketing". Grey marketing is an illegal arbitrage conducted by an unauthorized third party. If MNCs set different prices for different markets, an unauthorized third party may buy their product at the low priced market and sell it at the highly priced market. If MNCs believe there is a high chance for this kind of illegal activity because of the geographic proximity or relatively low tariff among the markets, you may need to set uniform price to avoid this undesirable business practice.

Differentiated Pricing

However, in many cases, it may be inevitable for MNCs to set the different prices in different markets. First of all, the market in the host country can be significantly different from other markets in terms of demand and supply conditions, consumer preferences, national culture and the level of competition. Another factor is the degree of brand name recognition in the host country. If you cannot enjoy strong brand name recognition in the host country, you have no choice but to reduce your price to sell your products. Another factor that makes it difficult to set the uniform price is the transportation cost. In some cases, the final product is so bulky and the geographic distance between host country and home country is too far. Thus, the transportation cost can be a serious burden when they set a uniform price. In this case, MNCs may have no choice but to set different prices to transfer this additional burden to the consumers in the host country. If MNCs see very little chance for grey marketing, they can also set different prices for different markets to maximize their profits. Finally, MNCs need to find out an optimal pricing method depending upon what kind of strategic objective they have in the target market. At this point MNCs need to clarify what strategic objective they want to achieve in the host country.

Objectives of Pricing

One objective that a company may want to achieve in the target country may be *Market Holding* where a company may have been selling in that market for a long time and knows the major players in the market. They may wish to simply maintain market share in a stable market. The pricing method used in this situation would be Normal cost plus pricing method. If they decide to apply this pricing method, it would identify all the cost factors such as fixed and variable costs, administrative expenses, R&D expenses and selling expenses and then add on some profit.

The objective of *Market Skimming* would be considered when a company has a monopolistic position and may be the only one selling a certain product and their supply capacity of that product is limited. Even under this kind of situation, you cannot set the prices too high, because if you do that, eventually that will hit the reflection point and the sales may start to decline. Thus, the maximum pricing method signifies the method to set the price as high as the market could bear.

If a company has a totally different agenda and has never sold their product in that market before, they may have an objective of *Market penetration*. In many occasions, when they try to penetrate into new market, pricing may be the only "p" that they can maneuver. This is the case since there would be no brand recognition for the new comers and it will be very difficult to establish a strong channel over the short period of time. In this case, the company might consider marginal cost pricing in this situation.

Marginal cost pricing is where only one component of cost, the variable cost, is covered in the pricing consideration. Under this method, the price is set to cover the variable cost plus some profit. This is originally applied to the extra output beyond 100% capacity output because any out produced beyond the 100 % capacity does not carry a burden to cover the fixed cost. Thus, for the extra output produced beyond the 100% capacity, the product can be sold if the price covers the variable cost and certain amount of profit. However, recently so many MNCs started to use this method even to the output produced below 100% capacity. This means their fixed cost is not covered anywhere and they lose their money. Then, the question is why would they want to do this? The rationale here is that they consider the fixed costs as **sunk costs**, which are already disbursed and can't be retrieved no matter what. Since the sunk costs are the costs you can not retrieve, it has nothing to do with pricing. The idea is that selling is better than not selling as long as the selling price covers the variables costs and some profit because even if they don't like the fixed cost from building the plant or buying the equipment, there is nothing they can do about it once it is disbursed. When they apply marginal cost pricing method, they would rather forget the fixed cost because there is nothing they can do about it. However, when they apply this method, what they really try to do is to lower the price first in order to penetrate the market. Then they gain market share and gradually raise the price to break even or at a point where fixed costs are recovered. Thus, when a company wants to apply this method to penetrate a new market, a long-term time horizon is needed for this pricing method. It will take a long time to break even when they apply this method and government subsidies are often used to get through the crucial periods by subsidizing the companies.

Factors that influence international pricing decision

It is a very difficult task to find out optimal price for foreign market because there are so many factors to be considered on top of regular factors, which would be considered for normal domestic pricing decisions. Several factors, which must additionally be considered for international pricing, are:

1- *Governmental intervention:* In many foreign countries, prices are strictly controlled by their government. A local government can set a maximum price ceiling to protect local customers from foreign firms when there is a sole supplier in the market. On the other hand, a minimum price floor could be enforced to protect local industries from foreign competition.

2- *Diversity of the market* can be another factor to be considered for international pricing because foreign markets can be so different from domestic markets. The perception and usage of the same product can be significantly different from country to country. An example would be that a bike is used in the U.S. for exercise and recreation, but may be a main source of transportation in another country. The competitive situation can influence the price in the target market. Price elasticity for the same product can be significantly different depending upon the level of national income. In high national income countries, even if price increases a little, people will still buy the product (Price Inelastic). However, in low income countries, if the price rises a little bit, the demand can decrease dramatically (more price elastic).

3- *Extra cost factors for exportation* must also be considered in international pricing. The long distribution channels usually means increased costs such as packing, loading, freight, insurance, or fees. Four of the most frequently used export price quotations are:

- FAS (Free alongside ship): The price covers all the costs up to the point within the reach of loading arm of the vessel that will carry your cargo to foreign destination.

- FOB (Free on board): The price will cover all the costs up to the loading of the cargo on the transporting vessel.

- C&F (Cost and freight): The price will cover all the costs up to the final destination including overseas freight to the arriving port.

- CIF (Cost, insurance, & freight): It covers all the costs up to final destination including overseas freight and insurance coverage. Current international regulations require that any products shipped by air must include insurance coverage.

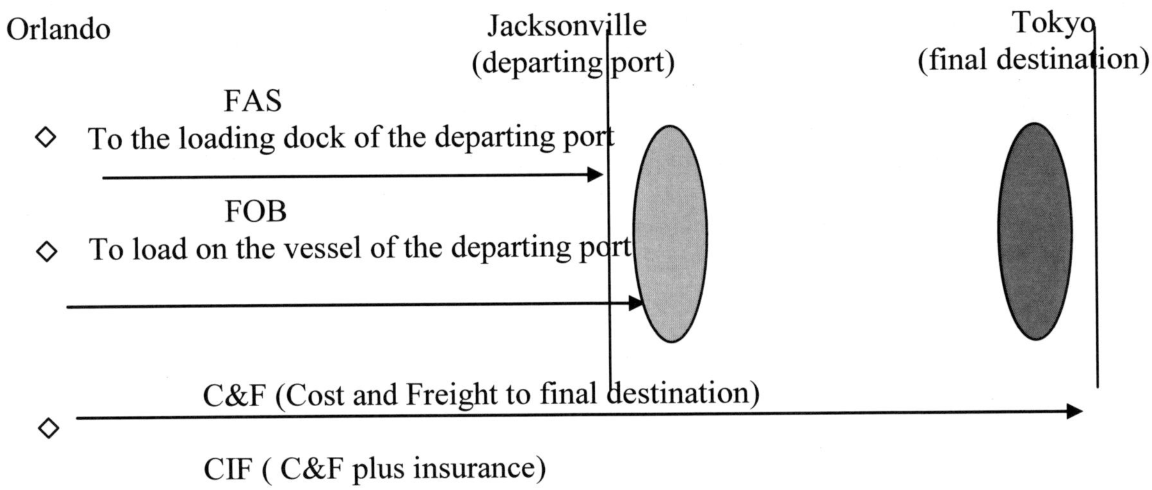

An obvious factor in international pricing would be the constantly changing *exchange rates*. This is an important factor as the trading companies are exposed to the risk of exchange rate fluctuations. For example, a company makes a contract with a Japanese firm to export a product of Y1,000,000 with 60 days credit. At the current spot rate of Y200/$1, the exporter would expect to receive $5,000. If in 60 days the future spot rate turns out to be Y250/$1, then the exporter would only get $4,000. The difference could easily reduce your profit and/or in worst case you may end up with a loss instead of a profit.

Lastly, a difference in *Foreign Pricing Practice* can be a serious problem. In many foreign countries, haggling is a generally accepted business practice. Since they expect some kind of haggling, sellers mark up their price significantly and give a large discount to make their customers happy. It is the international business manager's responsibility to understand these differences in pricing practices. This practice can be illegal in some countries but absolutely legal in many countries.

Freight Forwarder and custom-house broker

The international freight forwarder or custom-house broker acts as an agent for the importer/exporter in moving cargo in and out of the country. To differentiate between the two, the custom-house broker serves U.S. importers by handling U.S. customs regulations and documentations. The international freight forwarder handles the exportation of goods to foreign ports, including shipping arrangements and documentations.

Generally, the firm which is a custom-house broker also can fill the role of international freight forwarder. You should use an international freight forwarder to move cargo from your plant (or at least the port of shipping) to the port of entry overseas. This is because they are licensed by the Federal Maritime Commission and are familiar with the rules, regulations, and documentations connected with foreign trade.

Brokers (or forwarders) can assist with an order from the start by advising the exporter of the freight costs, port charges, consular fee, costs of any special documentation, and insurance costs, as well as their handling fees, which helps in the preparation of quotation. They also can recommend the type of packing necessary for shipment (including the selection /recommendation of a packing house, if necessary).

After the order is ready to ship, they will review a letter of credit to ensure that everything is in order. They then confirm the reservation of the necessary space aboard an overseas vessel or aircraft (which most likely was made earlier).

When the cargo arrives in the port of export, the forwarders make the necessary arrangements to clear it through customs and have it delivered to the pier (or loading ramp) in time for loading. They may also prepare the ocean bill of lading and any specific consular documentation that may be required. After shipment, they forward all the documents directly to the customer, or the paying bank, with instructions to credit the exporter's account accordingly. Then, if requested, as part of their service, they coordinate the goods' arrival with their foreign counterparts to ensure proper handling at the destination.

Freight forwarder's fees are minimal (often as low as $100) compared to the responsibility they assume, so you should make maximum use of their expertise. Many of their fees are fixed per transaction. Thus, their costs will be proportionately higher (i.e., as a percentage of the selling price) on smaller, less costly shipments. This might indicate that low-value shipments might be "bundled" or "consolidated" whenever feasible.

Promotion

The next marketing mix component is ***promotion***. Traditionally, we have two very different kinds of approach in promotional efforts. Those are;

1. Push: The product is "pushed" directly to the customer through direct sales or door to door selling.

2. Pull: The company tries to attract potential customers to the point of purchase with TV ads, radio, newspaper, magazines, etc.

There are several different factors that international marketers should consider to find out the most efficient way to make a promotional decision:

-One factor is the density of the population in the target country. If it is sparsely populated, the Push approach may be too expensive and pull approach may be more effective with minimal resources. If densely populated, the Push approach would be easy to use and more effective.

-The cost and availability of the promotional instrument is also an important factor. TV commercials can be extremely expensive in some countries and TV commercial time per day may be regulated by the government.

-The illiterate rate must be considered because if many people in the country can't read, any written promotional instrument such as advertisements in magazines and newspapers will not be effective.

-Also, the consumer's perception about a specific information source may be another factor. In certain countries people don't take TV commercials seriously. For example, while TV commercials do have high influence in the U.S., Europeans don't believe much of what they see on TV.

Advertising

One of the interesting and challenging aspects of international marketing is how to develop their advertisements for foreign market. International marketers always have a strong temptation to standardize their commercials and hope to use it simply by translating them.

The biggest advantage of standardized advertising is that it will be very cheap. You can save money by developing a couple of prototype commercials and use them by translating. It also helps the managers save time and energy allowing them to be more productive in other areas of their business rather than developing so many different commercials for so many different countries. Also the spillover effect can be a possible benefit when consumers can recognize a product no matter what country they are in.

However, there are several problems associated with the standardization of international advertising. First, the translation to another language makes it very difficult to reproduce a same nuance and image that a company wants to convey. One of the classic examples of this kind of problem is Chevrolet's car named "Nova", which was supposed to mean a bright "new star", but it sounds like "no go" in Spanish (no va). Similarly, the translated German version of Pepsi's 'Come alive" slogan was almost like "come out of the grave". To avoid the possible disastrous result like this incident, one may use a **back-translation** where the English version would be translated into the foreign language, and then back again into English to check the accuracy of the translation. Cultural differences can pose a problem too and can reduce the effectiveness of communication. For example, General Mills used kids in their cereal ads to appeal to other kids, but the same commercial didn't work in UK because in the UK, it is their parents who make a decision about what their kids will eat and not the kids. Lastly, legal factors may make it difficult to standardize ads. In the U.S., marketers use a certain commercial to criticize or slander their competitor's product, but it may be legally prohibited to do that in many other countries. Most of the foreign countries do have a "Fair Trade Act" under which the government prohibits a certain type of commercial such as the ones that used to heavily expose human body, etc. It is the international marketer's responsibility to understand all those local rules and regulations on the development of promotional aids.

Country of Origin Effect

One very unique factor that you can use as a way to promote the quality perception of your product is *Country of Origin Effect*, also known as the "Made In Effect". This is a kind of special a brand name effect. Being made in a certain country provides a positive impact on the quality perception. For example, for some reason, many American consumers believe that all Japanese electronic devices have top quality or all Colombian coffee has good quality. Many MNCs positively try to take advantage of this special brand name effect by contract manufacturing. For example, a Japanese company produces almost every part of their electronic devices in other countries and re-imports and assembles all the parts in Japan and put the label "Made in Japan".

Place (Distribution Channel)

The final marketing mix variable is ***Place (Distribution)***. There are two different channels of distribution to consider in international marketing; internal vs. external channel based on where your channel is located.

Internal Channel

The *Internal Channel* is a relatively passive form of channel located and operated in the home country.

Export agent is one form of internal channel that MNCs can use. It can provide export related services such as collecting information about the foreign customers, identifying the potential customers or conducting a promotional campaign in return of commission. However, just like any other agent, the export agents never buy or sell your product at their own expenses or risk. They never take title of the goods. They simply provide the related services in return of their services.

An **Export House** is another form of internal channel, which is commonly known as a "Trading Company". The Export House buys the goods from the seller (takes title) and then sells the goods at their own risk.

A **Resident Foreign Buyer** in a home country is another form of internal channel that you can use to reach foreign customers. Examples of resident foreign buyers are the branch offices or subsidiaries of the foreign firm operating the home country, often found in big cities.

Companies in the same industry can create an **Export Association** for the purpose of export promotion. Traditionally, the U.S. government has been very negative against any type of collaboration in the same industry. Anti-trust laws usually do not allow collusion in the same industry. However, the government decided to make some exceptions particularly for the U.S. export industry under the Web-Pomerene Act which allows U.S. export industries to get around the anti-trust laws for export purposes. Under this act the companies in the same industry are allowed to cooperate together to develop market in the foreign countries and promote their products jointly in other countries. An example is the U.S. movie and sulfur industry, which are now allowed to work together under this act.

Lastly, an **Export Trading Company** (developed in 1982 under the Export Trading Act) was developed especially for the U.S. to compete against a large Japanese trading company known as "Sogo Shosha" (general trading company). It is a group of six major trading companies in Japan, which accounted for the majority of Japanese international trade. One interesting aspect of this operation is that the trading company is always heavily financed by the affiliated financial firms such as banks and security firms, which has been traditionally prohibited in the U.S. By passing the Export Trading Act, the U.S. tried to make it a little easier for the U.S. financial firms to participate in and help export industry. It also gives the U.S. trading companies a way to compete as a large-scale trading company such as the Japanese Sogo Shosha. This act also gave the U.S. financial institutions the opportunities to get involved with merchant activity (import/export), which has not been allowed traditionally.

External channel

Another type of channel, which operates in the target country, is called an ***External Channel***. One type of external channel a company can use is an **Import Agent** who can perform such activities as gathering marketing information, promote advertising, etc., by providing services for a commission. However, like any other agent, import agents would never take the title to any of the company's goods.

A **Foreign Distributor** will take title to the goods, and will buy and sell at their own expenses and risk. The stronger form of External Channel would involve a company setting up their own operating units in the target country.

A **Branch** Office can be established by the parent company as an unincorporated business unit that is merely an extension of the parent company to operate on foreign soil. In other words, there is no legal distinction between branch and parent company.

Another option can be the establishment of a **Subsidiary**. It is an incorporated business unit legally established under the foreign law. It is legally independent from the parent company yet it would still be controlled by the parent company. The important difference between a Branch Office and a Subsidiary is that there are legal ramifications.

Factors to be considered for channel decision:

1) Market size and potential demand
Even if the current market is not big, the market is growing with high potential. We may need an external channel, which will enable us to exploit the market more aggressively.

2) The amount of experience a company has in a target country should be assessed and considered. An external channel requires a great deal of experience since it will operate on foreign soil.

3) The amount of resources available, in terms of both money and human resources, can dictate if an external channel would be the best option since it will require a lot of capital and well-trained employees.

4) The nature of the product should also be considered as such factors as the type of service or timely delivery may outweigh other factors. For example, if a company sells heavy construction equipment to a foreign country, they may want to have an external channel to facilitate the after-purchase service that would be needed for such equipment.

5) Strategic factors must be additionally considered. If a company plans to establish foreign direct investment in the future, they may have to collect a vast amount of confidential information before they commit large amounts of capital such as FDI. In this case one of their own organizations, like branch office or subsidiary, may be needed.

Review Questions

(Assessing potential demand)
Identify the various methods to assess potential demand in the target market.

Discuss the similarity and dissimilarity between the time series analysis and the cross national analysis.

(Product Policies)
Identify and discuss the conditions and assumptions of standardized product policy.

Discuss advantages and disadvantages of standardized product policy.

Identify and discuss the conditions and assumptions of localized product policy.

Discuss advantages and disadvantages of localized product policy.

Identify various factors that make it inevitable for MNCs to modify their product design?

(Pricing)
Discuss the necessary conditions for uniform pricing and market by market pricing.

What is “gray marketing” and under what kind of condition does it take place?

Identify three different pricing methods to achieve three different objectives (market holding, skimming and penetration).

What is “marginal cost pricing” and how it is applied?

What is “sunk cost”?

Identify the various factors that make international pricing more complex than domestic pricing.

Identify and discuss various terms for export pricing such as FAS, FOB, C&F and CIF.

Discuss the roles of International freight forwarder and custom-house broker?

(Channel)
Identify the various forms of internal and external channel and discuss the differences among them.

What kind of channel was created to emulate "Sogososha"?

What are the factors that must be incorporated when you make international channel decision?

(Advertisement)
What can be the potential advantages and problems when you using standardized advertisement?

What is the most desirable method to ensure the accuracy of translation?

Identify the various factors that make it difficult to use a standardized advertisement.
What is "country of origin effect"?

CHAPTER 16. INTERNATIONAL MANAGEMENT

Managerial Style

Many research have been conducted to investigate what kind of managerial style would be the most efficient and optimal one to motivate the employees. Traditionally, the researchers identify two different theories to motivate human beings. ***Theory X*** was developed with the assumption that a human being is idle and not self-motivated. They assume that employees tend to avoid the works whenever possible. Consequently, management needs to put pressure on their employees to make them work. The management style should then be formal with close and tough supervision and authoritative leadership is favored under this theory. ***Theory Y*** is based on the assumption that human beings are creative, eager to work, self-motivated and mentally programmed to motivate themselves to achieve higher level of needs. Underlying assumption of this theory is that when one level of need is met, a person will automatically move up to the next level of need following the need hierarchy (e.g. Maslaw's need hierarchy). The management style should follow broad guidelines and maintain informal supervision with democratic leadership.

Many researchers have investigated different types of managerial styles in many other countries in search of a more efficient managerial style that will improve the global competitiveness of the firms. Particularly, in the 1970's and 1980's, many researchers, after they witnessed the Japanese economic miracle, started to investigate why the Japanese achieved such a marvelous economic achievement over such a short period of time. Also, what are the major components of the Japanese managerial style and how is it different from that of the American managerial style. Ouchi and Jaeger found striking differences between these two managerial styles and they tried to find a new managerial theory by selecting the best parts of these two different managerial styles for MNCs. Based on various criteria's, they chose what they thought to be the traits from both management styles, and combined them to form Theory Z. The following table illustrates their choices by the ones marked (*) in **bold** letter:

	AMERICAN	JAPANESE
a. Employment 1. security 2. loyalty	Short-term – no long-term contracts provided. Low Weak	***Long-term*** – practice lifetime employment high strong
b. Decision making	Individual – personal decisions, usually one powerful individual	***Consensual*** - grass-root involvement (a.k.a. Ringgi Seido) - documents passed back and forth until all agree
c. Responsibility	***Individual*** – personal responsibility	Collective – group responsibility with lots of peer pressure
d. Way to evaluate & promote	Fast – fast to promote, but quick to dismiss employees too	***Slow*** – looking to develop the employee's potential over "lifetime employment"
e. Way to control	Explicit – written code of conduct, rules and policy must be very clear	***Implicit*** – unwritten code of conduct, more humane - insinuate because saving face is so important
f. Career path	***Specialized*** – individual productivity, easier to measure, no job rotations	Non-specialized – group productivity, frequent job rotation
g. Concern of management	Segmented – public concern, more worried about the public performance, functional relationship between employer and employee	***Holistic*** – personal & paternalistic care, closer human relationship between employer and employee

Global Human Resource Management

One of the most important issues in global human resource management for MNCs is who will run the foreign subsidiaries scattered all over the world. What would be the best way to handle this globally? MNCs have several choices when they select the manager who will run the foreign subsidiaries.

An MNC can hire a ***Host Country National (HCN) Manager***, or local manager to operate the foreign subsidiaries. There can be many advantages to this option. It would be less expensive than the parent country's national manager as they would not incur any relocation costs/costs of living adjustment/extra compensation for foreign assignments nor subsidizing education of the manager's children. An HCN manager would know the local environment, which could save a lot of possible serious mistakes. This individual could give proper managerial services due to the fact that they would be knowledgeable about the kind of care local employees need. A better public relationship could be established, especially if there is much government control on their business. Having an HCN manager can reduce the foreign image of a company and mitigate nationalistic attitudes. Also, having an HCN manager may be an incentive for other local employees to succeed.

However, having an HCN manager can also create problems. Poor communication with the parent company can pose problems. An HCN manager may require extensive training, as they aren't familiar with a parent company's business policies. Another potential source of the problem, which is very hard to detect would be a "split identity" due to multiple membership of the local manager-one as an employee of the foreign firm and one as the citizen of the nation state. HCN managers are often trapped in "the multiple loyalty dilemma" suggesting, if they are loyal to one party, it will make them disloyal to the other party. For example, if a parent company asks an HCN manager to manipulate a transfer price, he has a pressure to do it as an employee of the firm but he may develop a sense of betrayal because that can undermine his country's efforts to control their own economy. In other words, if he is loyal to one party, that makes him disloyal to the other party. This kind of situation can create an undesirable situation where their divided loyalties may lead them to deliberately not act at all (so called "intended inertia"). Limited transferability may also be a problem if an HCN manager does not want to relocate to other foreign countries.

Another choice is for a company to appoint a ***Parent Country National (PCN) Manager***, an individual from the parent company. This can allow for tight control over a subsidiary because the individual would be experienced with the parent company and they know exactly what the parent company wants. They can ensure more consistency and uniformity between the parent and subsidiaries. The communication between parent and subsidiary may be more effective with few serious problems. A PCN manager can be more easily transferable from one country to another country because foreign country A and B is still foreign to him.

A big problem with sending a PCN manager is the expense the parent company incurs. It can easily cost three times the normal cost due to home leave, relocation costs, costs of educating their children, cost of living adjustment, allowance for foreign assignment, etc. Unfamiliarity of the local environment may lead to a lot of costly mistakes particularly at the beginning of the assignment, some which can't be cured at all. An example is when an American manager was sent to an Asian subsidiary of a large corporation. The PCN manager decided to change the layout of the office by making individual offices. Rather than helping the productivity, this hurt the collective communication patterns of the local employees and consensual decisions characteristic of an Asian corporate culture. An ethnocentric PCN manager's condescending attitude can cause a serious problem even if it is not noticed in many cases. A gap may develop between locals and expatriates when there are many parent managers assigned to the subsidiaries. Another problem recently developed is the security of the American expatriate managers. Since the U.S. invasion of Iraq, anti-American rhetoric has been widely spread in many Middle Eastern countries and other Muslim countries. This kind of situation makes the American expatriate managers very vulnerable to terrorist attacks and kidnap for ransom.

A third choice would be to name a ***Third Country National (TCN) Manager*** such as in the case when Dow Chemical hired many Australian managers for the Pacific Asian countries. This may allow the company to get the best person globally available for the job. The cost may be less expensive than hiring a PCN manager as this person may be willing to work for less than typical American managers. A TCN can act as a neutral mediator between a parent company and the subsidiary when there are disputes between the parent and subsidiary. The only problem with this option is that a qualified TCN manager is often very hard to find.

Even if, in many cases, a TCN or HCN manager may be the idealistic option for the position (to run the foreign subsidiary), sometimes, MNCS have no choice but to send a parent company under certain conditions. Such conditions would be when strong control for the subsidiary is needed to ensure the conformity and uniformity between the parent and subsidiary. Another case may be when an MNC starts a new operation; the parent company needs to insure a smooth new operation with consistent rules. In some cases, there may be a serious fighting and racial conflict among the different ethnic groups within a country. To avoid serious multi-racial disputes in a subsidiary, a PCN manager would be called for. Also, an MNC wants to train future international managers as a part of management training program. In this case, they will send a parent manager to a country and rotate him from one country to another until he has enough experience in the area. If the parent company decides to send a PCN manger, what kind of qualifications are needed to become a competent manager and to finish his job successfully?

Qualifications for PCN manager in order to be successful are:

- Cultural adaptability; a manager should not have biased ethnocentric attitude.
- Knowledge of local environment.
- Ability to achieve goals with limited resources.
- Mental and physical strength.
- Efficient communication skills.
- Family support

Organizational Structure

Organizational structure requires incorporating two critical elements: (1) how to divide the organizational structure into subunits (2) where the decision for the subsidiaries should be made.

The Design of Organizational Structure

The decisions of the organizational structure of the firms are usually made on the basis of function, type of business, geographical area or product.

The structure of Domestic Firms

Even if most of the domestic firms begin with no formal structure and are run by one person or a small group of people, as they grow, the role of management become too complex for one person to handle. When a firm reaches this point, the organization is typically divided based on its functions such as production, marketing, R&D and sales, etc. These functions are normally coordinated and controlled by top management and most of the decision-making in this functional structure tends to be centralized. Functional divisions are popular among companies with very limited product lines. A typical organizational structure developed based on function is shown below.

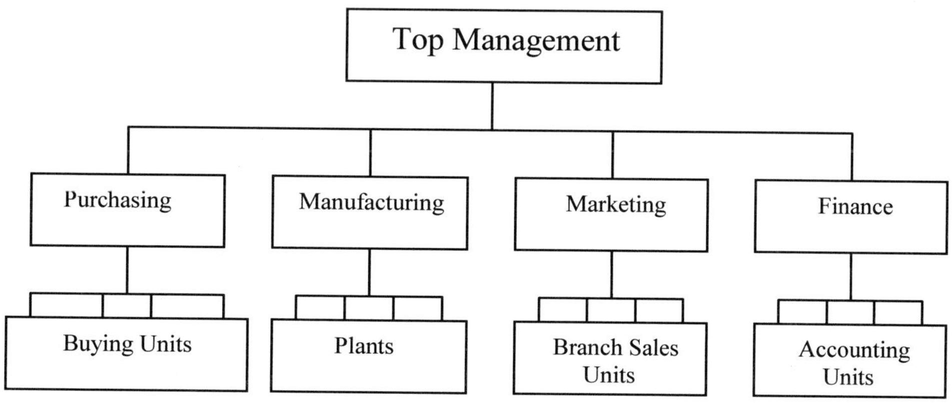

The International Divisional Structure

When firms' business activities overseas increase dramatically, they often group all their foreign operations under an international division based on the geographic location as shown below. Even if this structure is very popular for the firms that have expanded internationally, it also suffers some drawbacks. The dual structure it creates presents inherent potential for conflict and coordination problems between domestic and foreign units. One typical problem they found out with the structure is that the heads of foreign subsidiaries are not given as much autonomy and power as the heads of domestic unit. This can easily relegate each country's manager to the second tier of the firm's hierarchy, which is inconsistent with a strategy of trying to expand internationally with a separate independent international units.

International Divisional Structure

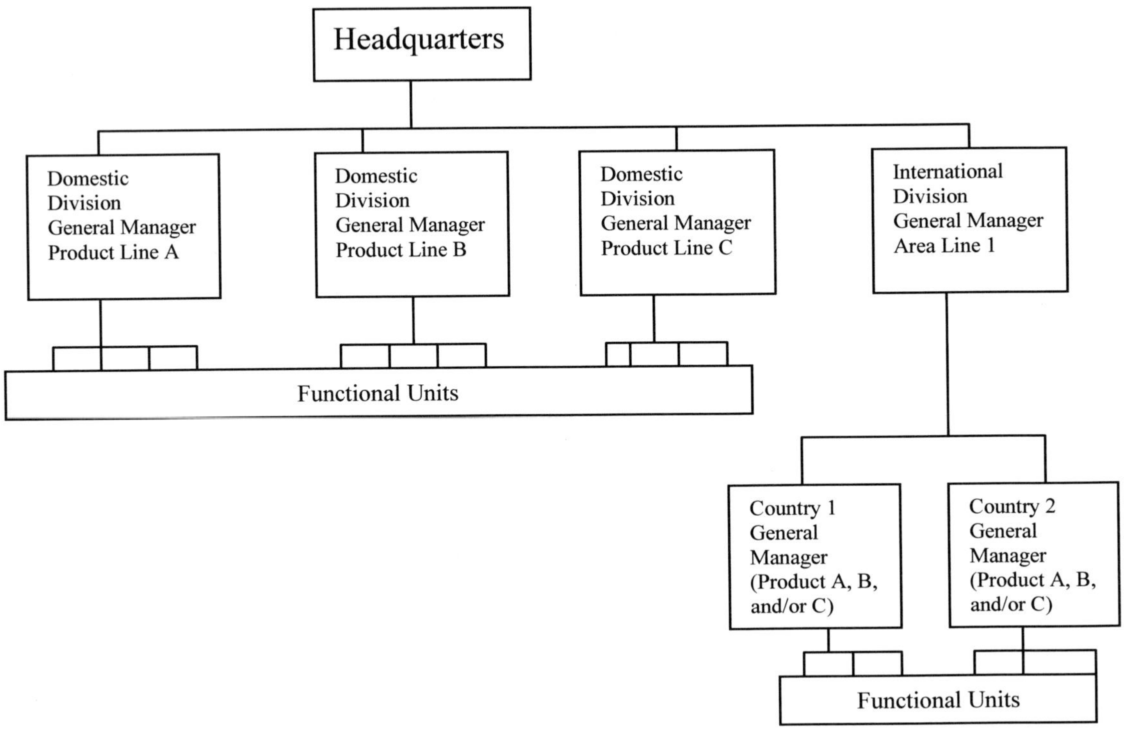

Another potential problem is the lack of coordination between domestic operations and foreign operations, which are isolated from each other in separate parts of the structural hierarchy. This can inhibit the global optimality of the MNCs. To deal with these problems, most of MNCs significantly expand their business globally and they replace this structure with the worldwide area structures as below.

Worldwide Regional Structure

Under this approach, the world is divided based on several regions. Each region is supposed to have an autonomy with its own functions such as production, marketing, R&D, human resources, and finance. Strategic decisions related to each of these functional activities are typically delegated to each area. However, the headquarters still maintains authority for the overall strategic direction of the firm and financial control. This structure is designed to ensure local responsiveness and flexibility. Because decision-making responsibilities are decentralized, each area can customize product offerings, marketing strategy, and business strategy in response to the local conditions. However, this structure can result in fragmentation of the organization into highly autonomous entities, which can make it difficult to ensure the uniformity and consistency between regions. This structure may present a problem if coordination and uniformity among the regions are more important than local responsiveness and flexibility. If this kind of problem persists, MNCs can choose the following structure called "Worldwide Product Divisional Structure."

A worldwide Regional Structure

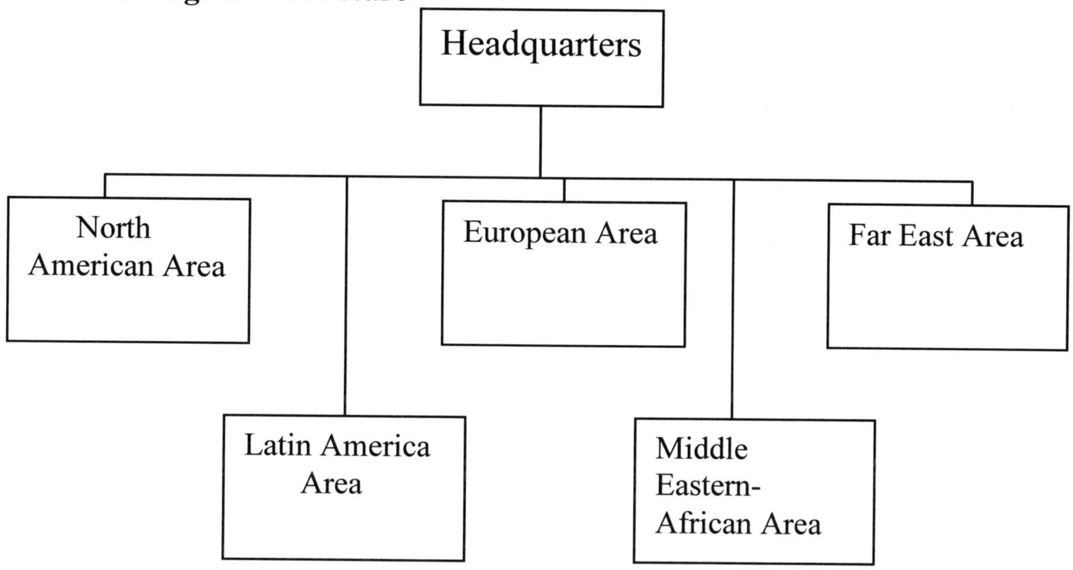

Worldwide Product Divisional Structure

This structure is designed to deal with the coordination problems that may arise with the worldwide area structure. This type of organizational structure is developed to enhance the consolidation of different business functions and also ensures uniform and simultaneous introduction of new business strategies globally. However, as in the case of international divisional structure, one problem with the structure is the limited authority and autonomy endowed to regional managers, since they are seen as subservient to product division managers.

A Worldwide Product Divisional Structure

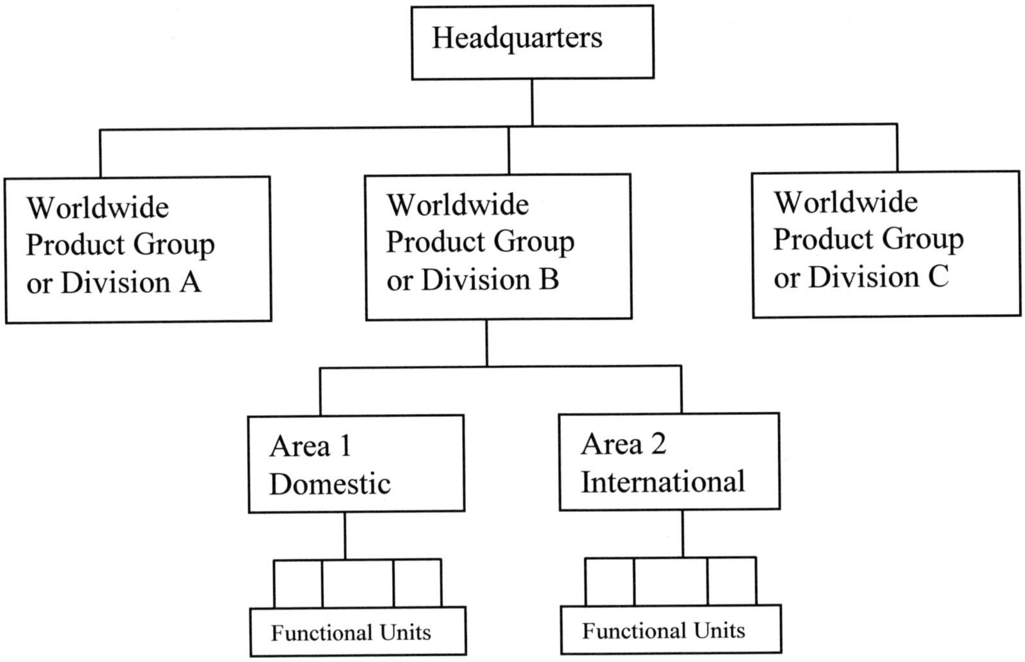

<u>Global Matrix Structure</u>

Both the worldwide area structure and the worldwide product divisional structure have its own merits and disadvantages. The worldwide area structure can ensure local flexibility and responsiveness. However, it can impede the coordination and uniformity among regions. The worldwide product division structure provides a better framework for pursuing global optimality in implementing strategies, but it is weak in local flexibility and responsiveness. Many MNCs have attempted to solve this problem by using a matrix structure as below.

A Global Matrix Structure

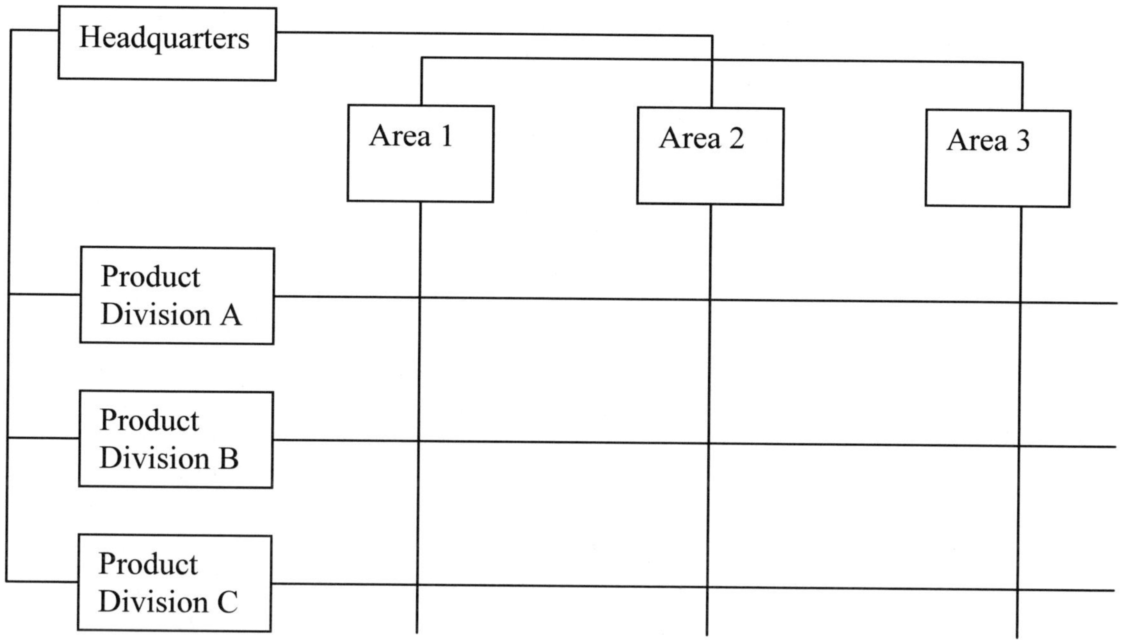

In a typical global matrix structure, organizational structure is designed based on two dimensions: product division and geographic regions. The reason for this design is that decisions for a particular product should be made jointly by the product divisional manager and the regional manager that the firm covers. This dual decision-making structure can help the firm reduce the potential problems such as lack of coordination among the relevant parties and to ensure the local responsiveness and flexibility. In this classic matrix structure, dual responsibility will be enforced by giving product divisions and geographical regions equal status within the organization. However, under this structure, one of the serious drawbacks is the fact that individual managers belong to two hierarchies (a divisional hierarchy and a regional hierarchy) and have two bosses (a divisional boss and an area boss). This can result in serious organizational inefficiencies and delay the decision making process and deprive the firms of their ability to make quick responses to market changes. One of the most serious problems arising under this structure is the difficulties to ascertain accountability. Since all the decisions are supposed to be made jointly between product division and regional division, when something is going wrong, they point fingers at each other. Because of these potential problems, many MNCs are recently trying to have an "invisible" matrix structure with more flexibility in decision making based on a more shared vision and nature of the business than on a rigid hierarchical design. The Dow Chemical is one example where the informal structure plays a greater role than the formal structure through its flexibility and intimacy.

Decision Making Responsibility: Centralization vs. Decentralization

A very critical issue for MNCs is where should the most crucial decisions, such as production, R&D and marketing decisions be made? Should all these crucial decisions be made at the parent company (centralized) or at the subsidiaries (decentralized)? Who will be in better position to make these decisions? There are some arguments for centralization and decentralization as below.

Argument for Centralization

There are four arguments to support the centralization frequently cited. First, centralization can facilitate cooperation among the different units in the same company. For example, consider a firm that has a component manufacturing unit in South Korea and an assembly operation in Mexico. A smooth flow of products from the component manufacturing to the assembly operation might be better achieved by centralizing production scheduling at the firm's head office. Second, centralization can help ensure the consistency of organizational objectives throughout the whole organization. When decisions are decentralized to the subsidiary level, they may make decisions, which are different from the objectives of the parent company. Third, by concentrating power and authority at the parent level, centralization can give parent staff the power and the means to bring about needed major changes and to control the subsidiaries. Fourth, centralization can avoid the overlap and duplication of similar activities carried on by various subunits within the organization and improves the efficiency of the limited resources available. For this reason, many MNCs centralize their R&D and productions functions at the parent company.

Arguments for Decentralization

There are several arguments for decentralization. First, parent management can become overloaded when decision-making authority is centralized, and this can result in poor decisions. Delegating more authority to the subsidiaries give parent managers more time to focus on critical issues. Second, as motivational research reveals, people are more motivated to work hard when they have a greater degree of authority and individual freedom. Third, decentralization provides a greater flexibility and adaptability – ability to rapidly respond to external and internal challenges – because decisions can be made at the local level by local employees who know the local environment and can access more relevant information better than the parent staff. Fourth, more autonomy by decentralization can increase the level of self control. Decentralization can be used to establish relatively autonomous, self-contained subunits within an organization. Subunits managers can then be held more accountable for their performance if the decision is made by themselves and not given from the headquarters.

Review Questions

(Managerial Style)
Discuss the differences in assumption and preferred managerial style between Theory X and Y.

Discuss the major characteristics of Japans managerial style and compare them with those of American managerial style.

What are the components of Theory Z by Ouchi and Jaeger?

(HR management)
Identify and discuss three different types of managers to operate foreign subsidiary in MNC.

Discuss the advantages and disadvantages of each type of manager.

What kind of conditions warrants the dispatch of parent country national manager?

What kind of qualifications is needed to become a successful parent country national manager?

CHAPTER 17. MODES OF INTERNATIONAL BUSINESS

Once a firm decides to enter a foreign market, the question arises: what would be the best mode of entry for the firm? Firms can use many different modes to enter foreign markets. Those modes include exporting (conventional trade and non-conventional counter trade), licensing, franchising, turnkey projects, management contracts, extract agreement, establishing joint ventures with a host-country firm, or setting up a new wholly owned subsidiary in the host country. Each entry mode has advantages and disadvantages. Managers need to consider these options very carefully when they want to get into a new market.

Exporting

Many manufacturing firms begin their global expansion as exporters. Later on they switch to another mode for serving a foreign market as they build up their experiences in the target market.

Exports can enjoy two possible advantages. First, it can avoid the costly FDI which requires a substantial amount of capital and risk taking to operate in a foreign country. Second, exporting by manufacturing at one centralized location may help a firm achieve economies of scale and a learning curve. This is how the Japanese automakers made inroads into the U.S. market, and how the South Korea firms such as Samsung gained market share in computer memory chips.

Even if exporting can give some advantages discussed above, it can also suffer a number of drawbacks. First, firms may not be able to utilize cheap production factors (such as cheap labor) available in foreign countries. Another potential problem is the fact that an exporter may not be in the best position to monitor the consumer feed back and reflect that in the product design because of the geographic distance between the consumer and the producer. Another problem can be the high transport costs. It is particularly true for bulky products, such as big plastic products or furniture. One of the most serious problems that exporters have to deal with is various forms of tariff and non-tariff trade barriers imposed by the host countries. This became a more serious issue recently because so many countries have established their own forms of economic integration (mutually exclusive economic blocs such as E.U. and NAFTA). One of the purposes of establishing these economic blocs seems to be to discriminate against non-member countries by imposing many different types of trade barriers. For this reason, many MNCs started to build production facilities inside of their target countries. A typical example is the Japanese automobile industry who gradually replaced their export to the U.S. with FDI in this country under an implicit threat by the U.S. Congress tried to impose high tariffs on imported Japanese cars. We can see a similar strategy recently adopted by South Korean auto makers such as Hyundai and Kia.

Non-conventional Trade (Counter Trade)

As the world economy becomes more globalized and complex, MNCs realized that with the traditional form of international trade they could not satisfy the varying need of so many parties involved in cross-border transactions. Furthermore, so many countries suffer a serious shortage of internationally acceptable hard currencies. They did not possess sufficient foreign "hard" currency to make purchases of crucial goods. That is why more creative ways to facilitate international transactions is needed and many MNCs are now using some form of non-traditional counter trade.

A Definition of Counter-trade

In the international market, it is very hard to define what counter trade is because counter-trade often contains a wide variety of complex arrangement among many different parties. However, it can be defined as "any international transaction that involves reciprocal commitment other than cash payment."

For the last several decades, the total number and volume of counter-trade has steadily increased. One reason for this trend is that the world debt crisis has made traditional international trade very difficult. Many heavily indebted countries could not afford buying foreign goods for the lack of internationally acceptable hard currencies. Counter-trade is also often viewed by some firms and nations alike as an alternative way to penetrate into new markets when normal marketing function is not working properly in your target market. Counter-trade also can help them establish a long tern and more stable relationship with the foreign customers because both parties know that it may be difficult to find a new partner and to replace the old one.

Types of Counter-trade

1. Barter

Historically, counter-trade was mainly conducted in the form of barter. In barter arrangements, goods are exchanged directly for other goods of approximately equal value with no money involved. Barter can encompass the exchange of a wide variety of goods – for example, oil for foods. However, such a straightforward pure form of barter becomes rare recently because of the difficulties to find two parties who are willing to make an exchange of goods of equivalent value at the same time.

2. Clearing Arrangement

Another form of barter is **clearing arrangement, which can be considered as an ongoing barter**. Under this arrangement, both parties establish open accounts and continue to exchange the goods with each other within the range of the originally stipulated amount. Each transaction will be recorded on either the debit side or the credit side. The account doesn't have to be settled immediately. Instead, at the end of the contract period, the difference between the cumulative debits and credits will be settled by using small amounts of currency. Frequently, the goods available for purchase with clearing account funds are tightly defined such as Pepsi syrup for Russia made Vodka. Sometimes, additional flexibility is given to the clearing account by permitting switch-trading, in which credits in the account can be sold or transferred to a third party.

3. Counter Purchase

Another form of counter-trade is the **counter purchase**. Under this mode, both parties involved in signing two parallel buy/sell contracts that stipulates the amount of goods and services to be exchanged in different time frames. In this way, one transaction can go forward even though the second transaction needs more time. This type of counter-trade can be particularly beneficial to both parties if delivery of the two products by two different parties requires different timing such as harvest of agricultural product in the future. In many cases, the value of the goods to be exchanged is not exactly equal value, which requires some amount of cash for settlement.

4. Buy Back

Another common form of counter-trade is **buy-back**, or compensation arrangement. One party agrees to supply technology or capital equipment that enables the other party to produce goods which will be used as a payment for the technology or equipment supplied previously. This kind of counter trade requires a lengthy amount of time for final settlement because payment will be made gradually as the other party produces the goods in the future. For example, an MNC from an industrialized country builds a fertilizer plant or to provide a technology to build the plant in a developing country and the developing country pays back for this technology in terms of the fertilizer produced by the developing country.

5. Offset

Another form of counter-trade is **offset**. This form of counter trade is arranged to provide any commensurate return or business right by one party for the goods and services rendered by another party to compensate for the value originally provided. For example, in return of a foreign investor's developing a certain region as a tourist zone, the host government grant a right to the firm to operate a casino in that area for a certain period of time. The Offset arrangements can take on many different forms such as extending exclusive business right, natural resource extracting right, and permission of sharing lucrative local business, subcontracting or participating in government procurement.

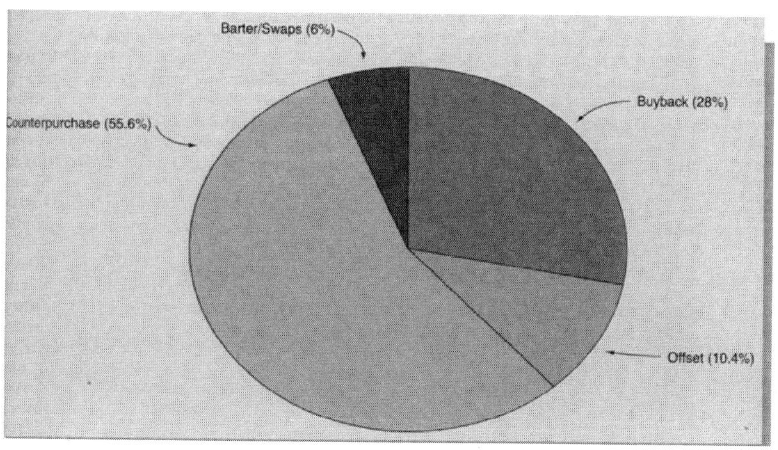

Licensing

A licensing agreement is an arrangement under which a licensor grants the rights to use intangible property to the licensee for a specified period in return of a royalty fee (normally a certain percentage of total sales value) from the licensee. Intangible property, which can be the objects of licensing agreement, includes patents, inventions, formulas, processes, designs, copyrights, trademarks and any sellable know-how.

Advantages

One of the advantages of licensing is that the firm does not have to bear all the costs and risks of operating and managing the units in foreign markets. All you need is to find out which foreign firms need your technology. Compared to other forms of international business such as FDI or Joint Venture that requires investment of large amount of capital, Another advantage of licensing is that it is relatively free from political risk that can result in the confiscation of the properties on foreign soil. Licensing is also often used as an alternative way to access a foreign market where direct investment is prohibited.

Disadvantages

Even if licensing has several advantages as discussed above, it also suffers some drawbacks. First of all, the licensor would not have the right to control the daily operations, manufacturing, marketing, and strategy that is required for realizing experience curve and economy of scale (as global and transnational firms must do). Since each licensee will establish its own production facilities and produce the goods at their own plant, MNCs as a whole can not get the benefits of economy of scale. Another problem associated with licensing is the risk of technology diffusion to foreign companies. Technological know-how constitutes the basis of many multinational firms' competitive advantage. However, when you do business under this mode and the contract expires, your previous licensee will learn every aspects of your technology or even develop better technology extended from your technology. This can present a serious problem to the licensor later and the previous licensee can become your serious competitor. Many firms have made a naïve assumption that they could maintain control over their know-how within the framework of a licensing agreement. However, there are always some undesirable illegal actions and legal loopholes that made it possible to transfer or leak any know-how to an illegal third party.

Franchising

One special forms of Licensing is Franchising in which the franchiser not only sells intangible property (normally a trademark) to the franchisee, but also assist the franchisee to ensure the smooth day-to-day operation. As with licensing, the franchiser typically receives a royalty payment normally based on the certain percentage of the franchisee's revenues. The most important aspect of any franchising business is how to ensure the standardized quality of the products and services. To this end, franchiser normally assists the franchisee by providing materials, operating manuals and undertakes promotional activities.

Advantages

The advantages of franchising as an entry mode are very similar to those of licensing. The firm is free from any burden, costs and risks of operating in a foreign market on its own. Instead, the franchisee typically assumes those costs and risks. In this sense franchising is relatively less risky for of international business. Accordingly, using a franchising strategy, a service firm can build a global presence quickly and at a relatively low cost and risk. However, one of the key elements of any franchising business is the reputation of the franchiser. Not all the firms do have this prestige to open a global franchising operation.

Disadvantages

As discussed above, the most important aspect of franchising business is that the firm's brand name and the standardized quality of their products or services. However, the geographical distance between the parent franchisor and its foreign franchisees and the cultural differences between them can make it extremely difficult to ensure standardized quality. In extreme cases, standardized quality may not even serve the best interest of the firms and they have no choice but to modify their product design or services to serve local markets more effectively. In this case, they may lose the major essence of the franchising business- standardized quality, and eventually the value of their brand name and firm's reputation.

Contract Manufacturing

Contract manufacturing is one of the most important tools for outsourcing. Under contract manufacturing, the whole product, or a certain part of the product, is made by foreign firms based on short-term contracts. Contract manufacturing allows the companies to separate the physical production of goods from the research and development and marketing as in the case of Nike. Most of the Nike products are made in foreign countries based on this type of arrangement. Nike does not own the production facilities in foreign countries even if the majority of their products are made in foreign countries. They simply use the foreign firms' facilities based on a short term contract. In Nike, they focus more on the high value-added activities such as R&D and marketing than day-to-day production management.

Advantages:

- Companies can utilize cheap resources such as labor without heavily investing their money to build a plant in other countries.
- It is politically less risky than FDI because the firms do not own the plants on foreign soil. If a firm has a physical presence such as a plant through FDI, it is always exposed to political risks such as confiscation/nationalization/expropriation when the host country and home country's relationship deteriorates.

Disadvantages:

-The risk of diffusion of technology may rise significantly when the parent firm gives their detailed specifications to the foreign firm when the contract expires. The previous contractor can make exact copy of your product and become your competitor in the future.

-Quality control is difficult under contract manufacturing (The foreign firm may not meet the parent firm's quality standards and delivery.)

O.E.M (Original Equipment Manufacture)

One type of Contract Manufacturing is ***O.E.M (Original Equipment Manufacture)*** where a company makes a contract with a foreign firm to buy their products and then sells them under its own brand name and through its own marketing channels. A typical example of this kind of arrangement is that occasionally Intel buys computer chips from Japanese chip manufacturer, Hitachi, and put their label on it and sell it through Intel's distribution channels. OEM is a special form of strategic alliance between an efficient manufacturer and an excellent marketer. This mode would be appropriate when;

- A company has an excellent brand name and recognition, but
- They have inefficient or limited production in its facilities, or
- It faces a sudden large demand increase beyond their production capacity.

However, if the company uses this method too extensively and fails to exercise tight control over the quality of the products, it may lose its most valuable asset: the brand name recognition and it can jeopardize their own operation over the long haul.

Turnkey Projects (project or plant export) Hill's 5th p488starts here

In a turnkey project, also called project export, the contractor agrees to build a large facility such as a utility plant or infrastructure for a foreign client, including the training of operating personnel. Upon completion of the contract, the foreign client is handed the "key" to a plant that is ready for immediate operation. Turnkey projects are most common in some industries such as chemical, pharmaceutical, petroleum refining, and infrastructure building industry (communication facilities and harbor, etc.) that require a substantial amount of capital and very sophisticated process technologies.

Advantages

This mode of business is particularly appropriate where FDI is limited by host-government regulations. Some countries want to explore their natural resources such as oil, gas and mineral. However, they don't have enough capital and technology to do this. Besides, they are still concerned about losing control of this industry to foreign firms because they maintain an imperialistic view of FDI. In this case, foreign firms simply build the facilities and hand them over when completed. A turnkey project is also relatively less risky than conventional FDI because you don't own any production facilities within the host country. Thus, you can be free from any political risk such as risk of nationalization or confiscation.

Disadvantages

The turnkey operation can suffer several drawbacks. First, the firm that is involved with a turnkey project may not be allowed to extend this opportunity to other business in the host country. It may be an easy way to get into the market but opportunity cost may be too huge if you simply build and hand it over and get out of the lucrative growing market like China or India. Another potential problem of doing business under turnkey operation is possible diffusion of the firm's process technology, which is the primary source of competitive advantage. Selling this technology under a turnkey operation is almost like selling competitive advantage, which can create a potential future competitor.

B.O.T (Build, Operate and Transfer)

A special form of Turnkey Operation is called ***BOT (Build, Operate & Transfer)***, where a firm builds plants or facilities such as a utility plant or a fertilizer plant in other countries at its own expense and in return they will have the right to operate and do business for a certain period of time. Usually the profits and operation is guaranteed by the host government until the company recovers its invested capital. This kind of arrangement is quite popular for the development of infrastructure in poor developing countries because they don't have any capital or technology to undertake such a huge project. This arrangement is mutually beneficial to both parties since the host government can have such facilities indispensable to their economic development without investing any money whereas the investor's profit is also guaranteed by the host government.

Usually when the investor successfully recovers their invested amount of capital, it turns over the facility to the host government.

Management Contract

Under this mode of international business, one party provides another party with managerial expertise for a specific period of time in return of a lump-sum amount or a fee in proportion to sales volume. In general, two types of expert services can be provided under management contract; technical know-how and management skills.

This mode is appropriate when;

- There are no qualified/trained human resources available in the host country,
- The local managers are in trouble or fighting each other.
- A property has been confiscated or expropriated by the local government. Thus, the host country doesn't have any previous experience of operating the facilities.

Extract Agreement

Extract Agreement is one of the oldest forms of International Business under which foreign firms agree to explore and develop natural resources at their own risk and expenses. This type of business mode is quite prevalent in the oil industry, mining industry and many other natural resource extracting industries. Usually the agreement calls for the extract output to be shared with the host government since the resources belong to the host country. Extract Agreements are appropriate when there are abundant natural resources in the host country but they have no capital or technology to explore and develop them.

International Joint Ventures

This mode of international business requires the establishment of a business entity firm that will be jointly owned by two or more partners. The most typical joint venture is a 50/50 venture, in which two parties equally share a 50 percent equity stock. However, some firms want to have a majority share to exercise tighter control over their subsidiaries. This mode of business has been one of the most popular forms of strategic alliance because it can offer so many benefits to all the parties involved. That's the reason many researchers predict the total value of joint venture will reach more than 50 trillion dollars in next 5 years.

<u>Advantages</u>

First of all, joint ventures can offer several advantages to the local partner. First, foreign partner can bring in much needed capital to establish the business unit. This is one of the reasons why many developing countries who do not have any capital accumulation want to induce joint venture. Foreign partner will also provide updated technological know-how and managerial and marketing skills to the local partner. And yet, this mode allows the local partner of host government to have a certain amount of control because they share the equity stock. This is another important reason why so many developing countries prefer this mode of business.

Joint venture can provide many benefits to the foreign investor, too. In many countries, joint venture is the only feasible entry mode allowed by the law. By sharing ownership with a local partner, firms can penetrate into host countries' markets that are otherwise impossible to access. These markets are difficult to access because the host government has a very negative view towards FDI. Another advantage of joint venture is the possibility of reducing risk. Since the risks of operating in an unfamiliar territory are very high, by having local partner, firms can share the risks derived from this new operation on foreign soil. Another risk that firms can hedge by having a local partner is the risk of being nationalized or other forms of adverse government intervention. Joint venture can also get the benefits from a local partner's intimate knowledge of the host country's business environment, culture, language and political systems and climate. This valuable knowledge helps the foreign partner to avoid a disastrous mistake. Another advantage closely related to the previous one is the possibility of building a better public relationship with other local business associates or government officials. This is very important when every aspect of a business is tightly controlled by the government. Next possible advantage of having a local partner in joint venture is to reduce the foreignness of the firms where the nationalistic resistance or anti-American rhetoric is very strong. It is particularly important after the U.S. invasion of Iraq. Another big advantage of having joint venture is the possibility of taking advantage of the various incentives provided by the host government such as tax exemption or low interest rate loan. Since this is the most preferred form of business mode by many local governments, as discussed earlier, the host government would provide a variety of incentive package to induce more joint venture.

Disadvantages

Even if a joint venture is one of the most favored forms of strategic alliances these days and supposed to provide a great deal of benefits to most of the parties involved, in reality, when you run this type of operation on foreign soil, you may encounter a series of problems in day-to-day operation. First of all, sharing control can be difficult since both sides must always get the other partner's approval first, even on small issues. The shared ownership can lead to conflicts and battles for control between the investing firms if their goals and objectives change or if they take different views as to what the strategy should be. The second issue is possible goal incongruence or conflict of interest when both companies have secret agendas. They may have covert goals and they may not be willing to disclose this covert goal to the other partners. In some extreme cases, one partner real goal is not to cooperate but to steal a technology or any other know-how from their partners. It is particularly true when two arch rival companies create a joint venture as we witnessed so often these days. For example, a Joint Venture was created by GM and Toyota. By creating this joint Venture, GM wanted to learn the technology to build a more efficient small engine and Toyota wanted to learn marketing techniques from GM. In this type of hostile joint venture, such conflicts tend to be triggered by shifts in the relative bargaining power of venture partners. Obviously anybody who learns the other's valuable asset first, will try to dissolve the venture. In this case, a joint venture will become a race to learn the other's competitive advantage first. Whoever learns faster will try to dissolve the venture and walk away with booty.

Another issue is the cultural and epistemological differences between the two partners that can eventually cause a difficulty to identify and solve problems. For instance, Japanese managers often take extended leisurely lunch hours, whereas U.S. managers would have a problem with that. More often than not, lunch time for the Japanese managers is very important work hours to forge a strong human relationship, which they hope they can use later.

Another potential source of problem is communication. The communication between the two partners and two different groups of managers-local and expatriate managers can be easily disrupted by different languages and "selective transmission" of the information. Each group tries to transmit only the information that they want to transfer. Each partner may develop their own communication networks and does not share all of the information with the other group.

Difference in managers' time horizons can also cause a serious problem in developing policy and strategy for the venture. For example, U.S. managers may want things to be done in a much shorter time while Asian managers may want to focus more on the long term project. This tendency has something to do with their term of employment.

Lack of cohesiveness amplified by the ethnocentric attitude of the managers with different nationalities can make it extremely difficult to create a sense of unity. A research indicates that people's ethnocentric attitude can be much more amplified under multicultural settings like joint venture than mono cultural settings like pure domestic or a wholly owned subsidiary. This can cause a serious dysfunctional and idiosyncratic behavior among joint venture managers. An interesting phenomenon is that Americans often become more American than the typical American and Japanese become more Japanese than the typical Japanese under multicultural settings like a joint venture.

As discussed above, even if Joint Ventures are supposed to be highly beneficial at the structural and macro level, it is a very difficult mode of business to operate at the micro level because of cultural and epistemological differences between the two partners.

Wholly Owned Subsidiaries

A wholly owned subsidiary entails 100 percent of the stock ownership which enables the parent company to exercise perfect control over its subsidiary. A wholly owned subsidiary can be established in two different ways. The first one is to set up a new operation which is often called green-field investment. The other way is to acquire an existing firm already operating in the host country.

Advantages

The fist advantage of having a wholly owned subsidiary is to exercise a tight control over the subsidiary's operations in different countries. In some organizations, this is so critical for global strategic coordination because each subsidiary should accept centralized decisions for global optimality even if the decision may not serve the best interest of the unit. Another potential advantage is to ensure the uniformity and conformity between the parent and the subsidiaries and among the different units scattered all over the world. Another advantage of having a wholly owned subsidiary is to reduce the risk of technology diffusion and losing control over the other core competence of the firms such as marketing and managerial skills. In other words, you still can "internalize" the foreign market without losing those core competences while producing the goods in foreign country.

Disadvantages

Operation of a wholly owned subsidiary is the most costly and risky way of serving a foreign market. MNCs operating their business under this mode in the host country should solely bear all the costs and risks derived from this mode. You may be able to reduce this kind of risk through acquisition of the existing venture. However, acquisitions can open up a series of other problems. You may have to deal with local employees accustomed to different corporate cultures and systems and there may be serious unknown and hidden problems carried over from previous operations. These problems may present even more problems than any benefits from acquisition of an existing unit.

Review Questions

What is counter (compensatory) trade and why is it so popular these days?

Identify and discuss the various forms of counter trade.

Identify and discuss different forms of strategic alliances other than counter trade.

Discuss the advantages and potential problems of licensing.

Discuss the advantages and potential problems of contract manufacturing.

What is O.E.M. (Original Contract Manufacturer)?

Discuss the advantages and potential problems of Turnkey Operation.

What is B.L.T. (Built, Operate and Transfer)?

Discuss the advantages and potential problems of Joint venture.

Discuss the advantages and disadvantages of wholly owned subsidiary.

Interesting WEB sites to visit:

1) Country information

https://www.cia.gov/cia/publications/factbook

http://highered.mcgraw-hill.com/sites/0072973714 : general information about the countries

www.infoplease.com/world; general information about countries

www.kidon.com; International media-link

www.unwire.org : International News

www.wri.org ; World Resources Institute (environment & energy)

www.odci.gov/cia/publications/factbook; CIA World fact book

http://www.esc.edu/library/ibol/travel.htm; International travel information

2) Cross Country Research data;

http://www.harzing.com/

www.worldbank.org ; world development report, etc.

www.r0.unctad.org: FDI and Trade data

www.un.org; ditto

www.oecd.org; ditto

3) Foreign Currency Information:

www.xe.com ;

4) Cross-cultural Training;

www.intercultural.org; intercultural communication and training

5) UCF Study Abroad program;

www.international.ucf.edu; UCF study abroad program

6) How to join the Peace Corps.

There are ample opportunities to get involved with Business Development programs in the Peace Corps for you. Two years of service in a Peace Corps business project could provide excellent experiential education in an international setting for you straight out of college and help you get ready for serious employment in the future. Click on this link to learn more about the Peace Corps Business Programs:

http://www.peacecorps.gov/index.cfm?shell=learn.Whatvol.busdev_01

7. International job listings;

www.rileyguide.com; The Riley Guide

http://ohrm.doc.gov/jobs/student/info.htm; US Dept. of Commerce internship program.

www.careers.state.gov/index.html; US dept. of State.

www.ifc.org; The International Finance Corporation of World Bank Group.

www.aiesec.org; Student-run Internship program with foreign companies.

www.oas.org/EN/PINFO/HR/gen_information.htm; Organization of American States.

www.ohiou.edu/studyabroad/internships.htm; Internship program offered through Ohio University.

www.montana.edu/wwwcp/national.htm; International Career Opportunities (University of Montana).

http://wiscinfo.doit.wisc.edu/globalstudies/goglobal/site-lists/external-centers.htm; (University of Wisconsin).

References

International Business; Competing in Global Market Place by Charles Hill, McGraw-Hill/Irwin, New York, New York. 2009.

International Business; Environments & Operations by J. Daniels, L.H. Radebaugh. Pearson Prentice Hall. Upper Saddle River, New Jersey. 2010.

International Business; The challenge of Global competition, by D.A. Ball, W.H. McCulloch, J. M. Geringer, M.S. Minor, J.M. McNett, 11ed. McGraw-Hill Irwin, New York, N.Y. 2008.

International Financial Management by Jeff Madura's, Thompson South-West, Mason. Mason, OH. 2008.

Culture, Strategy and Behavior by R.M. Hodgetts and F. Luthans, 4e, McGraw-Hill. 2005. Understanding Intercultural Communication by Jain, Samovar,Porter. Wadsworth, CA. 1981.

International Marketing by Subhash C. Jain. 3rd ed. PWS-Kent Publishing company, Boston. 1990.

International Management by Helen Deresky, 6th ed. Pearson-Prentice Hall, Upper Saddle River, New Jersey, 2008.

Multinational Business Finance by D. K. Eiteman, Arthur I. Stonehill, M. H. Moffett. 7th ed. Addison-Wesley publishing Co.,1995.

International Business By M.R. Czinkota, I. A. Ronkainen, M. H. Moffett. Hatcourt Brace and Company. 1999.

Multinational Financial management 5th ed. by Alan C. Shapiro, Prentice Hall, Upper Saddle River, New Jersey. 1996.

Culture, Leadership and Organizations; The GLOBE study of 62 societies, edited by R. J. House, P.J. Hanges, M. Javidan, P.W. Dorfman, V. Gupta. Sage Publications, Thousand Oaks, CA. 2004.

Global Corporate Finance by Suk Hi Kim, Copley Publishing Group, Acton, MA, 1991. Blunders in International Business by David Ricks, Blackwell Publishers Lt. Cambridge, MA, 1997.

Managing Cultural Differences by P.R. Harris and R.T. Moran. 3rd ed. Gulf Publishing Company, Houston, TX, 1991.

International Trade Theory and Policy by Miltiades Chacholiades, McGraw-Hill Book Company, New York, N.Y. 1978.

Comparative and Multicultural Management by Shimcha Ronen, Wiley, New York, New York. 1986.

Riding the seven waves of culture; Understanding the diversity in Global Business by Charles, Hampden-Turner and Fond Trompenaars. McGraw-Hill. 1997.